Empire and After

EMPIRE AND AFTER

Englishness in Postcolonial Perspective

Edited by

Graham MacPhee

and

Prem Poddar

Berghahn Books
New York • Oxford

Published in 2007 by

Berghahn Books

www.berghahnbooks.com

©2007 Graham MacPhee and Prem Poddaer

Library of Congress Cataloging-in-Publication Data

Empire and after : Englishness in postcolonial perspective / edited by Graham MacPhee and
Prem Poddar.
    p. cm.
Includes bibliographical references and index.
ISBN 978-1-84545-320-6 (hardback : alk. paper)
1. National characteristics, English--History. 2. Great Britain--Colonies--History. 3. Nation-
al characteristics, British--History. 4. Postcolonialism--Great Britain--History. 5. Great
Britain--Civilization. 6. Imperialism. 7. Nationalism--Great Britain--History. 8. Nationalism-
-Great Britain--Colonies--History. I. MacPhee, Graham, 1968- II. Poddar, Prem.

DA118.E487 2007
320.5409171'241--dc22

2007018806

British Library Cataloguing in Publication Data

A catalogue record for this book is available from the British Library

Printed in the United States on acid-free paper

978-1-84545-320-6   hardback

CONTENTS

This volume is dedicated to all those fighting to restore
the legal rights of the British residents currently imprisoned
without charge at Guantánamo Bay.

Acknowledgements

We would like to thank Linda Colley for her interest in the project in its early stages, and Ian Baucom for his support and advice throughout. Thanks are also due to David Johnson, Shane Moran, Anne MacPhee, and Emma Barker for their helpful suggestions.

Graham MacPhee would like to thank Conor McCarthy, Christopher Wood, Erica Fleming for her help with indexing, and Cheryl Wanko, Anne Herzog, and the Department of English at West Chester University for their support. My greatest debt is to Sally.

Prem Poddar would like to thank Cheralyn Mealor, Dominic Rainsford, Jenny and Leela. I would also like to acknowledge my debt to the Danish Institute for Advanced Studies in the Humanities for allowing me time to visit the Public Records Office at Kew Gardens in London.

Nationalism beyond the Nation-State

Graham MacPhee & Prem Poddar

> In theory, there is an abyss between nationalism and imperialism;
> in practice, it can and has been bridged . . . .
> —Hannah Arendt, *The Origins of Totalitarianism* (1951)

Local and Global

In recent years there has been a sustained renewal of interest in British national identity at popular, political, and academic levels, and strikingly a common feature in each case has been the concern to differentiate between "British" and "English" and define a distinct sense of Englishness. The English flag (the cross of St. George as opposed to the flag of the United Kingdom, the Union Jack) has gained a currency inconceivable even ten years ago; politicians and media pundits have devoted extraordinary amounts of time to arguing about the nature of English identity, or listing which characteristically local landscapes, persons, objects or architecture best stand as icons of Englishness, and lengthy academic studies have been devoted to establishing the distinction between Britishness and Englishness and charting their historical emergence and applicability. For many beyond the shores of the British Isles, the terms "England" and "Britain" appear to be interchangeable synonyms, and such debates may therefore seem parochial and even eccentric. It is the claim of the present volume that far from being idiosyncratic or self-involved, the question of Englishness and its relationship to British national identity offers an important avenue for thinking about the politics of national identity in our postcolonial and globalized world.

A sense of the complex connection between local and global involved in these terms is evident when one considers the everyday difficulties involved with the terms "English" and "British." Far from being straightforward synonyms, these terms are bound up in a range of distinct but overlapping meanings for inhabitants of the British Isles. Thus, for example, to describe the United Kingdom as "English" may well be a source of

---

discomfort for inhabitants of Scotland, Wales, and (even more problematically) Northern Ireland, who may object that this confusion reflects the subordination of other national traditions and the unacknowledged and illegitimate predominance of the English within this "nation of nations." And while many would prefer "British" in this instance, significant numbers in each of these locations would reject this term outright in favor of an alternative national appellation (Scottish, Welsh, Irish). Conversely, in the face of a limited measure of devolution for Scotland, Wales, (and again, even more problematically) Northern Ireland, a widely reported current of opinion has argued that a distinct English identity is required as a response to these other nationalisms. However, the acceptability of such an English identity for all those born in England is by no means straightforward or unproblematic. In certain contexts, the description "English" within popular discourse may connote "white," while to certain speakers a person of South Asian descent born in England, for example, might be described as "Asian." Thus, for many members of ethnic minorities, often the descendants of citizens of the former British Empire who emigrated in the postwar period, the term "English" retains a racial or ethnic coding that makes it inappropriate for them, whereas "British"—often conjoined as in Black British or British Asian—is seen as more inclusive and open. Yet this term is by no means straightforward either: while for non-Europeans the "British" are "European," for many inhabitants of the United Kingdom the terms "British" and "English" are at some deep level opposed to a European identity that is conceived of as distinct and alien.[1]

Two contradictory visions of the relationship between local and global, or the internal and external, emerge from these everyday terminological sensitivities. The first is manifest in those statements which claim to find a common sense certainty in designations of national identity, but which do so by defining it as an internal *response* to a threat that is *external*: thus, the exercise of British sovereignty is seen as threatened by EU integration, with its unaccountable, faceless, and fundamentally foreign bureaucracy; calls for a renewal of English nationalism are seen as a response to the assertiveness of Scottish, Welsh, and Irish nationalism; while demands for a return to a properly British (or sometimes English) culture are presented as a response to the "invasion" of alien cultures brought by migrants who refuse to assimilate and so threaten the national character. From this perspective, the integrity and strength of the "inside" paradoxically derives from the vitality and agency of what is "outside."

A different kind of relationship between global and local, internal and external, is suggested by those more avowedly problematic statements of identity, as for example in the difficulties surrounding the self-identification as English by members of ethnic minorities, even if born and raised in England, or indeed the claim for British national identity by many unionists in Northern Ireland, even though geographically its six counties are not part of Great Britain. In each case, the problematic nature of such identification points to the involvement of an ostensibly "internal" identity with what is assumed to be "external," and of the "local" with the "global." In the case of many descendants of citizens of former colonies, the difficulty lies in the persistence of racial designations and hierarchies inherited from the British Empire, designations which remained informal and at arm's length while the empire remained intact, but which since its demise have maintained a powerful hold both institutionally and in terms of popular political discourse. In the case of the unionist community of Northern Ireland, on the other hand, the anxiety expressed by the claim to Britishness has more to do with the perceived need for differentiation from the Irish identity prevalent on the island which they share, as it is to do with a claim of affiliation with the inhabitants of the English shire counties or the suburban boroughs of London. If such troubled articulations suggest that the "external" history of colonialism and imperial expansion continues to inhabit the "internal" space of the nation, so too do these ostensibly confident accounts of British or English identity; for each is premised upon the threat of the foreign and external, indicating that the very "externality" which proves so threatening is somehow already bound up in British and English identity.

What emerges in the slippage between these confident and problematic statements of British national identity is a worrying disavowal of the relationship between local and global, internal and external, in public discourse in the United Kingdom. Contemporary conceptions of Britishness, and perhaps still more Englishness, seem to imply a profound blindness with regard to the involvement of global and local, a blindness which Paul Gilroy argues is premised on an amnesia associated with empire. "Once the history of the empire became a source of discomfort, shame, and perplexity," Gilroy writes, "that unsettling history was diminished, denied, and then if possible, actively forgotten." (Gilroy 2005: 90). Gilroy terms this amnesia "postcolonial melancholia," and argues that it has two disastrous effects: first, "the error of imaging that postcolonial people are only unwanted alien intruders without any substantive historical, political, or cultural connections to the collective life of their fellow subjects" (2005: 90); and second, "the mysterious evacuation of Britain's postcolonial conflicts from national consciousness," which, as Gilroy notes, include not only Palestine, Malaya, Korea, Kenya, Suez, Cyprus, and Ireland, but also two wars in the Persian Gulf within the last decade or so (2005: 89).

If this disavowal of the involvement of local and global has its roots in British imperial history, it is by no means simply a historical phenomenon. A striking example of the contemporary operation of this denial occurred in the wake of the bombings on the London transport system in July 2005. The bombings followed the US invasion of Afghanistan and Iraq in which the UK participated as a subordinate ally, and were initially framed in terms of 9/11 as an incident in the larger "war on terror" declared by the Bush administration. But when it transpired that those responsible for the July bombing were British Muslims, young men who had grown up and participated in the broader multicultural society of the Midlands and North East of England, public discussion was immediately focused by establishment politicians and the mainstream media on the alleged failure of multicultural society in Britain and the need to reassert a unified British identity. This extraordinary turnaround sought to cast the violence as a purely "internal" matter whose cause and remedy are *cultural* rather than *political*. The extent to which the event came to be framed as exclusively domestic was made evident by British Prime Minister Tony Blair's fantastic claim that there was no relationship between the bombings and the participation of British military forces in the invasion of Iraq, despite widespread incredulity and mounting evidence that the bombings took place in the shadow of both internal racism and international policy. As Osama Saeedm of the Muslim Association of Britain observed, public discussion erased "Britain's explicit role in creating the injustices in the Muslim world—from the mess that colonial masters left in Kashmir to the promising of one people's land to another in Palestine." He urged journalists and politicians alike to remember that "[w]hat happens abroad matters to British Muslims as much as what happens here" (Saeedm 2005).

The palpable irony here is not that British Muslims have sought to bring "foreign" and "external" concerns into the domestic arena; after all it was Prime Minister Blair who overrode all political, military, and legal obstacles to pursue the invasion of Iraq and the American "war on terror," arguing that it was central to both international *and* domestic security (see Sands 2005: 174-204). Rather, the irony is that Blair could dismiss this apparently overriding global context at the drop of a hat, as a mere irrelevance beside the wholly internal woes of the beleaguered national community. What powerfully emerges in this instance is the way in which local and global are played off against one another in British political discourse, so that national prestige is gauged in terms of global reach, yet the nation itself is conceived as primary and fundamentally removed from this larger world. At one moment, Britain is at the forefront of a struggle that is understood to be both altruistic and in the national interest; in the next, attempts to trace the very international relationships upon which such an understanding would depend are rendered abstract and tendentious when set against the "common sense" dissatisfaction of middle England with the demands of multicultural society. Here the global serves to obscure the discontents of the local, while the local in turn serves to obscure a global involvement that continues to shape the lives of millions of human beings, albeit as a subordinate partner.[2]

The claim that motivates this volume is that the confusions and anxieties surrounding British national identity—and which emerge in the slippage between "Britishness" and "Englishness"—are not simply historical curiosities, but may be more broadly illuminating in an era when the intersection of local and global is at once more pervasive than ever and yet acknowledgement of this fact proves increasingly unpalatable within the national polity. British identity is of course not the only European identity powerfully informed and inflected through its colonial history, but it is perhaps unique in registering the continuing relevance of that history in its enduring terminological and conceptual confusions.

Isolating Englishness

The current academic concern with a distinct and identifiable Englishness has grown out of revisionist histories of British national identity, most notably by Linda Colley (1992). What makes this work on British history relevant to the slippage between Britishness and Englishness is its emphasis on the role of the external in the development of a specifically British national identity in the eighteenth century: as Colley writes, "men and women came to define themselves as Britons—in addition to defining themselves in many other ways—because circumstances impressed them with the belief that they were different from those beyond their shores." Colley's extensive historical account points again and again to the role of what are perceived as alien and external entities—whether in the form of French Catholicism or the supposed "savagery" of Native Americans—in the crystallization of a highly flexible, discontinuous, and even contradictory British identity which nonetheless proved to be powerful, popular, and enduring. Indeed, as she explicitly insists, it was "*not so much consensus or homogeneity or centralization at home*, as a strong sense of dissimilarity from those without [that] proved to be the essential cement" (1992: 17; emphasis added). In these terms, the unifying power of Britishness came from its commitment to expansion, a commitment it was able to sustain precisely because its unifying appeal did not require the kind of relinquishment of tradition and local rootedness necessarily demanded by a uniform and centralized identity.

While Colley's account focuses attention on Britishness, it has also had an important impact on the renewal of interest in a specifically English identity. Broadly speaking, there have been two ways in which this strengthened notion of British national identity has fed into discussions of Englishness, the first of which can be seen in Krishnan Kumar's *The Making of English National Identity* (2003), and the second in Ian Baucom's *Out of Place: Englishness, Empire and the Locations of Identity* (1999), and Simon Gikandi's *Maps of Englishness* (1996).

Kumar interprets Colley's emphasis on the connection between British national identity and the imperial expansionism of the eighteenth and nineteenth centuries as implying that Englishness proper—what he terms the "moment of Englishness"—could only occur with the prospect of imperial decline at the beginning of the twentieth century: it was "only when new commercial rivals threatened Britain's industrial supremacy and faith in the empire began to waiver," Kumar writes, "that a degree of self-consciousness began to emerge," so that "*for the first time* an inquiry into the character of the English people as a nation—as a collectivity . . . with a distinct sense of its history, its traditions and its destiny" was initiated (2003: 224; emphasis added). This approach commits Kumar to a strict and absolute terminological distinction between "English" and "British" and a strongly linear and unidirectional chronological scheme: Englishness and Britishness are distinct and should not be conflated or confused, while historically a discrete Britishness precedes an Englishness which only appeared on the scene once the imperial project was perceived to be on the wane. In this view, the terms designate alternate poles, and the one gains strength and currency at the expense of the other in a zero sum game.

At a deeper conceptual level, this approach also commits Kumar to a Britishness whose expansive and supranational commitment to civilization and modernity is fundamentally incompatible with the "narrowly conceived nationalism" signified by Englishness (2003: 194). Thus, while in other instances Kumar accepts that imperialism "can contain [nationalism] and at times be reduced to it," he argues that this was not the case with the British Empire. Rather, he maintains that "for the English, . . . empire offered an identity that lifted them above "mere" nationalist self-glorification," because "for the British generally, the empire was a force for good in the world [and] a means whereby all peoples—or at least many of them—might share in the material progress and moral enlightenment that were, so it was felt, increasingly characterizing Western nations" (2003: 193-94). According to Kumar, "in England . . . for much of the better part of the nineteenth century imperialism trumped nationalism" (2003: 193).

A different conception of the relationship between Britishness and Englishness is pursued by Ian Baucom, which does not envisage a neat separation of terms and epochs but instead locates the power of both terms precisely in their persistent conflation and confusion. Rather than seeing in Colley's account a demand for terminological precision and chronological sequence, Baucom interprets it as demonstrating "that Britishness . . . has consistently constituted itself through a rhetoric of disaffirmation" in which "English men and women simultaneously avow and disavow the British Empire, and in which Englishness, consequently, emerges as at once an embrace and a repudiation of what lies beyond it" (1999: 7). Focusing on place and its capacity to underwrite a specific and deeply rooted sense of identification, Baucom looks at how imperial conceptions of Britishness often involved the paradoxical displacement of characteristically English locations and spaces (such as the cricket field, an idealized English countryside, or the public school) from the imperial homeland to the colonial periphery. Thus, the situational specificity of English landscape and architecture—with its freight of experiential association, historical resonance, aesthetic value and political meaning—comes to stand in for and signify the supranational and ostensibly universal claims to progress, civilization, and modernity made by the British imperial project. At the fringes of empire, then, Britishness comes to be articulated through a lexicon of specifically English symbols, locales, histories, and meanings, so that the universal claims of empire are paradoxically narrated through the semantic and emotional particularity of Englishness. For Baucom, imperialism did not so much trump nationalism as merge with it in a deeply paradoxical way, so that imperialism becomes *both* an alternative to *and* a statement of nationalism, while nationalism becomes *both* an alternative to *and* a statement of imperialism.

Where Kumar would view this kind of conflation as a terminological error or conceptual weakness, Baucom instead sees it as enabling a flexible and "open" range of identifications and affiliations that nonetheless sustained a political and cultural hegemony that was decidedly English.[3] Thus, the Scots, Welsh, and Irish soldiers and imperial administrators could see themselves in this way as British (and therefore as also Scots, Welsh, or Irish), and—in some unacknowledged sense—as *somehow English*; and by extension, so too could the white colonists of Canada, Australia, New Zealand, and South Africa. However, for the myriad non-white colonial subjects of the colonies, protectorates and other territories, such an identification proved much more problematic.

The uneven and unequal character of this flexible and "open" conflation of identities is explored by Simon Gikandi in his *Maps of Englishness* (1996), where he recalls familial and communal memories of British imperialism in Kenya. As Gikandi demonstrates, while the identification with a Britishness was in some sense shared both by agents of empire and colonial subjects, its ethnic coding—the "Englishness" of Britishness—also meant that it was always experienced in very different ways. "[T]he Scottish missionary," Gikandi recounts, "would secure his British identity in the service of empire," bringing into alignment local and global identities, and allowing him to feel both modern (British/English) and rooted in tradition (Scottish): but for his Gikuyu congregation, for whom significantly "Scotland and England were the same thing," their accession to Britishness must be bought at the cost "of reading their local narratives not as stories about an autonomous African past but as minor and sometimes undesirable events that had now been transcended by a colonial destiny" (1996: 34-35). What Baucom would identify as the invisible ethnicity encoded in British imperial identity, thus allowed Britishness to remain substantially English while nonetheless accommodating (in this case) a Scottish identity whose historical markers and future interests were not (at least logically speaking) necessarily compatible with it. However, for those Gikuyu who sought such an identification—though as Gikandi points out, many *did not*—the ostensible universality proclaimed by Britishness was only accessible through the subordination of the particularity of one tradition to that of another.

The difference between the approaches signaled by Kumar on the one hand, and by Baucom and Gikandi on the other, turns on two different ways of conceiving the relationship between nation and empire. For Kumar, they are distinct and mutually exclusive: either empire incorporates nation or, as in the British case, "imperialism trump[s] nationalism." As such, nationalism emerges in the wake of imperialism, and therefore their interaction is *external* and *negative*, since the internal character of national identity is not substantially shaped or determined by the externality of empire, but is only inhibited in its expression and development. For Baucom and Gikandi, in contrast, empire and nation both conflict with one another *and* mutually inform, reinforce, and shape one another. As Baucom writes, following Arjun Appadurai:

> Englishness has been identified *with* Britishness, which in its turn has been identified as coterminous with and proceeding from the sovereign territory of empire, and . . . Englishness has also defined itself *against* the British Empire, first by retaining a spatial theory of collective identity but privileging the English soil of the "sceptered isle" or, more regularly, certain quintessentially English locales, as its authentic identity-determining locations; and then, intermittently over the decades of imperial rule, but programmatically from the 1960s onward, by largely abandoning spatial and territorial ideologies for a racial "discourse of loyalty" and coidentity. (1999: 12)

The conflation of nation and empire in British national identity generates a cultural discourse in which room is made for the *affective experience* of multiplicity, yet at the same moment, this multiplicity is denied or discounted by a unity that disavows its own act of denial. In this view, the transaction between Britishness and Englishness is not a one-time event—Kumar's "moment of Englishness"—but an ongoing process whose terms are constantly being renegotiated. Kumar is not wrong, then, in identifying *a* "moment of Englishness" at the beginning of the twentieth century, but in conceiving of it as the first and only such moment (2003: 176).

This concern for the conflation of imperial and national within British national identity speaks to each of the various moments and locations addressed in this volume; yet if it offers a valuable approach, Baucom is himself open about its limits as an interpretative framework. Arguing that "the dialectical estrangements of Englishness [must] become more than a banal metaphor for 'diversity,'" he concedes that a turn to "the local does not necessarily imply a turn to the emancipatory." Baucom's warning that the invocation of "multiplicity is not enough" returns us to the response to the London bombings mentioned above, in which the attempt to identify a political framework for this event was obscured by the insistence on its char-

acter as a *purely cultural* problem—the supposed failure of multicultural society—rather than the *political* question of Western involvement in the
Middle East (1999: 221). The point is not that the cultural must be subordinated to the political, but rather that the interrelationship of the cultural
and the political itself needs to be thematized. If each of the moments and
locations examined in this volume point to ways in which British national
identity allows an emotional or affective experience of particularity and
multiplicity while simultaneously denying it, then together they suggest
the need to examine the relationship between the immediacy of cultural
experience and the less immediate level of the political which the cultural
both illuminates and obscures. The remainder of this introduction will consider one attempt to think the political and economic coordinates of imperialism and the nation-state, namely that made by Hannah Arendt in *The
Origins of Totalitarianism* ([1951] 1973).

Nation and Empire

In *The Origins of Totalitarianism*, Arendt presents an account of the development of the nation-state in which imperialism is not an external factor
or an afterthought, but an integral and internally constitutive moment. In
contrast to Kumar's demand for a tidy conceptual separation, she identifies
the "confusion of imperialism and nationalism" as a key moment in the development of the European nation-state (Arendt 1973: 153). However,
within the framework of her understanding of the dynamic of imperialism,
this development at one and the same time marks "the decline of the nation-state" (Arendt 1973: 267).

The broader terms of Arendt's account are based on the intersection of
two antagonistic vectors. The first emerges from her understanding of the
nation-state as an (albeit adulterated) *political* space, comprising a relatively open if restricted public sphere.[4] Despite real limitations, the political space of the nation-state is characterized by formal structures of legality
that allow for an element of recognition and negotiation—even if uneven
and unequal—between a plurality of different political actors. To the extent that the nation-state approximates to what Arendt would conceive of
as a properly political space, it implies a level of respect for enduring patterns of social differentiation and some recognition of a "national" or public interest in contradistinction to the imperatives of the private realm.

The second vector emerges from Arendt's recognition that the nation-
state is at one and the same time a function of the emergence of the bourgeoisie as a class. For Arendt, the bourgeois are determined by economic or
"private" imperatives that are ultimately incompatible with the public interest of the national-political, yet they have an economic power with the
potential to subordinate the fragile political sphere of the nation-state to

these private imperatives. In contrast to the bounded character of the national-political, which requires the maintenance of discrete and enduring limits, distinctions, and borders (and therefore, albeit in a restricted form, of the plurality and particularity necessary for human community), the economic functions according to the imperative of "expansion for expansion's sake" (Arendt 1973: 126) whose "logical consequence is the destruction of . . . [the] stabilizing forces which stand in the way of constant transformation and expansion" (Arendt 1973: 137-38). Arendt's account of modern politics is thus underpinned by "the inner contradiction between the two principles" of nation and imperialism, where the latter is understood as marking the illegitimate and highly destructive importation of the economic into the political.

This picture is complicated in turn by Arendt's broader understanding of the social transformations incumbent on Western modernity. The economic imperative of expansion increasingly finds itself limited by the nation-state, and therefore seeks markets and opportunities for accumulation beyond the discrete borders that curtail the nation-state's jurisdiction and sphere of direct intervention. Yet at the same time, a range of contradictory developments collide in order to destabilize the national-political sphere and undermine its capacity to adjudicate the public interest, including the growth of class conflict, the social and economic atomization of market relationships, and the increasingly "national" character of the nation-state itself—i.e., the unfolding consequences of its ethnic self-identification, as opposed to the properly political basis of the "political state."

While the bourgeois had largely abstained from the public concerns of politics in favor of its "private" economic interest, the economic increasingly came to demand expansion, and in turn, the subordination of the state to the role of safeguarding this expansion. As a result, the privately minded bourgeois came to claim a "public" or "political" role. Despite the fundamental incompatibility of the national-political and the economic-imperial, the instability increasingly experienced by the nation-state led to a powerful propensity across different sectors of society to identify the *public* interest of the national-political with the *private* imperatives of the bourgeoisie. In the individual and atomized experience of modernity, the very privateness of the bourgeois economic imperative could paradoxically provide the appearance of universality, especially once articulated through the language of nation and race (Arendt 1973: 152-53). As a result, imperialism rapidly came to be regarded as the "panacea" for all the ills of the nation-state (Arendt 1973: 151). "In theory," Arendt writes, "there is an abyss between nationalism and imperialism"; but "in practice," she observes, "it can and has been bridged by tribal nationalism and outright racism" (1973: 153).

While Arendt sees these developments as having been operable across Europe in the nineteenth century, she sees them functioning in very different ways according to the social, economic, and political character of the different national polities.[5] The most consistent and logically coherent attempt to square imperialism and the nation-state emerged in France in the wake of the French Revolution. The drive to align the national-political with imperialism in France generated a sustained attempt to coordinate the formal legality of the nation-state with the expansionism of empire. For Arendt, it was preeminently the French who:

> attempted to develop the body politic of the nation into an imperial political structure, [and to] believ[e] that "the French nation (was) marching . . . to spread the benefits of French civilization"; they wanted to incorporate overseas possessions into the national body by treating the conquered peoples as "both . . . brothers and . . . subjects—brothers in the fraternity of French civilization, and subjects in that they were disciples of French light and followers of French leading." (1973: 129)

This characterization of the French attempt "to build an empire in the old Roman sense" is not, however, seen as having had benign consequences; indeed, the reverse. "The result of this daring enterprise," Arendt remarks ironically, "was a particularly brutal exploitation of overseas possessions for the sake of the nation," since it put the full force of the nation behind the imperialist project, while conversely placing the full resources of colonial possessions at the nation's call (1973: 129).

In contrast to the French experience, Arendt sees in British imperialism a more confused, rationally less consistent, but ultimately more "successful" model—successful, that is, from the viewpoint of the imperialists. The central distinction between them lay in the relatively greater separation between national institutions and the colonial administration. Thus, while the British colonial administrators were subject to the same predilection for "administrative massacre" and other "radical means of pacification" as the French, the stronger distinction between national-political and imperial-bureaucracy tended to restrain their full implementation, and they remained a relatively marginal, although by no means absent, method of colonial rule (Arendt 1973: 134).[6]

The point of Arendt's distinction here works at three levels: at the cultural, the political, and at the level of the future direction of decolonization. At the more familiar cultural level, this distinction between the domestic and the colonial shaped the self-perception of the universal, civilizing, and modernizing mission that was common to all imperial bureaucracies. But where French imperialism openly identified its modernizing and civilizing project with the nation-state, making the colonial subject at least theoretically French once they had assimilated into the French nation, "the British tried to escape the dangerous inconsistency inherent in the nation's attempt at empire building" through a highly contradictory and inconsistent set of strategies. A layer of its colonial subjects were encouraged to identify with British culture as civilized and modern, yet the possibility of full assimilation was effectively withdrawn since this very same culture was coded as racially and ethnically English. The majority of the "conquered peoples," on the other hand, were left "to their own devices as far as culture, religion and law were concerned," so that British administrators "stay[ed] aloof and . . . refrain[ed] from spreading British law and culture" (1973: 130). This "aloofness"—which Arendt saw as particularly dangerous (1973: 212)—allowed British imperialism to hold onto its claims to be "universal," "progressive," and "civilizing," while at the same time largely restricting British identity to colonial administrators and white settlers. Paradoxically, Arendt observes, "the colonies . . . were to become the very backbone of British nationalism," because "in the domination of distant countries and the rule over strange peoples" the colonial bureaucracy "discovered . . . the only way to serve British, and nothing but British interests" (1973: 154). Although her account does not employ the terminological distinction between British and English that we have used to designate the supranational and national, it nonetheless provides the terms of this paradox.

The political consequences of this "confusion of imperialism and nationalism" form the heart of Arendt's discussion of the political significance of imperialism in *The Origins of Totalitarianism*, for it is at this level that their incompatibility was most profound, and the retroactive power of empire upon the nation-state most destructive and enduring (1973: 153). Arendt is primarily concerned with two long-term processes, the first relating to the institutional and juridical reordering of the national-political space by imperialism, and the second relating to the resulting alliance between what she terms "capital" and "the mob." Together they constitute the powerful and highly damaging "boomerang effect of imperialism upon the homeland," a phenomenon that lead to the "decline of the nation-state" (Arendt 1973: 155).

According to Arendt, "The first consequence of power export" beyond the bounds of the nation-state "was that the state's instruments of violence, the police and the army, which in the framework of the nation existed beside, and were controlled by, other national institutions, were separated from this body and promoted to the position of national representatives" (Arendt 1973: 136). The redirection of public power to pursue the private economic interests of the bourgeoisie thus reformulates the very nature of public and private in the most damaging ways possible, corroding the legal supervision of the nation-state's increasingly massive capacity for violence and "liberating" the bureaucracies of coercion and surveillance associated with the police and military functions of the state. In these terms, the most powerful and dangerous instruments of the state increasingly become exempt from legal and political supervision, becoming instead the province of a largely autonomous and quasi-private bureaucracy operating for the most part beyond the purview of the nation's public sphere. The nation-state's commitment to imperialism therefore tends toward the etiolation of the legal and democratic elements of the national-political space and the growing autonomy of an expanding bureaucracy, so that legality is increasingly replaced by administrative regulation and bureaucratic decree (Arendt 1973: 215-16).[7]

The second consequence of the conflation of nation and empire for Arendt takes the form of a political alliance between the two "superfluous" sections of domestic society—the owners of capital, and those sections of all classes who no longer find a secure location within the national polity, or what Arendt calls "the mob" (1973: 155). What underpins the conflation of nation and empire, as we have seen, is the misrecognition of bourgeois expansion—which is for Arendt fundamentally private in character—as the *public good*. Consequently, the conception of "community" or "the public" which this misrecognition gives rise to is particularly impoverished at the political level, but compensates at the experiential level through its valorization of the mysterious, ineffable, and emotional character of national identity and belonging, a mystery that finds its ultimate expression in the fantasies of "race thinking" (Arendt 1973: 158-61).

Thus, although ostensibly expanding the remit of the nation, the confusion of imperialism and nationalism in fact results in the degradation of the substantive framework of the national-political characterized by legality, constitutionality, and publicity, the strengthening of the supranational force of the economic and of the extrademocratic and quasi-private power of the bureaucracy, and the increasing role of "tribal nationalism" and racism as a basis for national belonging (Arendt 1973: 153, 267). Together, these elements presage the "decline of the nation-state," which in certain circumstances—notably Germany, Italy, and France—would give rise to powerful fascist movements. According to Arendt, the British nation-state was "insulated" from the seduction of fascism by the comparatively wider separation between nation and empire, which "drew a sharp line between colonial methods and normal domesticate policies"; as a result, the "new alliance between the much-too-rich and the much-too-poor" which underwrote fascism "remained confined to overseas possessions" (1973: 155). Yet if the conflation of nation and empire generated the potential for "totalitarian government on the basis of racism" in the imperial possessions, Arendt finds to her surprise that this is not the likely course of British decolonization. "The stage seemed to have been set for all possible horrors," she remarks, but argues that while "British imperial rule sank to some level of vulgarity, cruelty played a lesser role between the two World Wars and human rights were always safeguarded." It is this "moderation in the midst of insanity" that underlies Arendt's anticipation that decolonization "may turn out to mean the transformation of the English nation into a Commonwealth of English peoples" (1973: 221).

However, Arendt's unqualified optimism here risks forgetting her own most powerful insights, smoothing them over within a progressive scheme that erases her diagnosis of the "decline of the nation-state." Rather than regarding decolonization as the end of the interplay between nation and empire, within the terms of her own account it must also be regarded as the moment when the separation of nation and empire—which for Arendt had been such an important barrier or "insulation" against the corroding effects of imperial expansion—is broken down, so that the reflux of empire is felt *more powerfully* within the bounds of the nation-state. In assessing Arendt's projection today we have of course the advantage of hindsight; but as well as factoring in the course of a history she was not privy to, we must also examine the consistency of Arendt's own thinking.

Arendt's optimism is certainly understandable. Not only did Britain escape the immediate appeal of fascism in the 1930s, but in the wake of the national sacrifice and struggle of war, a new sense of collective responsibility appeared to strengthen the public character of the nation-state while mitigating its purely "national" character—a collective responsibility expressed at home in the social democratic consensus and the welfare state, and abroad in active participation in building the new structures of international legality. But this renovation of aspects of the nation-state did not necessarily reverse the deepseated tendencies identified by Arendt in her account of the decline of the nation-state, whether at the institutional level or at the level of consciousness and affect. Just as the erosion of democratic accountability and the growth of the quasi-private military and security apparatus remained unchecked—and indeed accelerated under the imperatives of first the Cold War and then more recently the "war on terror"—so the habits of race-thinking and the imperial bureaucrat's mindset of aloofness were reimported directly from colonial periphery back into the space of the nation. And while decolonization involved the withdrawal of much of the colonial apparatus, it did not of course mean isolation from the global; if anything it meant the reverse. From the viewpoint of the Olympian British bureaucrat, the new global hegemony of the US is at once the scene of humiliation and the only opportunity for retaining prestige, while for the institutional investor it is more straightforwardly the prerequisite for maximizing profit. The incremental subordination of national policy to this vision of globalization over the last two decades has stripped away many of the gains made in rejuvenating the national-political in the immediate postwar period, while the resulting economic insecurity and social atomization threatens the very real achievement of an emergent multicultural society.

Arendt's account of imperialism in *The Origins of Totalitarianism* is valuable both because it suggests a way of relating the cultural to the political, and because it understands the inconsistent and contradictory character of national identity. However, Arendt's optimism about the future of decolonization forgets her own account of the decline of the nation-state, and uncharacteristically wagers that the erosion of the national-political can simply be wished away. But as she makes clear in *The Origins of Totalitarianism*, her analysis of imperialism was always motivated by a concern for the ways in which it would shape the future development of modern politics; indeed, she saw imperialism as a *beginning*, arguing against Lenin that it was not "the last stage of capitalism" but "the first stage in [the] political rule of the bourgeoisie" (1973: 138). In this light, we argue the contradictions, slippages, and inconsistencies in British national identity that are traced in different moments and contexts in this volume testify both to the deep-seated nature of the impact of empire and its continuing relevance for thinking British national identity.

Englishness and Invisibility

One way of thinking about the implications of Arendt's political analysis for the question of British national identity is in terms of appearance. Nationalism is always a curious configuration of appearing and disappearing, as Benedict Anderson indicates in his characterization of the nation as an "imagined community": for as Anderson observes, "the members of even the smallest nation will never know most of their fellow-members," they will not see them *"face-to-face,"* and "yet in the minds of each lives the *image* of their communion" (B. Anderson 1983: 15; emphasis added). The national flag exemplifies this combination of display *and* disappearance, for as a flag it signals *the* nation, and yet its apparent unity as image and object hides the multiple differences which inhabit the nation, and the many connections and relationships which reach beyond it.

In the case of the European conflation of nation and empire, this combination of appearance and disappearance carries a complex semantic and affective load, as Roland Barthes famously pointed out in his analysis of the "myth" of the French flag in "Myth Today" ([1957] 1982). In Barthes' example, what appears on the cover of *Paris Match* is not the flag itself, but the black soldier saluting it, an image whose mythic charge asserts "that France is a great empire, that all her sons, without color discrimination, faithfully serve under her flag, and that there is no better answer to the detractors of an alleged colonialism than the zeal shown by this Negro in serving his so-called oppressors" (Barthes 1982: 101-2). In Barthes' terms, this is a "myth" because it naturalizes—or makes invisible *while keeping in plain sight*—the contradictions of its "concept," which signifies the openness and universality of France-the-empire through the display of the exclusive character of France-the-nation. After all, the power of the image depends not on it picturing a French soldier saluting the national flag, but on the fact that it is a "French soldier" who is *visibly* "not French." In the Union Jack (which combines the crosses of St. George, St. Andrew, and St. Patrick), the particularity of England is at once displayed in the cross of St. George, and disavowed in the visual equality accorded to the crosses of St. Andrew and St. Patrick, which so visibly contradicts the cultural and political inequality that structures the United Kingdom.

This configuration of appearance and disappearance, visibility and invisibility, is not static, but presents a highly mobile and deeply contradictory pattern of permutations which, in the case of British national identity, is not reducible to a neat conceptual distinction between British and English. In the present context, the resurgence of English nationalism does not simply replace a properly British national identity, but functions in tandem with it in order to generate new configurations of appearance/disappearance. In particular, it plays a powerful role in the forgetting of empire by narrowing the horizon of national memory to that of a "medium-sized European nation," an England of the local and the particular as against the globally expansive British Empire. The false modesty of this gesture, in which Britain is reinvented as a number of "colonially innocent" locales from which empire and decolonization have been evacuated, enables Englishness to assume the pose of victimhood: no longer representative of mastery and power but the perennial loser at the hands of Scottish, Welsh, and Irish nationalisms, the bureaucrats of the EU, and the "bogus asylum-seekers" whose presence on "our" shores is as unexpected as it is unwanted. Under the guise of this "new Englishness," British nationalists can now "be like everybody else" in the sense that they can imagine the postimperial state as the innocent victim of the unjust and unprovoked oppression of external power, while at the same time reveling in Britain's status as one of the best armed and largest economies on the earth, whose continuing global political power is institutionalized in a seat at the UN Security Council.

An exemplary articulation of this "new Englishness" is provided by a speech to the Institute for Public Policy Research, entitled *A New England: An English Identity within Britain*, by the British MP and former minister David Blunkett, which cites Kumar's account of the beleaguered and neglected status of English nationalism as its occasion and justification (Blunkett 2005: 6).[8] Its description of the English as "an open, trading and enterprising people who have traveled the world and given it great science, literature and sport" at once claims too little and too much, airbrushing away the history of imperialism through an understatement whose modesty is exorbitantly egotistical (Blunkett 2005: 12). More worrying still is the fact that through a rhetorical sleight of hand, cosmopolitanism and the commitment to multicultural society have become "extremes" against which a common sense "new Englishness" stands as a bulwark (Blunkett 2005: 4). Unmentioned in the speech, however, are the implications of this new nationalism for the nation-state's residual political architecture of rights, legality, and constitutionality, even though as interior minister in the Labour government Blunkett presided over the Anti-Terrorism, Crime and Security Act (2001)—which as A. Sivanandan points out "effectively abolished habeas corpus for foreign nationals" (2005)—and the Nationality, Immigration and Asylum Act (2002), which was judged by the cross-party parliamentary Joint Committee on Human Rights and the United Nations High Commissioner for Refugees to contravene provisions of the UN Refugee Convention of 1951 (Joint Committee on Human Rights 2004). The new nationalism, then, not only obscures the ongoing erosion of the national-political—in the form of the attack on fundamental domestic rights and the incremental privatization of the public sphere—but also the degradation of the nascent structures of international law. This suggests that Arendt's assessment of the decline of the nation-state gains a renewed significance in an increasingly globalized environment, where a hollowed-out "nationalism" at once undermines the national-political, while at the same time restricting the purview of popular concern so that emerging international legal structures—which might safeguard human rights across nation-states—are framed as external to the national debate.

However, the contradictions in the postimperial state of the nation are nowhere more evident than in the extraordinary identification in Britain at both a popular and a bureaucratic level with American military power. And it is here that the paradoxical and irrational character of nationalism as both a cognitive discourse *and* an arena of affective investment appears most starkly. For example, as George Monbiot notes, British involvement in a European Union military force—in which the UK has extensive political input and decision-making powers, including elected members of the European Parliament—has faced widespread and often hysterical condemnation as presaging the collapse of British national sovereignty in the nationalist media.[9] Yet, according to the then defense minister Geoff Hoon, the new British strategic doctrine requires British armed forces to be "structured and equipped" according to American strategic requirements because "it is highly unlikely that the United Kingdom would be engaged in large-scale combat operations without the United States." As Monbiot points out, although the new strategic logic formally requires that the British "military [should] become functionally subordinate to that of another nation" within which the UK has no constitutional, institutional, or democratic decision-making role, there has been no outcry from the nationalist media or the traditionally nationalistic Conservative party (2003). More recently the Labour government has railroaded through the renewal of the Trident "independent" nuclear weapons system, which Britain buys from the US, while offering Yorkshire as a key location for the US National

Missile Defense System. Far from representing isolated incidents, this conflation of British nationalism with the global power of the US is codified by an editorial in *The Daily Telegraph* of London as the ninth of "ten core values of British identity," which declares that the attacks of 9/11 "were not simply an attack on a *foreign nation*; they were an attack on the *anglosphere*" (2005; emphasis added). In the context of the paper's wider coverage, this mysterious neologism presumably refers to the US and the UK (and perhaps Australia), rather than say Jamaica or those other nations which according to the same editorial once "prospered under colonial rule," but whose people are unhappily no longer "infected by the self-belief of the British Empire" (*Daily Telegraph* 2005).[10]

In the light of Arendt's account of imperialism and the decline of the nation-state, the contradictions underlying this "nationalist" identification with the global military hegemon can be recognized as the continuing legacy of the conflation of nation and empire. "Only when exported money succeeded in stimulating the export of power could it accomplish its owners' designs," Arendt writes; but conversely, "[o]nly the unlimited accumulation of power could bring about the unlimited accumulation of capital" (1973: 137). Thus, once the spatially limited nation is subordinated to the limitless expansionism of empire, identification with the national is in turn subordinated to *identification with power itself*. Now that the promise of unlimited power held out by the British Empire has drained away, the "new Englishness" seeks to sustain this identification with power in the guise of a "modest" and "responsible" nationalism that is ostensibly compatible with the language of universality associated with freedom, democracy, and human rights. But as the *Daily Telegraph*'s identification of "all . . . who believe in freedom, justice and the rule of law" with "the anglosphere" indicates, such "universality" remains ethnically and racially coded.

The essays collected in this volume do not present a unified thesis or adopt a single theoretical viewpoint, nor do they offer encyclopedic coverage; yet each in some way engages with the conflation of nation and empire signaled by Englishness and its coding of British national identity. The first part deals with the experience of that conflation at various locations and at different moments during the epoch of imperialism itself. Thus, for both Enda Duffy writing about Ireland and Vivian Bickford-Smith writing about South Africa, the neat distinction between "British" and "English" collapses into a highly contradictory—yet for that, an extremely powerful—discourse of identification which not only defines the Britisher but also the "other" in complex and unexpected ways. Prem Poddar focuses on a significant moment—the reflux after the Indian Rebellion of 1857—when the contradiction between nationalism and imperialism is brought to a head over the issuing of a British passport to imperial subjects, generating an anxious attempt to straddle universalism and xenophobia that powerfully anticipates contemporary hypocrisy over asylum. Geoffrey Nash, on the other hand, scrutinizes the physiognomy of this contradictory Englishness for fissures that might enable an identification with the "other," in the shape of the emergent Middle Eastern nationalisms of the early twentieth century. Graham MacPhee questions the insights into imperialism of that self-identified Englishman, Joseph Conrad, by reading the disappearance of the Irish context of political violence in his novel *The Secret Agent* (1907) in the light of Arendt's conception of the erosion of the national-political and the increasing opacity of the security apparatus.

The second part focuses on the postcolonial and postimperial world, where the contradictions between nation and empire can no longer be kept overseas but penetrate the homeland with increasing violence. Sheila Ghose examines two different attempts to manage or assimilate the specter of disenchanted British Asian youth in the wake of the London bombings of July 2005. Comparing the tabloid discourse of the "Brit Bomber" with the homegrown fundamentalist of Hanif Kureishi's fiction, she finds that while Kureishi's liberal perspective may seek to counter the aggressive fantasies of right-wing populism, it remains tied to notions of British national identity that cannot accommodate the experience it seeks to narrate. Bridget Byrne and Colin Wright both examine the unfolding contradictions of British national identity, with Byrne focusing on the lived experience of Englishness by women in London, and Wright focusing on the political rhetorics of the Labour and Conservative parties. Fittingly, Matthew Hart concludes this volume by shifting the analysis of British national identity to the Financial District of New York, where he explores the increasingly prevalent strain of mourning within Englishness as instanced by the proposed memorial garden for British victims of 9/11. Hart argues the memorial is primarily concerned to elide the economic and political inequalities that characterize the so-called "special relationship" between the US and UK, and so the memorial tailors its representation of British national identity to fit this larger, supranational imperative.

Notes

1. For a fuller exploration of the intricacies of the ethnic and racial coding of British national identity, see Parekh (2000) and Bridget Byrne's essay in this volume.
2. This incident should serve as a warning against the tendency—best exemplified by the writings of George Orwell—to fall back on an English "localism" to set against what are simplistically conceived as the "abstractions" of state and nation: such a "local" is of course no less abstract in its own way. For a perceptive critique of Orwell,

see Williams (1981), and for a critique of Williams in turn see Viswanathan (1991).

3. Which is to say, a restricted and class-bound notion of Englishness.

4. Like Hegel, Arendt's thought distinguishes between the "nation-state," based on an ethnic or linguistic identity, and the "political state," within which membership is a political act rather than simply an inherited condition. While the nation-state involves a political realm, for both Arendt and Hegel it is significantly compromised by its national character, and therefore the properly political state is to be preferred; see Tsao (2004). This important distinction associated with Hegel is largely ignored in English speaking accounts of nationalism and the modern state.

5. Arendt's focus on the second half of the nineteenth century tends to downplay the significance of the European slave trade for the interaction of nation and empire, which has significant repercussions for her engagement with the US; see MacPhee (forthcoming).

6. Arendt's judgment needs to be qualified in the light of ongoing historical research into British colonial violence. For example, recently there has been considerable scholarly interest in the extent and systematic nature of British violence in Kenya in the postwar period; see, for example, David Anderson (2005) and Elkins (2005).

7. Specifically, in the British context Arendt identifies "imperialism [as] the chief cause of the degeneration of the two-party system into the Front Bench system, which led to 'a diminution of the power of opposition' in Parliament and to a growth of [the] 'power of the Cabinet as against the House of Commons'" (Arendt 1973: 153). Thus, the substantive degradation of democratic structures which Arendt has in mind may well occur without necessarily affecting the appearance of *formal* democracy and legality, at least for the majority of its citizens.

8. This is not to say that Kumar's argument is designed intentionally to endorse the positions of Blunkett and other "new English" nationalists; it is, however, to point out that unless conceptual categories are thought through carefully they will, in Walter Benjamin's words, "allow factual material to be manipulated in the interests" of those seeking to undermine legality and constitutionality (Benjamin 2002: 101-2).

9. This is not to underestimate the democratic deficit in the European Union, and in particular the marginal status of the European Parliament in contrast to the power of the EU Commission and the Council of Ministers.

10. The neologism "anglosphere" echoes Niall Ferguson's awkward euphemism for imperialism, "Anglobalization," which he defines as "globalization as it was promoted by Great Britain and her colonies"(2002: xxiii); on this logic, the transatlantic slave trade might become "labor mobility as promoted by Great Britain and her colonies." Like Roland Barthes' myth, Ferguson's rebranding of British imperial history both displays and obscures its tendentious character through its contracted form.

Bibliography

Anderson, Benedict. 1991. *Imagined Communities: Reflections on the Origins and Spread of Nationalism.* London: Verso.

Anderson, David. 2005. *Histories of the Hanged: Britain's Dirty War in Kenya and the End of Empire.* London: Weidenfeld & Nicholson.

Arendt, Hannah. 1973 [1951]. *The Origins of Totalitarianism.* San Diego: Harcourt Brace.

Barthes, Roland. 1982 [1957]. "Myth Today." In Susan Sontag (ed.). *A Barthes Reader.* New York: Hill and Wang.

Baucom, Ian. 1999. *Out of Place: Englishness, Empire and the Locations of Identity.* Princeton: Princeton University Press.

Benjamin, Walter. 2002. *Selected Writings,* vol. 3. Cambridge, MA: Belknap.

Blunkett, David. 2005. *A New England: An English Identity within Britain.* London: Institute for Public Policy Research.

Colley, Linda. 1992. *Britons: Forging the Nation 1707-1837.* New Haven: Yale University Press.

Elkins, Caroline. 2005. *Britain's Gulag: The Brutal End of Empire in Kenya.* London: Cape.

Ferguson, Niall. 2002. *Empire: The Rise and Demise of the British World Order and the Lessons for Global Power.* New York: Basic Books.

Gikandi, Simon. 1996. *Maps of Englishness: Writing Identity in the Culture of Colonialism.* New York: Columbia University Press.

Gilroy, Paul. 2005. *Postcolonial Melancholia.* New York: Columbia University Press.

Joint Committee on Human Rights. 2004. *The Nationality, Immigration and Asylum Act 2002 (Specification of Particularly Serious Crimes) Order 2004.* London: The Stationary Office.

Kumar, Krishnan. 2003. *The Making of English National Identity.* Cambridge: Cambridge University Press.

MacPhee, Graham. Forthcoming. "Recalling Empire: Anglo-American Concepts of Imperialism and the Decline of the Nation-State." *College Literature.*

Monbiot, George. 2003. "Our Fake Patriots." *The Guardian* (July 8). [Accessed 10 October 2005.] <http://www.guardian.co.uk/comment/story/0,,993465,00.html>.

Parekh, Bhikhu. 2000. *The Future of Multi-Ethnic Britain: The Parekh Report.* London: Profile Books.

Saeedm, Osama, 2005. "Back to You, Mr. Blair." *The Guardian* (July 23). [Accessed 23 July 2005.] <http://www.guardian.co.uk/attackonlondon/story/0,16132,1534715,00.html>.

Sands, Philippe. 2005. *Lawless World.* New York: Viking.

Sivinandan, A. 2005. "Why Muslims Reject British Values." *The Observer* (October 16). [Accessed October 16, 2005.] <http://observer.guardian.co.uk/comment/story/0,6903,1593282,00.html>.

"Ten Core Values of the British Identity." 2005. *The Daily Telegraph* (July 27). [Accessed 27 July 2005.] <http://www.telegraph.co.uk/opinion/main.jhtml?xml=/opinion/2005/07/27/dl2701.xml>.

Tsao, Roy. 2004, 'Arendt and the Modern State: Variations on Hegel in The Origins of Totalitarianism.' *The Review of Politics,* vol. 66, no.1:105-136.

Viswanathan, Gauri. 1991. "Raymond Williams and British Colonialism," *Yale Journal of Criticism,* vol. 4, no. 2: 47-66.

Williams, Raymond. 1981. *George Orwell.* New York: Columbia University Press.

PART 1

Nation & Empire

CHAPTER 1

"As White As Ours"

Africa, Ireland, Imperial Panic, and
the Effects of British Race Discourse

Enda Duffy

Re-cognizing the Oldest Colony

The most controversial, and, in recent years, frequently quoted description by a Victorian Englishman of the Irish is the following:

> I am haunted by the human chimpanzees I saw along that hundred miles of hor-
> rible country. I don't believe that they are our fault. I believe that there are not
> only more of them, but that they are happier, better, and more comfortably fed
> and lodged under our rule than they ever were. But to see white chimpanzees
> is dreadful; if they were black, one would not feel it so much, but their skins, ex-
> cept when tanned by exposure, are as white as ours. (Kingsley 1881: 111–12)

This fantastic mélange of racism, travelogue, and imperial condescension,
all abounding under a veneer of righteous Victorian liberalism, may be
cited as the nadir of British racism directed at the Irish, extreme even by
mid-nineteenth century standards. Inserted, incongruously, in an account
of a fishing trip, it was written by Charles Kingsley, on the face of it a highly
unlikely source for such virulence. Kingsley, rector of Eversley, Hampshire,
was by 1860 a celebrated reformist clergymen, famous as the author of
Alton Locke (1850) and *Water Babies* (1863), forceful and effective exposés
of the conditions of child laborers and the urban poor in Britain. At this
symptomatic moment, however, he allows his reformer's zeal to escalate
into a rabid kind of othering. Written in 1860, only a year after Darwin's
Origin of the Species, he calls the Irish "white chimpanzees" with a shrill enthusiasm. Determined not to ignore the problems of the place in which he
was merely traveling as a tourist, the inevitable contradiction between his
tourism and his Christian socialism uncovers, rather, a pathological attempt to racially other those who, as he admits with something close to
panic, are of the same race as himself.

Notes for this section begin on page 52.

Kingsley's observations have, however, recently run the risk of becoming shop soiled, given their overexposure in debates about the status of relations between Britain and Ireland, and between British and Irish cultural productions, in the Victorian era. At least since L.P. Curtis, who in his pioneering book *Apes and Angels: The Irishman in Victorian Caricature* (1971), drew attention to the Victorian British habit of juxtaposing Irish and African figures, the rawness of Victorian British racism has been cited as proof positive that nothing less than the colonizer-colonized relationship is needed to characterize the British attitude to, and the reality of British power over, the Irish in the nineteenth century. By now it is clear that by far the most interesting work in Irish historical, literary, and cultural studies in the last quarter century has been produced by those who declared in advance that they considered that Ireland had been a colony of Britain, so that the Republic of Ireland, which gained its independence from Britain in 1921, should be considered a postcolonial nation. It may be claimed that the intellectual leap, made in such forums as the highly important Irish journal *The Crane Bag*[1] in the late 1970s, that Ireland's history and development be considered in a colonial and postcolonial paradigm, unleashed a series of insights whose power—and whose influence on contemporary Irish culture and even political developments both in Northern Ireland and in the Republic—has been unequaled since the intellectual and cultural work of the Gaelic Revival, which set the cultural conditions for the independence of Ireland in the first place. The Irish claim to colonial status has not, however, been without its doubters, and the strain of skepticism has recently seen a resurgence. It is in this context that commentaries such as Kingsley's have a renewed relevance. For example, in his polemical *Ireland and Empire: Colonial Legacies in Irish History and Culture*, Stephen Howe places himself at the vanguard of the opposition, castigating David Lloyd for using Kingsley's very lines in an essay in *Ireland after History* as a short-cut proof of the racism of British colonial rule in Ireland; Howe describes Kingsley's lines as overused and misunderstood (2000: 24). Overuse, however, is the point: to grasp the full implications of an emergent sense of Irishness in the late Victorian period, as I will show, one must take into account the burgeoning discourse on Ireland by British intellectuals at the same moment.

Rather than judge the worth of Lloyd's claim and Howe's counterclaim here in an essay on British attitudes to Ireland, I suggest that the recourse of both to Kingsley's observations shows that any attempt, whether within the ambit of postcolonial studies or otherwise, to understand the permutations of Irish modernity must take into account the agonistic, but nevertheless always more or less mutually aware, relations between intellectual developments in Victorian Britain and Ireland. The broadest terms of reference here are those of Hegel in his account of the master-slave relationship in *The Phenomenology of Spirit*: if one searches for the truth of the master, one will find it in the slave, while the truth of the slave will only be found in the study of the master. I believe that, at this juncture, Irish post-colonial studies needs to understand better how Irish nationalism was born out of a dialectical struggle with British discourses on Ireland if it is, first, to continue to have further interesting contributions to make to discussions on the nature of Ireland's version of modernity; second, if it is to have something valuable to contribute to the debates on postcoloniality in the world beyond the shores of Ireland; and finally, if it is to contribute meaningfully to a reimagining of the still prevalent narratives of the master—that is, if it is to be powerful enough (as it should be) to help reimagine Britain itself.

Irish postcolonial studies is coming under attack not because it lacks intellectual power or credibility, but rather precisely because it has been all too successful in convincing people of its validity and redirecting the course of nothing less than the history of the cultural formation—Ireland—which it studies. By now it is clear that this intellectual movement grew up in tandem with, and under the impetus of the shock of, the troubles in Northern Ireland since 1969. The Field Day Theater Company's location in Derry, from which it soon extended its influence with a pamphlet series and other endeavors, is a clue, as is the poet Seamus Heaney's very public and troubled reticence about whether he should be approaching the issues of the Northern troubles and what gave rise to them less obliquely in his poems. In this sense, those critics who disparaged Seamus Deane as the respectable intellectual arm of the Republican (that is, the ultra-nationalist) movement, and as a recycler of old versions of Irish nationalism under a new and more voguish critical aegis, were in the broader sense correct: the logic of the postcolonialist position has inevitably been that, as Northern Ireland is the last vestige of British imperialism on the island of Ireland, it should one day break free from its colonial master. By now, this has not come to pass, but the Good Friday Peace Agreement has cleared the way for a novel, if possibly provisional, experiment in quasi-postcolonialism. And this was effected not by any real changes in territorial claims, but by changes in culture and mentality—in part effected by the group associated with Field Day and more broadly with the cultural critics who spoke of Ireland in colonial and postcolonial terms. For, by recasting the old nationalism without losing sympathy with it, they succeeded, paradoxically, in diverting Irish attention away from an insular nationalism that could now be decried, as Deane did decry it, as an "atavism," and rechanneling Irish and Irish nationalist attentions to the ways in which any nationalism, including Ireland's, could be a worthy cultural expression of modernity rather than a narrow and sectarian archaic superstition.

The history of this striking achievement in such a marginal island as Ireland has yet to be written. What is clear at this juncture, however, is that, with the new stage of Anglo-Irish relations and the new possibilities for both Northern Ireland and the Republic of Ireland as postcolonial entities on the European and world stage, the intellectual movement which helped give rise to it risks falling into irrelevance. Irish postcolonial studies must enter a new phase. To continue its project it must, I suggest, determinedly fix its gaze outward, beyond Ireland. This reorientation might proceed on both the synchronic and diachronic axes: synchronically, Irish postcolonialism needs to forge links to other postcolonialisms if it is to continue to dispel the atavistic tendency that it condemned in the old "parochial" nationalism of Ireland. This work has already begun: David Lloyd has written eloquently of parallels between Ireland and the Philippines, while Joe Cleary has written strikingly of the nature of partition and opposition to it in Palestine and Ireland (Lloyd 1999; Cleary 2002). It also needs to reenvision Irish history; now, given the greater confidence that casting Ireland's case as the vanguard of twentieth-century anti-colonial movements has engendered, it can reexamine without any sense of threat the nature of the cultural relations which presaged, and precipitated, the anti-colonial insurgency. It is an experiment in such work that I practice here.[2] The turn to comparative work, and the return to a study of past relations, need not be mutually exclusive, but on the contrary, as I will show, to rehistoricize is to point to the inevitability of new kinds of comparison in the present.

The thesis of this chapter is this: what we think of as a construction of emergent Irish nationalism, modern Irish postcolonial identity, was in considerable part constructed in contestation with, and in reaction to, British discourses on Ireland as they developed in the course of the nineteenth century. On the face of it, this is not a controversial statement. It is a well known truism of modernity that although each nationalism is unique in the national features it celebrates, the structure of nationalism as an ideology is, nevertheless, everywhere the same. This structure of thinking and affect was largely developed during the nineteenth century in continental Europe, and the conduit through which it came to the attention of the emergent English speaking, Irish middle class, and the intellectual cadre within that class that emerged around the mid-century, was largely a British one. At the same time, partly in response to an interest in such thinking about nations (a sentiment that would become public policy in 1914 when Britain claimed to be fighting the First World War for "the freedom of small nations"), partly in response to events in Ireland, such as the Great Famine of 1845 to 1849, and particularly as developments in Irish politics affected England (through, for example, such violent episodes as the Fenian bombing which led to execution of the "Manchester Martyrs"), British discourse on Ireland was undergoing a massive change. My claim here, moreover, is that primarily this change did not have to do with Ireland at all. Rather, it was the result of Britain's growing awareness of itself as an empire; this, indeed, was what British culture itself took from the sense that each country must have a nationalism of its own, constructing itself as something greater than a nation in that it possessed colonies on the grandest scale. Now this sense of being "the empire on which the sun never set" was not developed in the course of attending to Ireland. Rather, I claim, it was worked out in the course of the nineteenth-century, largely in relation to two areas: the Indian subcontinent and Africa.

Here it is the British fascination with Africa which we will examine. This fascination led to a developing, continuously altering view of Africa and a continuous, dispersed, and changing discourse on "Africanness" in British culture, which provided a spectacular counterpoint to, and at the same time a guarantee of, Britain itself as an imperial nation. I contend that this Victorian discourse on Africanness was so strong that it provided in part the model for British thinking on other, possibly less strange, worlds else-where—and that the first of these was Ireland. If we read British accounts of Africa and Ireland throughout the century in tandem, we can discern a remarkable congruence in aspects of accounts of both. In this sense, it was the British themselves who first thought of Ireland as a colony, because they were thinking of their African possessions in colonial terms—and it was they who taught the Irish to think likewise.

Before we consider in detail the permutations of nineteenth century British discourse on Africa and Ireland, some words of caution are in order. First, the terrains of both discourses are vast and encompass within them an extraordinary range of opinions and ideological viewpoints: from Fred-erick Engels' claim, in a letter to Karl Marx after he had visited Ireland in 1856, that here was "England's oldest colony,"[3] to the more droll observa-tions of such novels as Trollope's *The McDermotts of Ballycloran* and Thack-eray's *Barry Lyndon*; from the romantic glamour of the Irish landscape evoked in Tennyson's "The Splendor Falls . . ."; to the anomalous, even grotesque evidential texts of the Anglo-Irish *fin-de-siecle*, such as the letters incriminating Parnell that became known as the "Pigott forgeries" of 1887, or the infamous "Casement Diaries" partly made public after Casement was condemned to death in a London court for his part in the 1916 Easter rebellion. Casement's diaries, however, could well serve as the final ex-hibits in this paper for they, perhaps more than any others in the archive of the modern British discourse on Ireland, embody at once the depths and ef-fects of the British attitude to Africa and to Ireland. The existence of the diaries alone directs us to think of these two discourses comparatively, and to search for trends discernable in both.

Second, we must not only keep in mind the interrelation of British dis-courses on Africa and on Ireland, but the ways in which British discourse on Ireland and what might be called the Irish discourse of self-creation were often intertwined, so that each developed through prolonged points of intercultural contact. In this intimacy, the Irish were continually "meet-ing the British," who set out not only to dominate them, but to tell them who they were. (Further complicating matters, part of the ostensibly British discourse on Africa was in fact Irish, particularly because a major recruiting ground for colonial administrators and officers was the younger sons and assorted members of the Anglo-Irish gentry. The poet Richard Murphy's recent memoir, *The Kick*, with its details of his childhood in the residency in Sri Lanka following those of his days in Mayo, is a late entry into this subgenre of imperialist writing; while, in the manner of many of his poems, it also manages a kind of desire for a postcolonial, anti-imperial future). The clarifying value of postcolonial Irish studies lies in its insistence on a firm distinction being maintained between Irish and British discourses on Irishness; it has been the cry of its adversaries, the so-called "revisionists," to remember that in practice, partitions between the two traditions, when they existed, were permeable in the extreme. What is needed is a model of intercultural contact which preserves the distinction as a working one, but which is always aware of the interaction.

An effective way to characterize this discursive *agon* for a postcolonial critic might be as follows: the Irish could (even if, in fact, they rarely did) answer back. In one of the earliest interventions in postcolonial literary criticism on a global scale, a group of Australians characterized worldwide writing in English by people from former dominions of Britain as "the Empire writes back" (Ashcroft et al. 1989).[4] The point is, however, that, as far as Britain and its empire went, this was a belated exercise, reliving a trauma in order to exorcise it, a textual exercise temporally disjunct from the presently existing political order. The difference in the Irish case was that, to a limited degree—limited by the few possibilities for the Irish themselves to participate in the public sphere even in Ireland, let alone in Britain—the Irish could respond to British characterizations. An awareness of this possibility always underlies British pre-independence discourse on Ireland. On the other hand, since there was virtually no possibility that the subjugated African could respond to characterizations of Africa and its people, colonial and racial fantasies of the most extreme sort were given free rein. It was these fantasies and tropes of otherness and domination, developed on a terrain that could not answer back, that were then applied to Ireland. Some of them, indeed, turned out to have been tried on the Irish earlier. It is this African-Irish discursive intersection that I will map in more detail now.

Ireland *in Media Res*

What one discovers in a survey of a broad range of books on the African colonies, and almost as many on Ireland, written between 1830 and the end of the century, as well as all of the articles on colonial matters and on Ireland in such major nineteenth-century British journals as the *Edinburgh Review*, the *Westminster Review* and the *Quarterly Review*, is this: there was a remarkable congruence in modes of British writing on colonial Africa and on Ireland in this period. These were the years in which sub-Saharan Africa was being discovered, traversed and written about in alluring detail by the likes of Dr. Livingstone, and, of course, mapped. Ireland, in the same period, was in a sense being rediscovered; it too had its own major mapping project in the Ordinance Survey—with the kinds of imperial ends in view that Brian Friel has made famous in his play *Translations*.[5] Ways of thinking and writing about Africa and Ireland grew more complex throughout the century in a remarkably similar manner.

The British effort to describe Africa in this period provides one of the greatest and most astounding archives for the study of cultural othering in modernity. By now, the mechanisms by which the various strands of this or any imperial discourse structure themselves to effect this work of othering are so familiar as scarcely to need citation, in particular through the work of Gayatri Spivak, Homi Bhabha, and, most of all, Edward Said. British nineteenth-century writing on Africa hovers above the actual enterprise of colonialism then rapidly being developed; it was most commonly subliterary writing that exists either as reportage, colonial propaganda, or the description of wonders. While the colonizers were busy staking out always more extended territories, the discourse of colonialism strained to push back the boundaries of what might be said. The goal of the discourse—especially as an *ad hoc* reporting of wonders and "discoveries" gave way to a set of protocols with the trappings of scientific inquiry—was ostensibly to completely "know" the "native," the intriguing other, her difference guaranteed as it were by the racial difference at the heart of each inquiry. What one senses in all of this colonial writing, the wonder-filled and pompous tomes describing African adventures and successes, is an ambivalent, dangerous astonishment at the fact of the native's existence. Here, ultimately, was an other who posed a threat, and whose otherness meant that they would never be absorbed.

In the complex efforts to know this "other," Ireland and its peculiar natives became a privileged locus of discussion in British writing. As Fenian terrorism and the varied attacks that came to be known as "outrages" made very clear, Ireland, in very concrete, immediate ways, was much more of a threat to British well-being than the otherness of the African could ever be to the British sense of self. Ostensibly, however, Victorian liberal guilt, rather than the African narrative of colonial adventure and derring-do, dominated British discussions of the "sister island," which was officially absorbed into the United Kingdom by the Act of Union of 1800. Ireland as a familiar, yet acknowledged strange and "other" territory, became in this period a *media res* between Britain and her new territories. Ireland was a ground on which new discursive tropes might be tested, and a resting point at which writers who had absorbed the more full-bodied discourse of

African colonialism could apply their patterns to a territory that was less problematic and less strange.

British writing about Africa is most extensive in the years of initial expansion into the continent from 1830 to 1870; this period also saw the greatest transformation in the British discourse on Ireland and its inhabitants. In both cases, three broad stages can be discerned. The first, early writing on "The Dark Continent" is a discourse obsessed with and aware of limits, remarkably tentative in the information which it imparts, often not organized but relayed episodically, and with the note of wonder still intact or even accentuated. Many of the volumes from these years are travelogues and accounts of voyages; they are the memoirs whose tropes would be rifled toward the end of the century in order to put together the popular imperial adventure novels that became the earliest pulp fiction: the books by John Buchan and Karl May. These early travelogues, coming soon after the abolition of slavery in England, which itself had been cast as a liberal rationale for British expansion into Africa, often constructed their narratives around the trope of the relation between master and slave. In English writing on Ireland in the same years (1830–50), there is a wealth of memorable travelogues too, from the wanderings of W.M. Thackeray, disguised as Michaelangelo Titmarsh, who opens his *Irish Sketchbook* with an account of his adventures in a very shabby Shelborne Hotel (1843), to the grandiose touring of Mrs. Hall, whose book, *Ireland, Its Scenery and Character* (1841), with its elegant plates, became a standard in gentry and genteel libraries. As in the African travelogues, even if the note of wonder is slightly muted and the comedy underlined, the style tends towards the impressionistic and the episodic, and information is primarily imparted through the anecdote.

The second stage is characterized by attempts to systematize much of the scattered information of the first. The pronouncements of science took over in this period. This was the era of ethnology, a study centered on the form of the human skull. Ethnologists outlined a hierarchy of the physical and mental attributes of the races described, beginning inevitably with the physically handsome, morally advanced Anglo-Saxon, and ending with the "Savage African" who was characterized by shortness of stature, protruding belly, and repulsive morality. In prose on Ireland in the two decades between the Famine of 1845 to 1848 and the Fenian rebellion of 1867, one can chart a remarkably similar progression. Characters like the Paddies and Judies of Mrs. Hall's novels contributed to the notion of the "typical Irishman,"[6] whose character had been limned, of course, by extensive English accounts of Ireland in the preceding centuries, most famously perhaps by Edmund Spenser's account of the "wilde Irish" in his *View of the Present State of Ireland*, written at the time of the Plantation of Munster, and given an added surge in the course of the "First Celtic Revival," as Seamus Deane has characterized it, in such strange texts as Caroline Lamb's *Glenavron*.

Despite the influence of the eighteenth-century infusion of Ossianism into the stereotype of the Irish, however, it was only in the mid-nineteenth-century, in such venues as learned, scientific articles in the *Anthropological Review*, that the Irish subject was scientifically recognized as "the Celt." This least regarded, because it was the least overtly incendiary, stage of mid-century British writing on Ireland was thus the most insidiously influential.

The third stage led the British discourse on Irishness into abstract and theoretical arenas, after the prevalence of concrete description in the first stage and the "scientific" analyses of the second. Now, a concern with the matter of Ireland became the business of the leading intellectuals of the day in England. By this point, colonial discourse, with its narrative trajectory, whether anecdotal or quasi-scientific, to know and then to categorize the native as other, had been accepted as a given. For figures such as John Stuart Mill, Thomas Carlyle, and Matthew Arnold, the worthwhile intellectual endeavor went beyond the categorization of the colonial other in relation to the self, to wonder if the homeland and Britishness itself might not be profitably redefined in the light of such diversities. In writing on Ireland, this stage centers on work called forth by the Fenian uprising of 1867. Carlyle had been the author of some reactionary polemics which compared the freed slaves of Britain's colonies in the Caribbean with what he considered the lazy Irish peasantry; the twin pillars of this phase, however, were Matthew Arnold's *On The Study of Celtic Literature* (1867) and John Stuart Mill's *Britain and Ireland* (1868).[7] With the publication of these essays, it could be said that Ireland was at the forefront of British colonial discourse as a whole. To England's "Victorian sages," Ireland's muted difference was more easily imagined than more exotic cultural landscapes and their inhabitants. Calls for a Chair in African Studies at Oxford did not immediately follow the calls for a Chair of Celtic studies (which Arnold championed); nevertheless, the acceptance of one would be an avenue for the eventual acceptance of the other.

These, then, are the three stages in the development of the last major phase of colonial discourse in Britain. I would now like to show how the influence of the discourses on Irishness and Africanness operated in practice upon one another. In doing this, one should keep in mind a series of questions. First, what effect did the discourse of African colonialism have on the development of the English image of the Irish in the same period? Next, assuming that there was such an effect, and adhering to the view that the (second) Gaelic Revival arose in part in reaction to the British views expressed about Ireland and the Irishness in these years, most famously responding to the work of Arnold, to what extent can we claim, therefore, that it was the permutations of the discourse which the imperial British developed to elucidate Africa to themselves, which gave rise, indirectly and in a kind of mirror image, to the Gaelic Revival in Ireland?

To what degree, and within the sightlines of what field of vision, should this transmission of an ideologeme across apparently enemy lines matter? For a revised history of the Gaelic Revival, should it not lead us to consider the achievement of that cultural movement to be less an imaginative self-styling which the Irish, taking a hint from Arnold, effected in these years—less the creation of a set of unique features that might constitute some credibly authentic self-made Irish identity—and more the engagement of a potential new Irish ruling class in a kind of strategic practice of self-stereotyping which mimicked the racist othering by the colonizer of the native peoples? This would be to read the Gaelic Revival in the light of Frantz Fanon's famous denunciation of the treasonous native middleclass. Further, might it not be claimed that if this racist othering of the Africans by the British turned out, historically, to be a prerequisite for the cultural nationalism created and developed in Ireland, then this racist othering exists too as a kind of unsaid in the new nationalist ideologeme? This would lead us to think of Irish nationalism's inability to deal with minorities within Ireland, particularly the northern loyalists, and its tendency to resent its minorities under the sign of the mechanisms of displaced abjection. The issue of parallels between African and Irish discourse on the part of British imperialists has the potential, therefore, to unsettle some of the most sanctified assumptions concerning the development and uses of Irish nationalism as expressed in the Gaelic Revival. Lastly, it might lead us to a theory of "comparative othering" as a key feature of the crucial imperial component in the rapidly evolving British nationalism in these years. Here, we will look in more detail at the interconnections of African and Irish othering by British discourses as we consider their effects.

Othering Duplicity/the Duplicity of Othering

When the *Quarterly Review* attributed the "elements of exaggeration," which it detected in Mrs. Hall's account of her Irish travels, *Ireland, Its Scenery and Character* (1841), to her "Irish extraction" it managed to stereotype the Irish from both ends (Anon. 1845: 505): it cited an Irish stereotype to suggest its falsity, but then blamed it on the very Irishness of the author of the book. Yet in one sense the reviewer is correct: the book *does* exaggerate. Yet this exaggeration is not merely a property of Irish travelogues; rather, it is the foremost attribute of British colonial travel accounts in these years. The texts in which the note of wonder and a carnival of exaggeration predominate are the numerous travelogues describing adventures in Africa. The colonizer-explorers in these books overcome difficulty after difficulty in order to reach yet another wonder, all reported excitedly as exaggerated spectacle. Works such as A. Cornwall Harris's sensational *Ethiopian Travels: The Highlands of Ethiopia Described* of 1844, H. Clapperton's *Journal of A Second Expedition into the Interior of Africa* (1829) and Richard and John Lander's *Journal to Explore the Course and Termination of the Niger* (1830) are generally willing to celebrate the use of force among the natives who are wholeheartedly portrayed as "others," mostly revealed as liars and often as thieves.[8] The first major British book in this genre of explorer-adventurers in "savage Africa" had been Mungo Park's *Travels in the Interior Districts of Africa* (1860), which appeared as early as 1799. Repeatedly excerpted and reprinted in the following century, it was the inspiration for countless explorers and the model for their writings; the edition now most commonly available comes from 1860.[9] Against this glut of wonder-filled, first-stage racist texts, let us examine two episodes from journals of travel to Ireland in this period.

The Irish travelogues transformed the sweating adventurers into respectable Victorian travelers, and the "African savages" were replaced by mere "Irish natives," but the drama of contact, and the stereotypes delineating otherness betray a striking consistency. The episodes I chose to consider are recounted by Thomas Carlyle and the Halls. The first is Thomas Carlyle's reaction, as described in his *Reminiscences of My Irish Journey*, to some begging children he encounters on the bleak road to Ballina, County Mayo, in the west of Ireland; the second, the Halls' reaction to the Achill Island Mission, an effort by evangelical Protestants to aid and convert the impoverished inhabitants of the extremely poor and remote island of Achill, off the coast of the same County Mayo. Carlyle's coach-and-four passes children who stand half-naked outside their parent's cottage, begging from the passing coach. The sage's reaction: he wonders if their mother has told them to "strip and beg" (Carlyle 1882: 154). Mrs. Hall tells of the proselytizing mission in best journalistic fashion by recounting the story of "a poor wretched-looking boy about thirteen years of age, clothed in rags, who had been dismissed from the orphanage" (Hall & Hall 1841: 394). The first factor which structures these accounts is the tacit awareness of a governing master-slave relationship between visitor and native which is at the heart of every colonial travelogue at this stage. In the Irish cases, each of the authors turns to teenage children as representative natives: on the verge of independence, but clearly in no sense even ready or equipped for self-reliance. The character tacitly contrasted to each of these is the author, a well-dressed Victorian potential-philanthropist viewing this fixed, static and childish misery from the high, and moving, perspective of their carriage. Each account begins as a "tale of wretchedness," implying that it will concern Irish poverty, but is transformed in the telling into a "tale of deception," of native lying. Carlyle's beggar children, he claims, are possibly not as poor as they look; Hall's vagrant (she reminds us of her suspicion) may be lying. The master-reporters excuse themselves for this suspicion by making the real lie be the one they always expect from the person who at the outset they portrayed as a victim.

The pathos of the children, then, turns out to be exaggerated only in order to heighten the pathos of the lie which they, it is revealed, have themselves concocted in advance. The greater the pathos the narrators illicit for their victims, the greater their own credibility, within the economy of the telling, in calling these subjects liars. This is a discourse deeply concerned with lying, in which what is substituted for African wonders, that is, the appalling spectacles of the "condition of Ireland," are constantly, and explicitly shown as lies, the revealed lies of the native inhabitants. Ireland's otherness, in this way, is constantly revealed as a mirage; in fact, the only real otherness of the country is located in these texts in descriptions of nature, scenes denuded of their inhabitants. In this sense, the work of othering the Irish, whether in the text by the reactionary Carlyle or the liberal Mrs. Hall, turns out to be staged as a failure. First, the lies invariably and repeatedly imputed to the natives find their reflection in the suspicion, even on the part of such early readers of these texts as the *Quarterly Review* reviewer, that the authors themselves at least exaggerated as well. Thus, this strategy of imputing lies relies on the authors generating a rhetoric of suspicion to propel their texts, a suspicion which spreads virus-like to undermine every certainty in each text. These Irish travelogues turn out to be unstable texts, undermined by suspicion and alert for lying, in which the attempt to fix the Irish as other is undermined by a textuality of deceit.

Ireland, in fact, precisely because it was, as Engels would put it writing of *his* visit, "England's oldest colony," turned out, in terms of the discursive task of othering that was the cultural arm of imperialism, to be England's Achilles heel. Ireland was the place where the colonial stereotypes would not stick, as much as the travel writers, casting themselves of explorers of the wild regions of Ireland, tried to make them do so. What occurred was that British writing on Ireland could not maintain the absolute dichotomies—White/black, civilized/savage, cultivated/wild—on which writing on the colonies, and very especially writing on then-being-discovered Africa, needed to rely. As such, the discourse on Irishness posed a threat to the imperial othering discourse as a whole. It was partly in response to the threat that that discourse's certainties might altogether evaporate that, at the mid-century, the next stage of imperial discourse on the other rapidly developed. Its certainties would be less open.

In constantly suspecting a lie on the native's part, and hence a native secrecy, the first stage of imperial discourse suggested the way to further questions, even if it testily suggested it could answer them from the confines of its reinforced egocentrism. Moreover, as the readership at home became jaded by wonders, whether they were African feasters (regarded suspiciously as "cannibals") or Irish beggars (read, with equal suspicion, as fakes), a more subdued second stage of colonist discourse—the first steps in a questioning one—came into being. For this second stage of colonial discursivity, the focus would be more fully on the "native," rather than on the native merely as a feature in, and obstacle to moving across, territory. Interrogativity would be the prevalent idiom, and inquiry, with all its scientific and measuring trappings, rather than mere reportage, would be the engine of the narratives. The questioners often operated under the aegis of learned societies, such as the Anthropological Society of London. Examples from Africa are the famous *Travels and Researches*, as he insisted on calling them, of the explorer Dr. Livingstone (1857), whose work marks a bridge between the earlier notion of the uncovering of wonders and the new systematization of facts.

Works of this type were concerned to perform the following tasks: to describe the differences between tribes, to describe in detail their behavior and (to the extent that they could be gleaned) their customs, and, very often, to evaluate their capacity for fighting. The principle of comparison, not only between tribes, but, ultimately, between the "free African," as the natives began to be called, and the Englishman (or, on a very few occasions, English woman), undergirded the language of classification. Much of the writing of this stage, despite its veneer of scientific certitude in arriving at a truth through patient description, classification and inquiry, in fact vacillates unpredictably between a yearning for a known past in which the dichotomy between savage native and civilized colonist was clear and provided vast scope for both missionary and colonist, and the more nervous dreams of a utopian future. Thus, if one of the symptomatic nightmares of this stage was the disapproval, which crops up regularly, of the idea of "going native," the new persona of the imperialist tended to be closer to that of the missionary rather than the adventurer. The future, for the new stage of imperialist discourse inflected by missionary language, would be based on "the capabilities of the Negro for civilization;"[10] meanwhile, certainties could be reinscribed upon the present, and the work of othering ensured, by applying to Africa, and eventually to Ireland, "the true principles of inquiry into human origins."[11]

This was the task of the pseudo-science of ethnology, which, centered on the measuring of bodies and in particular of skulls, went to enormous lengths to classify and sub-classify every people, ethnic group and tribe in the world. However, if the missionary talk of civilizing the natives gave rise to the traumatic notion of an eventual sameness between natives and Britisher, thus once again leading to the breakdown of the imposition of otherness, the science of ethnology in its certitudes contained the implication of such a potential erasure of difference as well. Ethnology classified people on a principle of degrees of difference, and this difference was thought of in terms of historical time: that is, westerners were thought of as more developed, the natives as primitive. This effectively displaced the anxiety about potential sameness on to the diachronic axis, pushing it onto the conveyor belt of time, where it might be safely assumed that the African other might never catch up. Here again, however, the Irish proved a disquieting inbetween "race," clearly further back on the line of development than their neighbors, but whose backwardness was, as it were, liable to slippage. Between Englishman and African, the marginal peoples of Europe could be cast as a bulwark, at once reassuring to racist othering impulses and comforting to professed missionary desires to colonize. Irishness, more vehemently than Welshness or Scottishness, seemed at the same time to represent the impossibility of the project of imagining an ideal "Britishness," a project which implicitly equated Englishness and Britishness, but which might have been willing to imagine a more inclusive subject-citizen of the Union.

Anglo-Saxon Revival?

The Irish enter the tables of the ethnologists, then, along with the Welsh, the Scots, the people of the Balkans, and every other marginal European territory, as "aboriginals," whose previous primitivism could be quite easily imagined when one had qualms about imagining one's own: "Prichard assures us that the aborigines of Europe were in a more degraded state than the Negroes now are..." (Hunt 1864: 42). As the Irish came to be read through the ethnologist's eyes, the concept of "the Celt" rapidly assumed contours that had a clarity and predictability which the scientists found difficult to detect in the contours of the Celtic skull. "It seems a suitable undertaking," said the *Anthropological Review* in 1860, to determine "the typical form of the modern Celtic cranium; but the results have hitherto been of very indefinite character." The writer forged on, notwithstanding:

> They [the Celts] have a head rather elongated, and the forehead narrow but slightly arched. The brow is low, straight and bushy; the eyes and hair are light, the nose and mouth large, and the cheekbones high. The general contour of the face is angular and the expression harsh. (Wilson 1865: 63)

Even in the scientific journals, the distance between observation and moralistic judgment was negligible; ungainly physical characteristics were invariably taken as the keys to "character," so the race itself could be assigned a character through observation of its members. Just as we saw in the case of the first "explorer" discourse, where a vision of wretchedness could become the basis for a moral judgment—that the native was a liar—so too even more seamlessly in this stage, the observation of the physical appearance of the native became the template for the anthropologist to make a judgment, inevitably derogatory, about the condition of this native's "race":

Why does the wretched man cling to the filthy hovel and scanty patch of ground? It is natural to his race. The Celt clings with tenacity to his patch of ground, because he has no self-confidence, no innate courage to meet the forest and the desert; without a leader he feels lost. He is entirely wanting in those qualities of enterprise and self-reliance which make the Saxon *par excellence* the colonizer of the globe . . . . With the Saxon, all is order, wealth, comfort; with the Celt, disorder, riot, destruction, waste. (unsigned review, *Anthropological Review*, vol. VI, 1868: 137)

It was this image of "the Celt," validated by extensive pseudo-science, that was then popularized as the simianized Irishman. This figure, with prognathized features, apish gait and torn clothes, who leers from the pages of Punch cartoons, and later from the cartoons of the new yellow journalism, was inevitably rife in times of "unrest" in Ireland; it reached a frenzy with the Fenian rebellion of 1867, and again during the "Land War" of the 1880's and after.[12] In these cartoon depictions, the British imperialist discourse on Africa and on Ireland is rendered as one, under the sign of popularized versions of the new science of Darwinism. Both Irish and African natives could now be shown as ape-like; in the new popular press, the Irish-African analogy was played up with a vengeance to insult both sets of subjects. Othering as jingoism in the penny papers clearly had no trouble at all with the notion of Ireland as a colony on a par with Nigeria or "British West Africa."

Therefore, while in the broad new field of popular culture the comparison of Africa and Ireland in the British imperial consciousness was becoming a given, an intellectual sea-change was occurring among the most distinguished British intellectuals in their level of attention and attitude to Ireland. It has been remarkably seldom asked why this was so. A provisional answer, I suggest, is that the ambivalence opened up in each case by the application to Ireland of the first two stages of Victorian British discourse on Africa left an anxiety which gnawed, in a fundamental way, upon the Englishman's own sense of national selfhood, an ostensibly supranational or inclusive Britishness that was in fact fundamentally reliant on English or "Anglo-Saxon" ethnic identity. Certainly Matthew Arnold, in his most famous work on the Celts, *On The Study of Celtic Literature*, the text of a series of Lectures given at Oxford University in fulfillment of his duties as Chair of Poetry there in the years 1865 to 1866, turns to the Celts as a counterpoint to his preoccupation with what he attacks as the "philistinism" of Saxon—that is, British—culture. Here too we can see the desire to imagine a "British" identity which could possibly include ethnic elements other than those of Englishness alone. Yet in Arnold's writing one can understand that the vehemence with which the othering of colonial natives was carried out, whether by the early explorer-adventure narratives or later by the pseudo-scientific ethnographers, has as its impetus a desire to transform for modernity the British national-imperial sense of self. Arnold's tincture of liberal guilt about the Irish, therefore, is always contained within a larger concern for the reform of the British "character."

Arnold, under cover of apparently praising the Irish "faery dew" as a counterpoint to the British stolidity he decries, in fact acts as the intellectual arm of the imperialist project, ready to rifle the colonies—the first being Ireland—for their cultural resources if these can be made to enrich the culture of the imperial metropole. He is ostensibly campaigning for a Chair of Celtic studies at Oxford, but this will be a Chair of dead Celtic languages, because, as he is happy to report, with considerable approval, as living, spoken languages these have all but died out (Johnson 1996). As John Kelleher has pointed out, his essay is in no sense an attempt to understand the essence of the Irish; his very examples, as Kelleher notes, betray his ignorance of his subject (1950: 197–221). Rather, accepting the ethnological racism of the second stage of Victorian colonialism at face value, and apparently, as the critic Dillon Johnson remarks incredulously, believing it, Arnold managed, no doubt under the influence of the remaining strands of romatic Ossianism from the first Celtic Revival, to transform the negative and derogatory stereotypes of the Irish as violent, ape-like, and untrustworthy, into positive ones. Arnold's language in praise of the Celts, therefore, walks a kind of knife-edge: when he tells us they are "turbulent . . . ariel . . . titanic . . . full of ardor, rebellion, Romanism, superstition . . . hauntings . . . a passion for revolt" and in "indomitable reaction against the despotism of fact," we can see how his language takes the familiar terms from a stereotype of the Irish as violent (even as terrorists, certainly as Fenians) and shifts their register slightly to recast them as terms within a lexicon of the sublime (Arnold 1867: 116, 102).

Arnold's brilliant ruse, in the iteration of these types of words, is to keep the old stereotype as a memory behind the new praise. He keeps the two attitudes in contention at once, the old, violent one barely concealed behind the screen of the other. As such, he manages with considerable grace to model by sleight-of-intellect a standard imperialist bifurcation, in which a rabid condemnation of the native could cohabit with a meager admiration for the exotic quality of their otherness, which would subsequently be the feature of many varieties of imperial discourse. All of this is, all the while, resolutely put at the service of enhancing British resources and British culture. Arnold in effect keeps the master-slave rhetoric of the first stage of imperial discourse, allies it to the ethnological distinctions of the second, and creates a metaphor of "Celtic magic," but only as an entity theorizable as a desirable element in a superior British psyche. This in turn, he believes, will end the "unrest," for the Irish themselves, doomed to become more British under the inevitable pressure of progress, will keep a whiff of their Celticism just as the British will absorb it also, until "they are part of ourselves, the composite British gent" (Arnold 1867: 116).

While the gall of this, to an Irish reader at any rate, is astonishing, it should not blind us to the self-serving success of its ideological work. What Arnold appears to achieve, in his juggling of the old stereotype and his overt valorization of the new one, is to close down the ambivalence which had marked the two earlier discourses. Or does he? What he hopes to do, I suggest, is to neutralize Irishness as the weak point of Britain's cultural project of imperial othering, by recasting Irish "turbulence" as a wholly desirable extreme factor of his own "sweetness and light." Absorbing this turbulence, once Arnold has revamped it as an ethereal spirituality, will, he claims, leave the British more refined. The irony would seem to be that no one believed him but the intellectual avant-garde among the Irish themselves. As has often been acknowledged, Arnold's work was a major influence on Yeats, Wilde, and the whole cultural project of the second Celtic Revival; in Seamus Deane's essay, "Arnold, Burke and the Celts," he traces the whole Revivalist project back to Arnold's essay (1985: 17–27). Surely the fact that the major cultural plank underpinning modern Irish postcolonial nationalism originated in a pillar of the British intellectual establishment at the height of Victoria's reign should give us pause. As Declan Kiberd puts it in his magisterial *Inventing Ireland*, "The strategy of the [Celtic] revivalists thus became clear: for bad words substitute good, for *superstitious* use *religious*, for *backward*, say *traditional*, for *irrational*, suggest *emotional* . . . . The danger was that under the guise of freedom, a racist slur might be sanitized and worn with pride by its very victims" (Kiberd 1995: 32). What exactly, we must ask ourselves, is the danger to which he refers?

Disappearing Complicities

Keeping in mind each of these three stages of British imperial discourse on Africa, and the parallel discourse on Irishness, one can better understand the specific force of the horror which underlies the observations of Charles Kingsley on his visit to Ireland—the observations which opened this paper. I have argued here that Irish travelogues for British audiences from 1830 onwards employed the tropes of otherness that had been so successfully and so unselfconsciously used in the numerous accounts of African exploration published in the same years. However, in the case of Ireland, attempts to render that colony as a succession of wonders and to portray the Irish as unquestionably other were undermined by a rhetoric of suspicion and accusations of lying. The British, in other words, failed to convince themselves that the Irish were as fully and completely "other" as they succeeded in convincing themselves was the case with the Africans. They failed to make the Irish, in their eyes, black. It is an unselfconscious awareness of precisely this, and a horror of its implications, that animates Kingsley's prose, rendering it a real example of imperialist panic. Kingsley very literally wants the Irish to be black: "To see white chimpanzees is dreadful; if they were black . . ." (Kingsley 1881: 112).

It traumatizes Kingsley to admit that the skin of the Irish is "as white as ours." It is this trauma which Arnold assuages, with the invention, for the Irish case, of an emollient brand of Irish primitivism. The Irish intellectuals and writers of the second Celtic Revival took Arnold at his word, for them too the word *violent* would always be behind the word *turbulent*, just as the word *superstitious* would always be behind the word *religion*. Even more, behind the wholesale adoption of Arnold's positive stereotype, was the history of the stages of the attempt to racially "other" the native Africans, and the native Irish, as a way to enable a sense of British superiority. To jettison, along with Arnold, those negative stereotypes was to deny the chance to hate their oppressor's tradition properly, to deny in fact that Britain had any say (apart from the case of a few distinguished liberal friends of Ireland such as Arnold) in creating to a substantial degree the identity that fostered Irish nationalism. It was also to refuse to see to its fullest extent the kind of cultural subjection which the Irish held in common with the peoples of Britain's other colonies. It was in a real sense to smooth over, in the cause of an apparently idealized version of Irish culture, the most profound cultural distortions and malformations in the Irish-British relation. In an attempt to cauterize the wound of racism, it meant a tacit agreement to be silent about it, even where, as in the Irish case (as in all cases of racism) there was a deep ambivalence (as the Kingsley quote exemplifies) at the center of the racist enterprise. Arnold's lectures glorified British identity even as he appeared to scold it; the Gaelic revivalists, by taking Arnold on his word about Celtic passion, effected suppressions—of race, of otherness, of subalternity—which would haunt the Revival, the anti-imperial rebellion, and above all, the culture of the postcolonial state to which it gave rise.

Provocation: Meeting the British

> We met the British in the dead of winter.
> The sky was lavender....
> They gave us six fishhooks
> And two blankets embroidered with smallpox.
> Paul Muldoon, "Meeting the British"

When the Irish accepted this gift of imperial race discourse from the British as the basis of Irish national identity, most of the consequences, inevitably, accrued to the idea of Irishness alone. The glaring exception concerned British identity—as the Irish would come to represent it. One hears almost wholly, in this essay and elsewhere, of how the British stereotyped the Irish, but it is well worth turning the tables for a moment to look at how Irish writing of the Celtic Revival and since, and particularly recent writing from Ireland, represents Britishness. How did Irish culture look back at Britain itself? My thesis here is this: given the strongly racial element of the British colonial discourse of the "native," a strand of which, however apparently benign, the Celtic revivalists adopted as their own model of Irishness, these very revivalists and their literary heirs would inevitably look back at the British, and read them, through a discourse that was rife with racism itself. This was a reverse racism, a resentful race discourse from below. Further, since all racist discourse is a type of hate writing, I want to claim that Irish writing on Britishness is infused with no less an emotion than hate itself. This hate can be blamed on residual anger over the centuries of colonial oppression. This is the white-hot anger of which the psychiatrist and theorist of the Algerian anti-colonial revolution Frantz Fanon wrote so passionately in *The Wretched of the Earth,* when he spoke of how the native detests the imperial oppressor with a venom which the oppressor, even in their most liberal and missionary mood, should never underestimate (1968: 35–106). In the Irish case, however, this never-to-be-underestimated hate is generally repressed, giving the nagging awareness, always present, that the dominant postcolonial version of Irish subjectivity was accepted as a gift from the colonizer; it should be seen as more muted, but certainly no less intense, for all that.

What we can discern again and again in Irish fiction are scenes of encounter between Irishness and Britishness, where the English, bearing gifts, are regarded resentfully by the Irish. It is as if the final major drama of cultural contact in the late-colonial period—that imaginary occasion where the definition of Irishness generated by Arnold was accepted with open arms by Yeats and the revivalists—is repeated compulsively because of an awareness of its compromised qualities. These repeated, staged encounters are deeply ambivalent, but they show the newly independent Irish looking upon the British with an eye of utter withering contempt. Seldom are specific reasons for this contempt articulated; the lack of specification is the point mostly being made. These British figures of fun and worse are hated with a sullen fury often merely because they are British. In what follows, I will first show how the pattern of these scenes of resentful encounter were developed, and then compulsively reiterated, in the works of the author of the postcolonial moment who, on the face of it, most overtly rejected Celtic revival pieties: James Joyce. I go on to show how, in the early years of the new Irish state, it was the sons and daughters of the Anglo-Irish gentry, the authors of the so-called "Big House" novels, who, in an exercise of deeply ambivalent imitation-reverse-racism, colluded in casting the British (whom they felt had let them down) also as pathetic buffoons. My example here is Elizabeth Bowen's 1929 novel of the Irish anti-colonial guerilla war of independence, *The Last September*. It is in Irish fiction of the last quarter of the twentieth century, however, that this anti-Britishness has become a commonplace. In many cases, wrath against the British, on the part of Irish writers, has fallen upon the heads of Irish immigrants to Britain, especially when encounters are represented between members of this huge group and the Irish who remained at home in post-independence Ireland. I examine two such moments, in novels by John McGahern and Patrick McCabe. It is upon a writer who is the inheritor of each of these strands, however, an Anglo-Irish figure who has written both on the Big House and on the immigration of the Irish rural poor, who often deals with emigration from post-independence Ireland and who lives in England, that the weight of this persistent anti-British feeling has fallen most profoundly: William Trevor. With Trevor, perhaps the greatest living Irish prose stylist, the ironies posed by this reverse racism weigh so heavily that they give a cast of melancholia to every sentence of his work. In some of his stories and novels, an apparently placid and polished surface belies an ambivalence-riven textuality, which can issue in the most vehemently negative attitude to the British available from any Irish source other than IRA propaganda. To show how this works, I briefly read *Felicia's Journey* (1994) in which an absurdly innocent, pregnant Irish country girl falls into the clutches of a caricature of a British psychopath.

The revivalists themselves were fundamentally deeply respectful of Britain. Even if Yeats's fumblers "in the greasy till" of "September 1913" are referred to as "shoneens," that is, servile imitators of British modernity, and if Douglas Hyde's "The Necessity of Deanglicizing Ireland" (1894) similarly turned its back on modernization as represented by Britain, it was nevertheless they who had adopted the Arnoldian, British-made, version of themselves. Even in "Easter 1916" Yeats has the naiveté, and the temerity, to point out that "England may keep faith/ For all that is done and said" (1996: 83–5). The cultural revivalists quarreled only with a Britain which they constructed as an abstraction: it was (again, they took this from Arnold) a cypher of the unmitigated modernity they would abjure. It was left to the more properly postcolonial writers, those who hailed from the middleclass, and worked primarily around the historical phase that saw the ushering in of the new nation state, to apply to the British the raw race discourse which the British had long used in considering them.

The poet and critic Tom Paulin, in a hard-hitting essay, has called it "The British Presence in *Ulysses*": to the extent that this suggests army patrols, aggression, and the fear and silences that go with them, this is an accurate shorthand for the feelings aroused by Britishers whenever they appear in Joyce's texts (1984: 92–101). The signal moment is the apparently inadvertent encounter of Stephen and the (British) Dean of Students in *A Portrait of the Artist as A Young Man*—Stephen's silent, somewhat sullen rumination that "The language in which we are speaking is his before it is mine" (Joyce 1992: 200–6). "How different are the words *home, Christ, ale, master* on his lips and on mine!... My soul frets in the shadow of his language" have become a touchstone-text for critics writing about the self-alienation of Irish writing in the English language (1992: 205). At the very end of the novel, Stephen, who evidently worried over the encounter, discovered that the word which had caused these thoughts, the infamous "Tundish" (which might have been from the Gaelic as it is the word Stephen advances in place of the dean's more prosaic "Funnel") is in fact "English, and good old blunt English too" (Joyce 1992: 274). The multiple layers of irony here are nevertheless passed over; they resurface as altogether more livid anti-Britishness in the opening episode of *Ulysses*.

At the opening of *Ulysses*, when Stephen encounters the young Englishman Haines outside the Martello tower, itself a compelling symbol of British defensiveness, Joyce lays down the gauntlet of a new Irish postcolonial aggressiveness. He has just described Irish art as "The cracked looking glass of the servant" (Joyce 1986: 6); the attitude to Britishness displayed throughout *Ulysses* may be read as a compulsively reenacted interrogation of the first implication of that description—what it means for the way the Irish will look at the British. As Irishman and Englishman part, Stephen's ire does not subside. When Haines—whose name approximates to the French *la haine*, i.e., hate, and who has spent the morning condescending to all things Irish, including Stephen, even as he professes to greatly admire them—smiles, Stephen notes to himself that Haines "Smiles at wild Irish;" that is, he feels that he is secretly thinking of the Irish as interesting savages. In return, Stephen offers a silent riposte: "Horn of a bull, hoof of a horse, smile of a Saxon" (1986: 19). This is the answer to an old riddle: "What are the three things an Irishman should most beware of?" Just as the "tundish" haunts *A Portrait*, Haines haunts this book: he crops up later with Buck Mulligan in the Dublin City Bakery, and in the "Oxen of the Sun" episode he is laughed at and very literally seen as a ghost when he gets to be the ghoul-apparition who stars in the portion of the text written as a parody of literary gothic. *Ulysses'* attitude to Haines can be summed up as one of gothic comedy: that is, here the Britisher is the butt of the Irish joke, but the laughter is inscribed in a context of the fear and loathing that are the discursive trajectories of the gothic. In the postcolonial moment—remember that this book was written, as its final dateline tells us, between 1914 and 1921, *the* key dates of revolution in Ireland's modern postcolonial history—any fear transmutes itself into an open feeling that can easily be called hatred. In a materialist register, the *ressentiment* of the subaltern, which erupts in the revolutionary moment into insurrectionary anger, is now scattered into the currents of culture.

With this in mind, we can turn to what is possibly (there are a number of competitors) the most controversial review of a work by Joyce ever written, H.G. Well's famous attack on the novel in a contemporary review. Wells, in a judgment that has never been satisfactorily answered, engages at once with what he, speaking unequivocally as an Englishman, discerns as the hatred for the British in Joyce's work:

> A thing of immense significance is the fact that everyone in this Dublin story, every human being, accepts as a matter of course, as a thing in nature like the sky or the sea, that the English are to be hated. There is no discrimination in that hatred . . . . It is just hate, a cant cultivated to the pitch of monomania, an ungenerous violent direction of the mind . . . these bright, green young people across the Channel are something quite different from the liberal English in training and tradition and absolutely set against helping them. (Wells 1970: 86–88)

This may certainly be ascribed to a less brilliant author's jealousy, or to the general antipathy of the British towards the Irish, or to the increased bad press the Irish received in Britain after 1916, when the 1916 rebels were seen to have "stabbed Britain in the back" for rebelling while the mother country was fighting the First World War. What, however, if Wells is right, and if the novel—its anti-Britishness thoroughly mild compared to the directness of the issue in *Ulysses*—is a thinly veiled text of anti-British hatred? For one thing, it helps explains the famous British critical antipathy to Joyce, from Virginia Woolf's extraordinary detestation in the midst of her secret admiration onwards, all the way to the days of the Colin McCabe controversy (C. McCabe 1978). I submit that Wells' commentary is extraordinarily perceptive, one of the best examples in modernism of a backhanded tribute from a lesser author to a major one. The simmering resentment evident in the whole of Joyce's *oeuvre*, for those Irish who took their cultural definitions of themselves from the British, is built upon a less overt but much more profound disdain amounting to hatred, I suggest, for the British themselves. And I want to defend such hatred as a proportionate response to the disrespect amounting to hatred which the British had for centuries bestowed on Joyce's "race" (as he had been taught to call it), the religion which he had disowned, and his class. (What is "the uncreated conscience of my race," which Stephen proposed at the end of *A Portrait* to articulate, if not in the first place an avowal of this hatred?) It is a proper hatred of the oppressor, that also must necessarily be a full-scale hatred of the cultural tradition in which this postcolonial author must necessarily participate.

All of which is to claim that Joyce is a much more radical writer than Yeats; the poet, at best ambivalently late-colonial; the fiction writer, fully postcolonial in ways few postcolonial writers have had the courage to imitate since. It is to infer, moreover, that the implications of this bitter Joycean anti-Britishness have never been taken seriously, not merely by his critics, but least of all by Irish writers since. It is the ambivalence of subsequent Irish fiction in the face of Joyce's version of hatred of the British that we will explore next.

Postcolonial Gothic

The gothic, as has been shown, for example, in the case of *Dracula*, is a form that may be read as the flip side, and the degraded, pulp side, of intense Gaelic revival romanticism; it has also been connected to the scandalous exploitation represented by Victorian absentee landlordism in late-Victorian Ireland. Hence, in a closely related genre, the Big House novel, there is always a gothic as well as dry-rot whiff to the decay of the ascendancy drawing room. Thus, when this genre too began to berate Englishness and the English, very much at the moment of Irish independence post 1921, its "twisting in the winds" of the gothic add an uncanny glow to what might merely have been a tic or an eccentric show of distaste. In other words, versions of Haines roam the drafty rooms and damp demesnes of all these novels; in a way, Haines is a character from a Big House novel who has wandered by mistake into *Ulysses*. The characteristic comic Englishman of the Big House novel is a member of a gauche lower (usually lower-middle) class whose failure is that he or she does not measure up to the novel's gothic overtones. This is snobbery writ large, but with a richly ambivalent reverse racism invoked at the same time, since every British character without exception and regardless of circumstance is likely to wither under its attentions. The snobbery comes straight from the Yeats-Hyde critique: these British are unspeakably "common." Displayed against the foil of Irishness, represented through the narrative expectations of high-end gothic, however, this commonness gets to be displayed in uncanny caricature.

In Elizabeth Bowen's *The Last September*, for example, the gothic tensions that arise in a plot which careens between domestic farce and a memoir about guerilla warfare serve to set off Gerald Lesworth, a Britisher so Rupert-Brookeish that he is described by another English visitor to the Big House at Danielstown, Leonard, as follows:

> And Mr. Lesworth is . . . rather pretty. He is like a photograph of a man in an advertisement putting on the right kind of collar. Doesn't advertizing develop—I sometimes wonder if I would not think of taking it up.
> (Bowen 1983: 54)

Lesworth, a British army officer over to fight the IRA during the guerilla war of independence (1919–21), is another Haines: his point that he fights the Irish rebels "from the point of view of civilization. Also, you see, they don't fight clean" (Bowen 1983: 92) echoes Haines' infamous formula "It seems history is to blame" (Joyce 1986: 17). There is no hate towards Lesworth in this novel; on the contrary, there is not even resentment. Yet, because he is no better than a figure in an advertisement, a cardboard cutout without any of the kind of (limited) depth that the Irish gothic can apprehend, (and possibly because this novel was published in 1929, after the Irish had won the war, and the rebel faction, led by Eamonn de Valera, had come back into power in the new Irish Free State) we as readers are made to mind relatively little, when, inevitably, he is killed. Like the thoroughly comic English officer's wife, Betty Vermont, he is little more than a pathetic figure of fun. When the Big House novel, that serial elegy for the Anglo-Irish as a class, becomes the stage for representing the British in disillusionment and death, and when this least likely of locales becomes the venue where they are displayed disdainfully as buffoons, then one can rest assured that no Britisher has any real chance of seeming honorable in any Irish fiction. Novels such as *The Last September* concern the downright refusal of even any real contact between the Anglo-Irish and the British: the British character gets killed off in case a meaningful encounter might occur.

Thus, downright resentment amounting to hatred, occurs in the case of Irish modernism in *Ulysses*;[13] downright disdain, amounting to rejection, occurs in such Anglo-Irish Big House novels as *The Last September*. Between these axes run the gamut of versions of Britishness in subsequent Irish high culture. Unsurprisingly, in Irish novels of the last quarter of the twentieth-century, Anglophobia persists most noticeably in representations not of the British themselves but of Irish emigrants to Britain. This is unsurprising, since just as standard-issue racism from above (in this case, the late-Victorian, and subsequent, British attitude toward the Irish) calls forth a reverse racism from below (Irish disdain for the British), so that this reverse racism finds as its first effect an operation that may be characterized as "displaced abjection," the disdain of the Irish themselves for a worse-off sub-group, the Irish emigrants to Britain. It was not enough that the Irish should detest the British heartily; this detestation turned its searchlights most strongly on those Irish who might become British, the Irish population in Britain. A new drama, which mimics the original othering of a subgroup, was thereby inaugurated. In a cultural logics whereby the Irish adopted part of the racialized version of themselves from the British as the basis of their own identity, and then turned this version of reading the race back upon the British themselves, the Irish immigrants were an ideal group, seemingly situated between British and Irish identities, to be cast as race traitors. They could be cast as "mixed middlings" in whom conventional nativist disdain for, and anxiety about, Ireland's own emigrants fit well upon its standard anti-Britishness. The bitter irony is that these very emigrants were also very much the victims, at the same time, of the old British othering of the Irish, still alive and well in multiple practical ways in British cities with Irish populations. The Irish writers, often well aware of this continuing racism, could nonetheless accommodate and even acknowledge it, rolling it deftly into their own ways of othering these same emigrants as well.

Two recent examples from many, taken from some of the most polished and ambitious recent Irish fiction: the character of Uncle Alo in Patrick McCabe's *The Butcher Boy* (1992), and the figure of Johnny in John McGahern's *By The Lake* (2002), published in Britain under the title *That They May Face the Rising Sun*. These are both, despite significant differences, extremely mannered novels, their overtly decorative styles busily working all the time as a lexical index of a local, closed community which each describes in detail. That community cannot fail to be read as a symbolic microcosm of the larger imagined community of the Irish nation. In *By the Lake*, the couple whose viewpoint readers are largely given in the novel, the Ruttledges, are themselves a returned emigrant and an Englishwoman. These two, however, work as the foil upon which the Irish emigrant who has chosen to stay in Britain, Johnny, is mercilessly pilloried in the book. Even before he arrives, his brother Jamsie, whose eccentricities the narrative holds dear, tells us of when Johnny took the emigrant train which led to Britain: "That was the move that ruined his life. He'd have been better if he shot himself" (McGahern 2002: 9). When the emigrant arrives on his annual holiday, his account of his lonesome life in London, working in the Ford factory canteen, all told with innocent enthusiasm, is clearly meant to reinforce the opinion of Jamsie, the brother who stayed at home "by the lake." Later, Ruttledge, the emigrant who came back, will claim of England: "I never feel its quite real or that my life there is real" (McGahern 2002: 23). As Johnny puts it with what is presented as a heartbreaking stoicism, "You get used to England. When you cut your stick and make your bed you have to lie on it." The Irish immigrant who will not return is, in McGahern's novel, not so much hated as refused an ontology. England's unreality must be decreed as a counterpoint to and guarantor of the authenticity of Ireland as pastoral, so that for an Irish community in Ireland to be belatedly imagined in McGaherenesque "Lake Isle of Inisfree" mode, the Irish emigrant to Britain must have his life vilified.

All of this is a vivid exploration of the immigrant experience—more usually, after all, told as a triumphant tale by those who emigrated. But undercurrents of resentment and a sense of inferiority inform it; these are held up more starkly in the surreal environs of McCabe's novel. Here the suited-and-tied Uncle Alo who will arrive on holiday from London is held up by the desperate child-hero's mother as the very image of what she would want from family life and that she is refused in her Irish town; Alo however turns out to be even more pathetic than Johnny. Still, in his cheap sharp suit, visiting his sister and her brutal husband who never left their grim rural town, he sings the maudlin songs, is insulted by his brother-in-law, and precipitates the breakdown, suicide, and, then, murder, which launch this novel enthusiastically into the well-trodden realms of Irish gothic once again. McGahern speaks of how some of the Irish country people by the lake had "an innate intolerance of anything strange or foreign" (2002: 26); the narrative's very deft management of the reader's sympathy, likewise, is ordered so that an admiration of the rural life depicted here, and the portrayal of it as real and authentic, is made dependent upon a rejection of those who have rejected *it* as somehow inauthentic. Moreover, these people are shown to suffer an intense and deep-seated alienation as the mark of that inauthenticity. McCabe's novel, awash with the gags of fifties comic-books, gives us an Uncle Alo who is no more than a caricature from such a comic-book—but whose arrival, nevertheless, is precisely what tips the lives of the villagers, and of Francie his nephew, into surreal horror.

Late-twentieth century Irish literature, here, turns its anti-Britishness on to representations of Irish people who, as it were, would become British. They have no intention of returning to Ireland. They get to represent all that still seems threatening in Britishness to the Irish, and they illicit from these Irish novelists, in fact, all of the anxieties which they have about the value of an inviolate Irish community. Even when the novels appear as scathing critiques of the Irish world they describe, as in the case of Mc-Cabe's novel, the Irish-British character who has committed the greatest sin of crossing over, marks the limit—as he exposes the limited quality of—that critique. Thus that character is invariably displayed as an innocent: a figure with the foolishness to admit, but without the discernment to pay heed to, what each work presents as the gruesome pathos of his situation. It is in the work of a writer who himself might well be said to have crossed over, that this issue of innocence, and the writerly strategy of seeking refuge in the gothic when depictions of the British are in question in Irish fiction, comes into the sharpest focus of all.

Forgetting Each Other

William Trevor, a writer whose style is decorously unassuming, manages in his fiction to be both a Big House novelist and a voice for Irish country people at once, to write some stories wholly about British characters and others wholly about Irish ones, who himself lives in Britain but (like Joyce before him) is clearly obsessed with Ireland. In *Felicia's Journey*, each of these influences is dramatically opposed. They clash against a background of the tradition of anxious anti-Britishness which has marked post-revival Irish writing. When Felicia, pregnant, implausibly innocent, and a native of an Irish country town, takes the emigrant route to the north of England to find her boyfriend (who has joined the British army and who clearly will grow up to be at best a Johnny or an Uncle Alo), she is sheltered by an hilariously morbid caricature of an English gent gone bad, Mr. Hilditch. Hilditch brings all of his deeply stereotypical Britishness to being evil: corpulent, dull, practical, reasonable, and above all helpful, he is the inhabitant of a gothic Victorian villa who invariably suggests another cup of tea as he lures Felicia into his serial-killer nightmare. He is a little-Englander who appears to have wandered out of a novel by a British writer of psychological thrillers such as Ruth Rendell and into an Irish gothic novel, where he can make your flesh creep within an altogether more historical and allegorical framework. Felicia, who gets the better of him, is the Irish Catholic would-be virgin who is if anything caricatured even more completely: convent-ridden, daughter of a rebel grandfather, rural, chaste, gullible, an over-the-top last romantic.

To what extent does the habit in Irish fiction of hating the British and jeering at Irish emigrants to Britain matter in the portraits of these two characters, each so exaggerated that we laugh even as we are horrified? The horror here is certainly Irish gothic, even if it is such gothic rudely transplanted on to a soulless British suburban landscape. One could plausibly claim that Trevor is sending up the ways in which Irish writers have portrayed both their British characters and young Irish women in their novels. Yet the novel's insistent tone of calm seriousness, enhanced by Trevor's characteristically unassuming style, belies any sense that here one is reading satire. Rather, the confrontation of near-racist stereotypes, in a novel that is both British thriller and Irish gothic at once, seems to me to stage an intense desire on the part of Irish high culture to erase both the British anti-Irish racism from above, and the resentful Irish anti-British response-racism from below, once and for all.

In what turns out to be a key symbolic scene in the novel, Felicia, in the midst of her entrapment, encounters an older homeless Irish woman from County Clare. This scene matters because this is what Felicia is destined to become: one of the many Irish emigrant members of Britain's homeless population. In the final paragraphs of the novel, Felicia's homelessness is presented as a salvation, and Felicia herself is strangely serene:

> She knows she is not as she was; she is not the bridesmaid at the Autumn wedding, not the girl who covered herself with a rug in the back of a car. The innocence that once was hers is now, with time, a foolishness, yet it is not disowned, and that same lost person is valued for leading her to where she is. Walking through another morning, fine after a wet night, she accepts without bewilderment the serenity that possesses her, and celebrates its fresh new presence. (Trevor 1999: 207)

Thus the novel reveals itself, in the thriller's last sleight-of-hand, as the story of how a woman becomes homeless. Meanwhile, the novel, as a text of Irish culture which once again stages the confrontation between the British and the Irish, attempts to follow Felicia into this space of pastoral-tinged calm. Yet the calm is plainly an assumed attribute, woven of literary artifice. Hilditch has killed himself, and Felicia is not only completely impoverished and alone, but is denied the sanctuary of either Britishness or Irishness now. Appropriately, her one memorable encounter in this last chapter is with an unnamed Indian shopkeeper—who has given her some rotting kiwi (Trevor 1999: 207).

This novel retells the story of the Irish "meeting the British," in the poet Paul Muldoon's phrase, in order to endow it with a serene outcome. Yet it implicitly admits in this last chapter that such peace would merely be wishful literary thinking. The British and Irish, when they meet in Irish fiction, seem doomed to struggle through further nightmarish gothic encounters for some time to come. What might bring an end to this repeated scene, where remembered resentment resurfaces as anti-British caricature? More peace in Ireland, perhaps. Or Irish culture's remembering more faithfully its emigrants—and its immigrants—and thereby fashioning more tenable versions of Irish community that would no longer feel threatened by the shadow of Britain. In the meantime, hatred of the British will resurface again and again as the prime generator of gothic nightmare in much contemporary cultural production from Ireland.

Notes

1. For a relatively early sampling of this work, see Seamus Deane et. al., *Ireland's Field Day*. Deane's own important essay in that volume, "Civilians and Barbarians," (1986: 33–42) echoes the "Apes and Angels" distinction developed by L.P. Curtis, which in turn comes from such earlier essays on the colonial manichean allegory as Mannoni's *Prospero and Caliban: The Psychology of Colonization* (1956).

2. Much of the groundwork for this study has been laid by a recent resurgence in Irish Victorian studies, led, in literature, by such scholars as Margaret Kelleher; see especially her *The Feminization of Famine* (1998). For a recent sampling of new work in Irish Victorian studies, see Terence McDonough's collection *Was Ireland A Colony? Economics, Politics and Culture in Nineteenth-Century Ireland* which includes an afterword by Terry Eagleton. Eagleton has in recent years been an extraordinary one-man powerhouse in Irish Victorian studies and in Irish studies generally; his *Heathcliff and the Great Hunger* (2001) is a brilliant and stunningly detailed study of episodes in the tangle of Anglo-Irish cultural and social relations from the time of the famine onwards.

3. Frederick Engels, letter dated 23 May 1856, reprinted in Marx & Engels (1960: 282). In the same volume see also Engels' "About the Irish Question" (1960: 229–32), and Marx's "Ireland" (1960: 239–56).

4. This book, predictably, does not discuss Irish literature.

5. Friel's play is a thoroughly characteristic Field Day document, within which the

Ordinance Survey represents the complications of the clash of British and Irish discourses on Ireland in the nineteenth century.

6. For example, see A.M. Hall's *The Whiteboy: A Story of Ireland in 1822* (1845) and *Sketches of the Irish Character* (1844).

7. One reply to this essay was a pamphlet by F.T.H. Blackwood, Marquis of Dufferin, *Mr. Mill's Plan for the Pacification of Ireland Examined* (1868).

8. For a later example of this genre, see W. Winwood Reade (1864).

9. See also Curtin (1985).

10. This is in fact the title of a book reviewed in an unsigned review, "Gupp and the Civilization of the Negro," *Anthropological Review*, Vol. 2, 1864, pp. ccix–ccxvi.

11. This phrase is taken from an unsigned article entitled "Types of Mankind," *Quarterly Review*, Vol. LXV, Jan. 1865, p. 196. An ethnologist named Morton was lauded as the founder of the "true principle of physical inquiry into human origins" and praised for having "amassed the largest and most complete collection of skulls ever formed."

12. See Curtis (1971). As Curtis makes clear, the Irish-African comparison was also pursued in the American press, especially at the time of the Civil War.

13. In his recent book, *Joyce's Revenge* (2002), Andrew Gibson speaks of this feature of Joyce's work more forthrightly than most. He however, refers to it as "Anglophobia." See Gibson 2002.

Bibliography

"African Discovery." 1861. *Quarterly Review* 217, (April): 259–77.

Arnold, Matthew. 1867. *On the Study of Celtic Literature*. London: Smith & Elder.

Ashcroft, Bill, Gareth Griffiths, and Helen Tiffin. 1989. *The Empire Writes Back: Theory and Practice in Postcolonial Literatures* . London: Routledge.

Blackwood, F.T.H. 1868. *Mr. Mill's Plan for the Pacification of Ireland Examined*. London.

Bowen, Elizabeth. 1983. *The Last September*. Harmondsworth: Penguin.

Carlyle, Thomas. 1882. *Reminiscences of My Irish Journey*. London: Samson, Low, Marston, Searle and Rivington.

Clapperton, H. 1829. *Journal of A Second Expedition into the Interior of Africa*. London : J. Murray.

Curtin, Philip. D. 1985. *The Image of Africa: British Ideas and Action, 1780–1850*, 2 vols. Madison, WI.: University of Wisconsin Press.

Curtis, L.P. 1971. *Apes and Angels: The Irishman in Victorian Caricature*. Washington D.C.: Smithsonian Institution Press.

Cleary, Joe. 2002. *Literature, Partition, and the Nation State: Culture and Conflict in Ireland, Israel and Palestine*. Cambridge: Cambridge University Press.

Deane, Seamus. 1985. "Arnold, Burke and the Celts." In *Celtic Revivals: Essays in Modern Irish Literature* London: Faber & Faber.

Deane, Seamus et. al. 1986. *Ireland's Field Day*. Notre Dame, IN.: Notre Dame University

Press.

Eagleton, Terry. 2001. *Heathcliff and the Great Hunger*. London: Verso.

Fanon, Frantz. 1968. *The Wretched of the Earth*. Trans. by Constance Farrington. New York: Grove Press.

Gibson, Andrew. 2002. *Joyce's Revenge*. Oxford: Oxford University Press.

"Gupp and the Civilization of the Negro." 1864. *Anthropological Review*, vol. 2: 209–16.

Hall, A.M. 1844. *Sketches of the Irish Character*, 2 vols., "Illustrated Edition," London: A. Nuttali.

―――― 1845. *The Whiteboy: A Story of Ireland in 1822*, 2 vols. London: Chapman and Hall.

Hall, A.M. & S.C. Hall. 1841. *Ireland, Its Scenery and Character, Illustrated by Distinguished Artists*, 3 vols. London: Chapman.

Harris, A. Cornwallis. 1844. *Ethiopian Travels: The Highlands of Ethiopia Described During A Residence of A British Embassy at the Christian Court of Shoa*. London: Longman, Brown, Green and Longmans, Paternoster Row.

Howe, Stephen. 2000. *Ireland and Empire: Colonial Legacies in Irish History and Culture*. Oxford: Oxford University Press.

Hunt, James. 1864. "On the Negro's Place in Nature." *Anthropological Review*, Vol. 2: 15–56

Hyde, Douglas. 1894. "The Necessity For De-Anglicizing Ireland." In *The Revival of Irish Literature*, Charles Gavan Duffy, George Sigerson and Douglas Hyde (eds.). London: T. Fisher Unwin.

Johnson, Dillon. 1996. "Cross-Currencies: Arnold, Yeats, Joyce." *The South Atlantic Quarterly*, 95:1 (Winter): 45–78.

Joyce, James. 1986. *Ulysses*. New York: Vintage.

―――― 1992. *A Portrait of the Artist as A Young Man*. London: Penguin.

Kelleher, John. 1950. "Matthew Arnold and the Celtic Revival." In Harry Levin (ed.), *Perspectives of Criticism*. Cambridge MA: Harvard University Press.

Kelleher, Margaret. 1998. *The Feminization of Famine*. Durham, NC.: Duke University Press.

Kiberd, Declan. 1995. *Inventing Ireland: The Literature of the Modern Nation*. Cambridge, MA: Harvard University Press.

Kingsley, Charles. 1881. *His Letters and Memories of His Life*, Vol. II, Tenth edition. London: C. Kegan Paul.

"Knox on the Celtic Race." 1868. *Anthropological Review*, vol. 6, no. 21, (April): 175–91.

Lander, Richard and John, 1830. 2005. *Journal to Explore the Course and Termination of the Niger*. Ann Arbor, Michigan: University of Michigan Library Scholarly Publishing Office.

Livingstone, David. 1857. *Travels and Researches in South Africa, Including a Sketch of a Sixteen Years Residence in the Interior of Africa*. London: John Murray.

Lloyd, David. 1999. *Ireland After History*. Cork: Cork University Press/Field Day.

McCabe, Colin. 1978. *James Joyce and the Revolution of the Word*. London: McMillan.

McCabe, Patrick. 1992. *The Butcher Boy*. New York: Dell.

McDonough, Terence (ed.) 2005. *Was Ireland A Colony? Economics, Politics and Culture in*

Nineteenth-Century Ireland. Dublin: Irish Academic Press.

McGahern, John. 2002. *By the Lake*. New York: Vintage.

Mannoni, O. 1956. *Prospero and Caliban: The Psychology of Colonization*. Trans. by Pamela Townsend. London: Methuen.

Marx, Karl and Frederick Engels. 1960. *On Colonialism*. London: Lawrence & Wishart.

Mill, John Stuart. 1868. *England and Ireland*. London: Longmans, Green, Reader and Dyer.

Muldoon, Paul. 1993. *Selected Poems 1968–86*. New York: Noonday Press/Farrar, Straus & Giroux.

Park, Mungo. 1860. *Travels in the Interior of Africa*. Edinburgh: Adam and Charles Black.

Pratt, Mary Louise. 1992. *Imperial Eyes: Travel Writing and Transculturation*. London: Routledge.

Paulin, Tom. 1984. "The British Presence in *Ulysses*." In *Ireland and the English Crisis*. Newcastle upon Tyne: Bloodaxe.

Thackeray, W.M. 1843. *Irish Sketchbook by M.A. Titmarsh*, 2 vols. London: Chapman and Hall.

"Tours of Ireland." 1845. *Quarterly Review* 85, (September): 505–10.

Trevor, William. 1999. *Felicia's Journey*. New York: Penguin.

Wells, H.G. 1970. "James Joyce." In *James Joyce: The Critical Heritage*, Robert Deming (ed.). London: Routledge.

"Types of Mankind," *Quarterly Review*, Vol. LXV, Jan. 1865, XXX–XXX.

Wilson, Daniel. 1865. "Inquiry into the Physical Characteristics of the Ancient and Modern Celt." *Anthropological Review*, vol. 3, (February): 52–84.

Winwood Reade, W. 1864. *Savage Africa: Being A Narrative of a Tour*. London: Smith and Elder and Co.

Yeats, W.B. 1996. "Easter 1916." In *William Butler Yeats: Selected Poems and Four Plays*, M. L. Rosenthal (ed.). New York: Scribner.

CHAPTER 2

Writing about Englishness

South Africa's Forgotten Nationalism

Vivian Bickford-Smith

Recovering Englishness in South Africa

Strangely, and despite numerous studies on African and Afrikaner nationalism in recent times, there is still very little analytical writing about the history of Englishness, the "prime nationalism of South Africa, against which all subsequent ones . . . reacted" (Ross 1999: 43). In other words, though England and the English are obviously present in an array of South African grand narratives—often as either largely unnuanced heroes or villains—there has been surprisingly little overt analysis of the inculcation, content or experience of this nationalism beyond a single article written twenty years ago (Sturgis 1982). As a consequence of this lacuna, we only have very piecemeal knowledge of how English nationalism was "forged" here from the early nineteenth century onward.

This essay attempts to give some sense of Englishness in South Africa both as process and experience. One point to make from the outset is that, in keeping with common South African usage throughout the period, Englishness is being used as a synonym for Britishness. Such a "supranational" use of the term Englishness was common practice even by people who could also, or at other times, see themselves as, say, Scottish or Welsh. Colls and Dodd persuasively suggested two decades ago that this was because Englishness in the colonies was primarily about "white skins, English tongues and, feelings about being free" (1986: 45). In other words, the sense of possessing these commonalities—in contradistinction to those "others" who actually or supposedly did not—generally (but not always) overcame potential metropolitan "national" divides, such as English in the narrower, "South British" sense versus Welsh, for example. Even those who challenged the above list of (supposedly appropriate) English commonalities—by suggesting, for instance, that you could be English and black—generally used English and British as synonyms.

Notes for this section begin on page 69.

Of course, Englishness was frequently used as a synonym for Britishness in Britain itself—even by someone who could also on occasion (or perhaps more frequently) see him/herself as (for example) a Scot (Colley 1992). Keith Robbins has argued this was because economic, demographic, occupational, and cultural integration or "blending" of the "multinational" constituents of the "Empire in Europe" was more complex and interactive than the simple and ubiquitous imposition of English (i.e., "South British") hegemony (Robbins 1988). Indeed the make-up of the Imperial civil service and armed forces (perhaps especially in the early nineteenth century) might even suggest that Scottishness was the predominant (or at least, proportionately overrepresented) ingredient of Britishness. Certainly it is still possible to identify specifically Scottish or English (South British)—or indeed Welsh or Irish—imagery, place names, institutions, histories, material culture or attitudes in colonial Englishness, even if this is not a focus of this particular essay.

The first section of the essay examines ways in which British imperialism begat varied and changing English (in the broader sense) nationalisms—as well as other major nationalisms—in South Africa, from the early nineteenth century onward. The second section suggests that writing about Englishness necessitates investigating three overlapping areas: Englishness as an (again, varied and changing) ideology; the forms or media through which the ideology of Englishness was inculcated and maintained; and the articulation of English identity—that is, the ways in which people expressed or demonstrated their (perhaps highly conditional) Englishness.

These thoughts come at the beginning of work-in-progress on what is intended to be an extended study of Englishness in South Africa from the early nineteenth century to the near present. Most of my writing on or around this topic thus far has been on the Cape, and most of my original research has been on Cape Town. The tentative comments here may well reflect this current limitation, but hopefully they will provide the possibility of comparing Englishness in South Africa with other Englishnesses analyzed in this collection. An enduring motive behind my exploration into collective identities, and one that informs this essay, is to demonstrate their constructed, situational, and conditional nature. Given essentialist notions of race and nation still omnipresent in political debate and popular discourse throughout the world, this seems as necessary now as in the days of apartheid South Africa.

If there is a lacuna surrounding the history of Englishness as practice, we are better off in terms of Englishness as experience—that is, in terms of the imaginings of Englishness among South Africans—and much of this work is excellent. However, most is confined to "loyalism" or "black Englishness" in the last decades of the nineteenth century or the first decades of the twentieth.[1] Certainly, we can acknowledge that Englishness was probably only a strongly held identity—with periods or moments of greater intensity (for example, during royal tours or wars involving Britain)—for a sometimes small minority of black and white South Africans. Geographically, they mostly resided in the eastern Cape and Natal, and larger towns like Cape Town, Durban, Kimberley, Port Elizabeth, Johannesburg, and (for a while) Bloemfontein. But Englishness affected many others, if only as an often interventionist "other" against whom they could define a sense of being part of an alternative "we."

British Imperialism and English Nationalism in South Africa

Whether as "we" or "they," Englishness was clearly perceived to be a matter of belonging to a national community. Like all collective identities, nationalism has proved to be a slippery object under academic scrutiny, and has generated a vast and often apparently contradictory literature. What we can currently agree on (can we?) is that particular nationalisms, like all collective identities, are: imaginatively created and experienced in particular historical contexts; subject to change through time (have to be at least partly recreated or reimagined); can coexist with other identities (including other forms of sub- or supra-nationalisms); but that, on occasion, they can also have a particular salience.

Yet we still have to deal with the problem that these "vertical divisions of mankind" have been imagined differently at different times and in different places, and that they continue to be so imagined. Debate on where those vertical lines should be placed continues to take place in South Africa—not least in ANC position papers on the "national question"—as it does in Britain, and in many other parts of the world.[2] Suffice it to say that nationalisms through time have seemingly been delineated by one or more of the following perceived or actual commonalities: loyalty to the state; culture; shared territorial boundaries; shared civic rights; shared history; or shared "race"/"descent."[3]

Understanding how these debates played out in South Africa in the nineteenth century, and for much of the twentieth century, requires some understanding of the relationship between the British Empire, English nationalism and other nationalisms: whether one calls these sub-nationalisms, counter-nationalisms or perhaps in the case of "Native"/African identity in the late nineteenth century, a proto-nationalism. It also requires some knowledge of how Englishness was simultaneously (and often similarly) created and imagined in the metropole, as well as in other parts of "the British world."

Predictably helpful is Chris Bayly's insight that the relationship between British imperialism and British nationalism was often tense.[4] And as Benedict Anderson reminded us many years ago now, empires in Europe—and indeed around the world—were dynastic, multi-cultural, and multi-territorial enterprises. Such enterprises came under threat from horizontally-imagined print-language communities—or nationalisms—in both the Americas and Europe from the late eighteenth century (Anderson 1983). A response in the case of the Hanoverian monarchs—as much to the threat from across the channel as from any within the empire in Europe—was not only to invent new and more ostentatious royal rituals and ornamentations, but also to emphasise their Englishness and actively pursue official nationalism—or the Anglicisation of subjects from above—in places like Ireland, India, and the Cape.

What arguably limited such efforts were both practical considerations—how possible it was to forge "Britons" out of all but a few of the millions of newly acquired subjects—and the concomitant anxiety that this might lead to expensive and unnecessary conflicts in far flung places. Many of these places (like the Cape—both in the 1790s and again in 1806) were acquired first and foremost out of strategic concerns rather than the thought that they would prove to be of much economic benefit. This may begin to explain the relative ease with which sub-nationalisms were accepted and representative institutions allowed.

Yet in the British Cape Colony, at least, there were also tensions around changing and contested ideas of how such Englishness should be defined and demonstrated. We know now that criteria of "descent"/"race" eventually predominated, but this was not apparent to many historical actors in nineteenth century South Africa, or even later. Teleological historical development is only ever obvious with hindsight. In the first half of the nineteenth century, acceptable Englishness appears to have been (predominantly) a matter of being loyal to the British monarch and colonial state, as well as adoption—whether willingly or less so—of elements of English culture: such as dress, appropriate behavior and language. But at least in the early years of British occupation, there seemed to be some contradictions even here between what one might dub aristocratic and bourgeois Englishness. The former was, for instance, relatively unbothered by whether you gambled or drank—arguably it actively encouraged these activities as part of forging loyalty. But the latter was more obviously evangelical, and required a reformation of belief and appropriately "respectable" behavior.

Ideas and debates about Englishness in South Africa were evidently closely related to ideas and debates about Englishness in the wider British World, not least the metropole itself. Such debates were informed by ideological and material considerations, as well as social conflict. They circulated around this world at the speed of available contemporary communications. One such debate was around the nature of English liberties: both more broadly on citizenship and on political economy. In the Cape, this resulted in inhabitants gaining newly reinvented "traditional"

English freedoms, notably of person and expression (if not without struggle and dissent). This latter freedom allowed members of the colonial middle-classes to imagine themselves as South African (citizens of a particular administrative unit of the empire, distant from other units), not least through the ability to imagine such a community through print (see McKenzie 1993 and 1997):[5] just as other colonial elites were imagining themselves as Australians or Canadians. But these colonial elites could also imagine themselves simultaneously as English South Africans, English Australians and so on. Sub-nationalism could coexist with English supra-nationalism, and vice versa, even if there had been (and continued to be) tensions which helped to explain the salience of sub-nationalisms.

The acknowledgement and encouragement of this possibility, together with crucial considerations of cost, was part of the reason London conceded representative and responsible government with reasonable enthusiasm. Also part of the reason, no doubt, was the memory of what happened when a different option was taken while dealing with the thirteen colonies in North America in the 1770s and 1780s. But also important was the understanding that the likes of Australia, New Zealand, and Canada were likely to be loyal—if representative institutions were conceded—because they (unlike the "dependencies") were already full of ready-forged Britons, albeit such identity still needed to be maintained through the likes of imperial ornamentalism.

The Cape, in this last respect at least, was a somewhat different case, since in the mid-nineteenth century already forged Britons appeared to be in a small minority. In granting representative government, the imperial authorities appear to have hoped that this would bring diverse colonists (whether British, "Dutch," "Hottentot," "Kaffir" or ex-slave) together at least as loyal subjects, while processes of both official and unofficial "anglicization" would help to forge more Britons in the longer term.[6] At this stage, such Britons could still be imagined both by London and some (white) colonists—and this was reflected in the Constitutions of 1853 (Representative Government) and 1872 (Responsible Government)—in terms of shared citizenship and appropriate behavior, rather than skin color or "race."

This definition of Englishness, and its Cape constitutional outcome, was contested—not least by white English-speaking settlers in Albany who had imagined and argued for their own Eastern Cape sub-nation, and whose English nationalism was enhanced by their involvement in frontier wars against Xhosas, but who could seem just as alien and dangerous as the French (Crais 1992; Keegan 1996). It would seem from work that exists on Eastern Cape settler identity, that their imagined Englishness was one in which white-skins—rather than Protestantism—as much (if not more) than culture or shared citizenship was central. They seem to have been joined in this view by English-speaking whites in other parts of southern Africa—whose numbers through immigration had been increased because of the mineral revolution—for a range of often locally and materially propelled motives. And, crucially, they were encouraged in this definition of Englishness by the fact that by the last few decades of the nineteenth century, it was shared by metropolitan historians, politicians, and imperial administrators, who hoped that a "kith-and-kin" empire-wide Englishness might help as Britain's economic and military prowess was being seriously threatened by other European powers (notably Germany) for the first time since 1815 (Colls 2002: 100–3). Mobilizing such nationalism to encourage or support imperial military intervention—whether in "defense" of, or to enhance, the interests of British subjects—occurred simultaneously in Britain and South Africa, most dramatically, of course, between 1899 and 1902.

Part of mobilizing white/kith-and-kin Englishness in South Africa was for print men, like the editors of Cape Town newspapers, to help some South Africans to imagine and define their (threatened? or destined to dominate?) Englishness in terms of biological descent, and to denounce the differences in other "races"/"nations"—whether dubbed as Boers, the Dutch, Afrikaners, Malays, Coloreds or Natives. This encouraged (if it did not entirely invent, because people used their "own cultural resources") a range of counter-collective identities ranging from the more clearly language/print based and largely "pirated" invention of Afrikaner nationalism to those identities based on the claim to equal citizenship: that of Native-ness/African-ness, which allowed a proto-nationalist self recognition as Native while still articulating the wish to be accepted as black English; and the Colored identity, which wished either to be accepted as Afrikaner or, more commonly, as English (Bickford-Smith 1995).

To ensure a loyal British South Africa, Milner wanted the ratio of "Britons" to Boers to be changed from 2 to 3 to at least 3 to 2. But his failure to achieve this end—either by importing sufficient kith-and-kin from Britain, or by imagining western educated, English-speaking black elites as properly English while arguing for an extension of the Cape Constitution northward—meant that Afrikaners were in the majority among the enfranchised under the Union of South African Constitution of 1910. In turn, this meant that kith-and-kin Englishness had a particular salience not only—and in keeping with other parts of the British World—during British wars or Royal Tours, but also during moments when in this part of the empire it continued to be particularly endangered: whether with the Afrikaner "apartheid election" victory of 1948; or during Afrikaner nationalist tampering with the constitution (to entrench power) in the 1950s; or with the establishment of a republic and South Africa's withdrawal from the Commonwealth in 1961. Yet this does not mean, of course, that white South African Englishness should be essentialized, or that there were not widely different variations in this identity.

What might one add about black South African Englishness in the twentieth century? I have written at some length elsewhere that the provisions of the Treaty of Vereeneging (1902) that ended the South African War and the exclusionary 1910 constitution were taken by many black English to be a decisive betrayal (Bickford-Smith 2004). However, this would not appear to have meant that black Englishness ceased to be an (at times) available and salient identity for some. Part of the reason was precisely because of both a constitutional and social rejection as acceptably (i.e. white) South African by their compatriots who racialized South African-ness, and themselves, in this way. But this did not mean, for all, an end to aspirations of black Englishness for at least part of their lives. Black Englishness does appear to have declined among South Africans racialized as "natives" after the Second World War: not least because of the replacement of mission schools by Bantu education.[7] But for some people racialized as "colored" in the Western Cape, the association of Englishness with "freedom" appears to have endured well into the apartheid years. Indeed it was perhaps given greater salience—a salience encouraged by English language newspapers—when the Afrikaner nationalist party rule entailed what appeared to be an active stripping of remaining British liberties: not only in the removal of the male-only limited franchise in the Cape, but perhaps even more painfully and dramatically, during group area removals (Bickford-Smith 1998: 56–59). As novelist Richard Rive put it:

> I remember those who used to live in District Six, those who lived in Caledon Street and Clifton Hill and busy Hanover Street. There are those who still remember the ripe, warm days…When I was a boy and chirruping ten, a decade after the end of the second world war . . . in those *red-white-and blue days*. (Rive 1986: 1; emphasis added)

District Six was a predominantly (but not exclusively) Colored inner city area that the National Party government declared was for "whites only" in 1966. Its inhabitants were forced to leave, mainly to the relatively distant and windswept Cape Flats, and most of their former homes were destroyed (Bickford Smith et al. 1999: 183–87).

The formal ending of British dominion in the 1960s, together with the ongoing and ever more dramatically illustrated political impotence of English nationalism in the face of its rivals, announced the latter's all but fatal demise by this decade. Afrikaner, African and, after 1994, a more Africanized South African nationalism continued with considerable efficacy to denounce, co-opt or destroy both the ideologies of South African Englishness and the forms through which these had been conveyed and marked. It is to these that we now turn.

Ideologies, Vehicles and Expressions of Englishness in South Africa

Writing about Englishness in South Africa requires an examination of three obviously overlapping and interactive themes or concerns. The first of these is to understand changes and continuities in ideologies of Englishness. Ranger argued, many years ago that "the 'theology' of an omniscient, omnipotent and omnipresent monarchy became almost the sole ingredient of imperial ideology as it was presented to Africans" (1992: 212). But this theology could be imagined as more than unconditional worship. For some at least, it involved the idea of monarch-above-the-barons or white colonial administrators/settlers, a monarch who—because he/she purportedly made no distinction of race among his or her subjects—might be appealed to in time of need against such barons. Equally, empire-wide ideas about progress, improvement, respectability, or the dichotomy between barbarism and civilization, were—as has been demonstrated at considerable alliterative length by the Comaroffs and others—part-and-parcel of refashioning many African lives at the level of the *quotidian* (see Comaroff and Comaroff 1991, 1997, and Elbourne 2002).

This was a matter of ideas translated into action, experienced in practice in changes in material culture or the gendered division of labor as much (if not more) than in consciousness. As such it may have allowed some of those beyond the more thoroughly westernized elites to imagine themselves, at least occasionally, as English, even though it was only the elites that were likely to write or make sophisticated speeches about being actual or potential possessors of English "liberties," as "civilized" subjects worthy of British citizenship. But putting lights in your windows on the occasion of a royal celebration, or naming your child Victoria, George, Edward or Nelson, or having a photograph of Queen Elizabeth on the wall of your room, may not have been purely (or cynically) strategic. And South Africa's glittering, often multi-media, array of underresearched ornamentalist royal parades and ceremonies, while conveying obviously hierarchical notions of how society was or should be ordered, appeared to demonstrate that you could and should include yourself as a British subject, and perhaps as a British citizen—even if this injunction was far more convincing in the mid-nineteenth century Cape than in any other time or location.

It is worth giving a thick description of an elaborate Royal celebration held in Cape Town in 1863 to demonstrate its sociological complexity. The festivities commenced with the ringing of church bells throughout Cape Town. The central event of the day was the Grand Procession, at once entertainment and a symbol of social order in the town, led by a band and the military, the ultimate guarantors of order. In the wake of the soldiers trooped municipal councilors, followed by members of parliament, civil servants, foreign consuls, and directors of banks and institutions. Then came the schools, and after, Education, Thrift, and Prudence in the form of the benevolent societies, tailed by the Dignity of Labor in hierarchical order—artisans, laborers, a life-boat crew, seamen, fishermen, boatmen and the fire brigade. Bringing up the rear was a carnival parade: floats included "Britannia in triumphal car attended by Tritons," "Lady Godiva," "Knights in armor," the giants "Gog and Magog," Bacchus and Bacchanals and "Jack-in-the-green." A motley throng of clowns, chimney sweeps, harlequins, and varlets made fun of the crowd. Winding its way slowly through the main streets, the procession started and finished on the Parade.[8] "The whole of Cape Town" watched or performed, and people from the country increased the audience, who "cheered and yelled almost to madness."[9]

Afterward came the feasting. The schoolchildren were fed in Greenmarket Square, in the center of which was a "lofty flagpole . . . . bedecked with evergreens to remind one of a Maypole." Members of the fire brigade were treated in the Town House and Breakwater workmen at Mr. Fuller's store. Other workmen, artisans, seamen, and soldiers, together "with the poor," were entertained on the Parade. There, a whole ox was roasted on a spit. After the first slice was ritually tasted by the governor, the meat was then distributed with copious amounts of free wine. When lunch was over, the Parade hosted "rustic sports"—climbing the greasy pole, catching the pig with a greasy tail, or wheelbarrow races—and athletics. After watching for a while, the governor and "the elite of the city and neighborhood" repaired to a marquee in the Botanic Gardens for a late, but splendid, subscription lunch. In the evening, the gardens—illuminated with lanterns—became the venue for a fete and "fancy fair," with boxing, marionettes, a mock Chinese astrologer and Christy minstrels. Bonfires were lit on Lion's Head, Lion's Rump, and Robben Island. At 10 PM there were fireworks on the Parade, while a Grand Masquerade Ball commenced at the circus.[10]

There was a predictably wide range of forms in which ideologies of Englishness were conveyed and maintained. One of them was, of course, this South African "ornamentalism." Understanding such ornamentalism requires an examination not only of changes and continuities in rituals of royalty through time, but also of the chronological development of English "logos," like place names—Cradock, Caledon, George, Grahamstown, Albany, and Somerset were just some of these markers already established in the Eastern Cape before the 1820s—statues and monuments, postage stamps, pillar boxes, or the publishing of maps covered with pink bits in school text books (Canadine 2003; Anderson 1983: 171–75). A related vehicle of Englishness was the oral, written, and electronic discourses concerned with England and its empire that helped inculcate Englishness, and so allowed people to imagine themselves as English: whether this was in the form of English history in school text books, the grand canon of English literature, or South African created cinema-of-empire films like *Symbol of*

Sacrifice (1918), set during the Anglo-Zulu War of 1879. The cast list of the latter read in part:

> Preston Marshall: A Young Englishman, owner of a farm. Affianced to Marie. [Marie Moxter, daughter of "Dutch" farmer].
>
> Private Tommy H'atkins of 'Ighgate 'Ill: A decided type of cockney soldier. About 30.
>
> Private Geordie M'Gluskie o' Glasgie and Everywhere: A typical raw-bones Scotch soldier of about 35.
>
> Gobo. A faithful old Zulu servant who served the Moxter family since childhood.
>
> Aleta. Marie's Cape girl maid. She's fat, forty and bare-footed, but in so far as possible apes her young mistress in the doing of her hair and trying to show a slender waist line
>
> Tambooki: A finely built Zulu warrior...his attire and accoutrement would be of the finest Zulu type.

The opening shot consisted of the following words superimposed over a Union Jack:

> I am the flag that braves the shock of war
> From continent to continent and shore to shore
> Come weal or woe, as turns the old earth round,
> Where hope and glory shine, there is the symbol found.
> Look! Sun and moon and glittering star,
> Faithful unto death, my children are!
> You who for duty live, and who for glory die,
> The symbol of your faith and sacrifice am I.
> (Cited in Davies 1996: 135–7)

Another way in which a sense of Englishness was conveyed or maintained was through the replication or importation of recognizably English material culture, including the architecture and spatial arrangements of British urban landscapes as well as such English things as Dover stoves. A range of institutions also played a crucial role in inculcating or maintaining Englishness. Of central importance in this respect were the established and dissenting British churches and missionary societies. They were overtly responsible for the reformation of many elements of behavior (not least the appropriate behavior of the sexes) in an acceptably English direction, and their efforts have already received considerable academic attention (Bickford-Smith 1998). But also significant were the likes of loyalist associations and a variety of associations modeled on their English counterparts, whether these were (elite or working) men's clubs, sporting organizations, schools, temperance groups, trade unions, friendly societies or the Girl Guides.[11]

As evidenced most obviously in diaries, biographies, oral testimonies, and the literary and visual arts, Englishness was overtly demonstrated and expressed in a similarly diverse number of ways, and with predictable variations according to such factors as region, class, and gender, to name but a few. Sensitive reading of such sources, particularly but not exclusively those generated by black South Africans, requires that one remembers, as Bill Nasson put it while writing about the acceptance and rejection of British loyalism around the time of the South African War, "that such expressions of patriotism should not be interpreted as the product of a simple, unmediated absorption of an imperial creed." Instead, we should recall that "To this process people brought traditions, acquired or inherited social identities, practices and skills, and whatever they could marshal from their native cultures and the colonial cultures to which they were now continually exposed" (Nasson 1991: 8–9).

Varieties of Englishness

After perusing a very large number of such historical sources, it is hard to accept that there was a simple bifurcation between a "strategic" black (or white?) Englishness and a sincere, genuinely internalized white (or black?) one. Certainly, from the pen of a white South African, one can point to the paean to kith-and-kin Englishness that is contained in the likes of Francis Gerrard's *Springbok Rampant* (Gerrard 1951). But in the case of other "whites," Englishness is expressed or demonstrated in often highly complex ways: whether, for example, in *Memoirs of a Socialist in South Africa*, the autobiography of Wilfred Harrison, a South African War veteran and member of the Social Democratic Federation (Harrison n.d.); or through the complicated twists and turns of Laurence van der Post's life and self-identity as described by J.D.F. Jones in *Storyteller*, wherein the ex-British army officer and future godfather of Prince Charles could also project himself as the "doughty and dogged Boer" of British imaginings when deemed necessary (Jones 2001); or in the ostensibly uncolonial musings of the young (Sir) Nigel Hawthorne growing up in mid-twentieth century Cape Town (Hawthorne 2003).

Similarly, black Englishness should surely not be seen simply or always as inauthentic "mimicry," in other words, denounced in terms reminiscent of the racism of Richard Burton commenting on the Creoles of Sierra Leone in the nineteenth century, as seems perilously close to being the case even in some academic analyses.12 This amounts to the "othering" of dead black Africans, whose authentic or inauthentic voice twenty-first century academics unconvincingly claim to be able to detect. As such, it is unpleasantly reminiscent of the simplistic and racist categorizations of kith-and-kin Englishness of whatever century.

My own prejudice is that the academic project should challenge essentialist definitions of any given nationalism, even if one takes the postcolonial theoretical point that such notions were, and might still be, wielded for understandable and avowedly progressive "strategic" reasons. Indeed, one happily accepts that not only English ideologies but also individual English identities are subject to change, including overt rejection thereof. Such rejection could be personally (and collectively) liberating, as was the case with an implicitly former black Englishman like Nelson Mandela who wrote somewhat self-mockingly about how he was anglicized through his schooling in the Eastern Cape:

> The principal of Healdtown was Dr. Arthur Wellington, a stout and stuffy Englishman who boasted of his connection to the Duke of Wellington. At the outset of assemblies, Dr. Wellington would walk on stage and say, in his deep bass voice, "I am the descendant of the great Duke of Wellington, aristocrat, statesman, and general, who crushed the Frenchman Napoleon at Waterloo and thereby saved civilization for Europe—and for you, the natives." At this, we would all enthusiastically applaud, each of us profoundly grateful that a descendant of the great Duke of Wellington would take the trouble to educate natives such as ourselves. The educated Englishman was our model; what we aspired to be were black Englishmen. (1995: 35–6)

Mandela's reflections remind one that Englishness is not something that is conferred on you in the womb: rather, like any other identity, it has to be taught and (partially?) learnt or unlearnt: Mandela became an "African" nationalist, but retained not only his English tongue but also his Methodist faith. And the precise content of taught or learnt Englishness might, of course, vary considerably according to a particular teacher or pupil. Equally, individuals may not experience a simple (or one off) "acceptance" or "rejection" of Englishness as against any other available "national," "racial" or "ethnic" identity. We should instead allow for the fact that individuals can have (simultaneously held) multiple and ambiguous identities—despite the implicit or explicit ideological argument to the contrary of (in our instance) kith-and-kin Englishness.

And yet, it would seem, categorization and concomitant essentialist notions of nation and/or race—purportedly a product of the European Enlightenment, conveyed to South Africa by the Dutch and the English, and condemned as such by many postmodernist and postcolonial theorists—continue to haunt academic and popular discourse. Such essentialist notions—even when ostensibly harnessed in a progressive cause—need to be continually and consistently challenged because they can still potentially (or actually) lead to destructive othering. Thus, in an attempt to correct the wrongs of the past, South African affirmative action or "equity" legis-lation today continues to divide the population into categories uncomfort-ably akin to the National Party's apartheid Population Registration Act of 1949, which was modeled on categorizations employed by British colonial administrators in the nineteenth century: African (previously "Native"), Indian (previously "Asian"), Colored and White. Consequently, South Africans, whether they wish to be or not, continue to be encouraged by government espousal of colonial racial categorizations to view themselves in these terms rather than, say, those of relative economic advantage. It would be ironic indeed if this proves to be an enduring legacy of nine-teenth century Englishness in South Africa.

Notes

1. A review of existing historiography on Englishness in the British colonial Cape is given in Bickford-Smith (2003), which is also published in Bridge and Federowitch (2003).
2. See the most recent ANC position paper on "The National Question" (2005).
3. Work on nationalism that has obviously influenced this essay include, for instance: Anderson (1983), and Hobsbawm (1990). Less obviously, and offering less well known insights are Chatterjee (1993) and Piper (1998).
4. My argument in this and the next paragraph is clearly drawing on Anderson, Bayly and Colley.
5. Saul Dubow (2006) has also just completed a book-length study on this topic in which he has examined, *inter alia,* the establishment of colonial institutions such as the South African library and South African museum.
6. Sturgis (1982) looks at official policies aimed at anglicizing the "Dutch." These included anglicizing the civil service, local government, and the law—and making English the language of government and the law—as well as assisted immigration from Britain, the (partial) Anglicization of education and the encouragement of British religious institutions (e.g., by state subventions of salaries). In Bickford-Smith (2003), I argue that studying Anglicization requires looking at how all colonists were affected by this process, and that Sturgis was unable to say much about what he called "informal cultural transfers" of Englishness not directly attributable to British colonial officials at the Cape: e.g., in terms of popular culture.
7. Also part of this process, quite clearly, was the adoption of a more Africanized and more (consistently) populist African nationalism by the likes of the ANC Youth League and the PAC. See Lodge (1985).
8. *Cape Argus* 14.5.1863. Much of this thick description, and some further analysis, appears in Bickford-Smith et al. (1998:152–53, 190).
9. *Cape Argus* 16.5.1863.
10. *Cape Argus* 16.5.1863 and 21.5.1863.
11. For an initial attempt at saying something about this particular element of the inculcation of Britishness, see Vivian Bickford-Smith (1998/9).

12. See, for instance, Elleke Boehmer who, in an often insightful monograph—particularly on the connections between anti-imperial nationalist movements and individuals—nonetheless deems Sol Plaatje guilty of "colonial mimesis" and at "one level . . . [of being] . . . an ill-adjusted parodist" and talks of "the dangerous imitativeness, which was to mark the Rolong people's relationship with South African society in general" (Boehmer 2002: 132, 134).

Bibliography

Anderson, Benedict. 1983. *Imagined Communities.* London: Verso.

Bayly, C.A. 1989. *Imperial Meridian: The British Empire and the World, 1780–1830.* Harlow: Longman.

Bickford-Smith, Vivian. 1995. *Ethnic Pride and Racial Prejudice in Victorian Cape Town.* Cambridge: Cambridge University Press.

———— 1998. "Representing Cape Town on the Eve of Apartheid" *Urban History* 25, no. 1.

———— 1998/9. "Leisure and Identity in Cape Town, British Cape Colony, 1838–1910" *Kronos* 25: 103–28.

———— 2003. "Revisiting Anglicization in the Nineteenth Century Cape Colony" *Journal of Imperial and Commonwealth History* 31, no. 2: 82–95.

———— 2004. "The Betrayal of Creole Elites." In Sean Hawkins and Phillip D. Morgan (eds.), *Black Experience and the Empire.* Oxford: Oxford University Press.

Bickford-Smith, Vivian, Elizabeth Van Heyningen and Nigel Worden. 1998 *Cape Town: the Making of a City.* Cape Town: David Philip.

———— 1999. *Cape Town in the Twentieth Century.* Cape Town: David Philip.

Boehmer, Elleke. 2002. *Empire, the National, and the Postcolonial 1890–1920.* Oxford: Oxford University Press.

Bridge, Carl and Kent Federowitch (eds.). 2003. *The British World: Diaspora, Culture and Identity.* London: Frank Cass.

Chatterjee, Partha. 1993. *Nationalist Thought and the Colonial World.* Minneapolis: University of Minnesota Press.

Colley, Linda. 1992. *Britons: Forging the Nation, 1707–1832.* New Haven: Yale University Press.

Colls, R. 2002. *Identity of England.* Oxford: Oxford University Press.

Colls, R. and P. Dodd (eds.). 1986. *Englishness: Politics and Culture 1880–1920.* Beckenham: Croom Helm.

Cannadine, David. 2003. *Ornamentalism.* London: Penguin.

Comaroff, Jean and John Comaroff. 1991. *Of Revelation and Revolution: Christianity, Colonialism and Conciousness in South Africa. Vol. 1.* Chicago: Chicago University Press.

Comaroff, Jean and John Comaroff. 1997. *Of Revelation and Revolution: The Dialectics of Modernity on a South African Frontier.* Chicago: Chicago

University Press.

Crais, Clifton. 1992. *White Supremacy and Black Resistance in Pre-Industrial South Africa*. Cambridge: Cambridge University Press.

Elbourne, Elizabeth. 2002. *Colonialism, Missions, and the Contest for Christianity in the Cape Colony and Britain, 1799–1853*. Montreal: McGill-Queen's University Press.

Davis, Peter. 1996. *In Darkest Hollywood: Exploring the Jungles of Cinema's South Africa*. Johannesburg: Ravan Press.

Dubow, Saul. 2006. *A Commonwealth of Knowledge: Science, Sensibility and White South Africa 1820–2000*. Oxford and Cape Town: Oxford University Press/Double Storey.

Gerrard, Francis.1951. *Springbok Rampant*. London: F. Muller.

Harrison, Wilfred H. n.d. *Memoirs of a Socialist in South Africa 1903–1947*. Cape Town: published by the author.

Hawthorne, Nigel. 2003. *Straight Face*. London: Sceptre.

Hobsbawm, E.J. 1990. *Nations and Nationalism since 1780: Program, Myth, Reality*. Cambridge: Cambridge University Press.

Jones, J.D.F. 2001. *Storyteller: The Many Lives of Laurens van der Post*. London: John Murray.

Keegan, Tim. 1996. *Colonial South Africa and the Origins of the Racial Order*. Cape Town: David Philip.

Lodge, Tom. 1985. *Black Politics in South Africa since 1945*. Johannesburg: Ravan Press.

McKenzie, Kirsten. 1993. *The South African Commercial Advertiser and the Making of Middle–Class Identity in Early Nineteenth Century Cape Town*. MA thesis, UCT.

McKenzie, Kirsten. 1997. *Gender and Honour in Middle-Class Cape Town: the Making of Colonial Identity, 1821–1850*. PhD thesis, Oxford.

Mandela, Nelson. 1995. *Long Walk to Freedom*. Johannesburg: Abacus.

Nasson, Bill. 1991. *Abraham Esau's War: A Black South African War in the Cape, 1899–1902*. Cambridge: Cambridge University Press.

"The National Question." 2005. *Umrabulo 23*, (June): 1–6.

Piper, Nicole. 1998. *Racism, Nationalism and Citizenship: Ethnic Minorities in Britain and Germany*. Aldershot: Aldgate Publishing.

Ranger, Terence. 1992. "The Invention of Tradition in Colonial Africa." In Eric Hobsbawm and Terence Ranger (eds.), *The Invention of Tradition*. Cambridge: Cambridge University Press.

Rive, Richard. 1986. "Buckingham Palace," *District Six*. Cape Town: David Philip.

Robbins, Keith. 1988. *Nineteenth Century Britain: Integration and Diversity*. Oxford: Oxford University Press.

Ross, Robert. 1999. *Status and Respectability in the Cape Colony 1750–1870: A Tragedy of Manners*. Cambridge: Cambridge University Press.

Sturgis, James. 1982. "Anglicization at the Cape of Good Hope in the early nineteenth century," *Journal of Imperial and Commonwealth History 11*, no. 1: 5–32.

CHAPTER 3

Passports, Empire, Subjecthood

Prem Poddar

"Do not shoot," it shouted. "I am a British object!"
—David Malouf, *Remembering Babylon* (1993)

Banner of England, not for a season, O banner of Britain, hast thou
Floated in conquering battle or flapt to the battle-cry!
Never with mightier glory than when we had rear'd thee on high
Flying at top of the roofs in the ghastly siege of Lucknow
....
Handful of Men as we were, we were English in heart and in limb,
Strong with the strength of the race to command, to obey, to endure,
Each of us fought as if hope for the garrison hung but on him
....
Praise to our Indian brothers, and let the dark face have his due!
Thanks to the kindly dark faces who fought with us, faithful and few,
Fought with the bravest among us, and drove them, and smote them, and slew
That ever upon the topmost roof our banner in India blew.
—Lord Tennyson, "The Defense of Lucknow" (1879)

Race, Territory, and Belonging

The first page of any British passport "requests and requires in the name of Her Majesty all those whom it may concern to allow the bearer to pass freely without let or hindrance and to afford the bearer such assistance and protection as may be necessary." However, as a *Guardian* reporter notes, for those who hold such a passport but fall under the category of British Dependent territories citizenship or British Overseas citizenship, "the freedom from let or hindrance comes to an abrupt end if they choose to approach our own island shores" (17 April 1991: 18). As a promise from the sovereign of "safe conduct," passports could be issued to people of all nationalities (see e.g., PRO 1992). Since 1794, passports have always been granted by the Secretary of State in the UK, but it was not until 1858 that the UK passport became available to UK nationals only. The document consequently became invested with the sign of belonging specifically to the British nation-state and, more problematically, to the empire. My ar-

Notes for this section begin on page 83.

gument in this essay is that the growing awareness of the presence of colo-nial subjects hastens the surfacing of nationality as a territorial affection. In other words, the equation between people and territory must be found in the emergence of certain notions about British/English nationality in rela-tion to empire. "What—besides power and a congealed state of affairs," asks Mehta, "made an Inuit in the upper reaches of Canada, a gentleman in a borough of London, a Bhil tribesman in the hills of Rajasthan, and a Maori in New Zealand—all subjects of an empress in a small island in the Atlantic Ocean?" (1999: 115).[1]

With the coming into effect of the 1981 British Nationality Act, the term "British subject" takes on a more constricted meaning. This Act prioritizes parentage over geography and places it within the postwar discourse of blood and family, rooting for a familial understanding of Britishness.[2] Its ap-plication is now restricted to those who retain some kind of subject-status in relation to the British Crown, but who do not come into the ambit of the new classifications of "British Citizen," "British Dependent Territories Citi-zen," "British Overseas Citizen" or "Commonwealth Citizen" (Part IV and Schedule 2, British Nationality Act 1981). Prior to the Act, all citizens of the United Kingdom and Colonies were Commonwealth citizens and British subjects, and Commonwealth citizens were also British subjects.[3] Earlier still, all those born within the "allegiance of the Crown"—that is, within ter-ritory controlled by the Crown—were British subjects (see Dummett and Nicol 1990). Lord Diplock in DPP v. Bhagwan in 1972 states in unequivo-cal terms that a British subject had "the right at common law to enter the United Kingdom, without let or hindrance when and where he pleased and to remain here as long as he liked" ([1972] Ac 60: 74).

In 1950, Labour Home Secretary Herbert Morrison declared that "no one has a legal right to a passport," that all passports remain the property of the issuer and can thus be impounded at will (Parliamentary Debates (Commons), 5th ser., [1950], v. 474, c. 1895). He drew from a precedent that dates back to at least the seventeenth century, when a court ruling known as Calvin's Case determined how British subjecthood was acquired and the obligations of its subjects. No provisions for subjects' rights were made. At a stroke, the "feudal law of lord and subject," which guaranteed rights and obligations on both sides, was legally dispensed with, formally signaling the erosion that had been going on for centuries (Dummett and Nicol 1990: 62–67). Privileges of nationality or free entry into the country have since been subject to the whim of Parliament or the government of the day. The common understanding is that until 1962, all Westminster governments preferred to stress equality by treating all British subjects the same. This, it is held, was irrespective of where in the British Empire they habitually resided.

Before the term "British Subject" found an amplified resonance during the heyday of empire, documents were carried by adventurers to places that had no diplomatic ties with Britain as a sort of safeguard. John Jourdain in 1611, for instance, who was engaged by the East India Company to open up trade, was traveling armed with a letter of introduction from King James I. By the time Jourdain arrived in India after many adventures, on the heels of the Portuguese who had established a foothold on the west coast of India, he had already lost his letter. In order to secure a safe passage, he applied for an audience with the Moghul King Jahangir. The king gave him a safe conduct, as Jourdain wrote in his journal, but makes the point that such a paper was not absolutely necessary in his kingdom:

> Soe at the daie appointed wee went, where as soone as the Kinge came forth and was sett on his throne, he called us to him, demandinge what our desire was. Wee told him that wee had lost ship and that wee weare desirous to travaile to gett home for our countrie by the waye of Cambaia and Suratt; desiringe His Majestie that hee would favour us with his passé as well for our quiette travellinge as alsoe passing of our stuffe without custome. He answered that his passé to travaille was needlesse because his countrie was a free country for all man, notwithstanding wee should have his passe as wee desired . . .
> (Foster 1905: 42)

Around this period the East India Company was setting up four trading posts in India, and by the middle of the eighteenth century, it had obtained the *Diwani* (or financial control) of Bengal, Bihar, and Orissa. In 1775, Oudh was being turned into a dependency and by 1801 it was partially absorbed by the Company.[4] In contradistinction to the flow of capital and goods controlled by European powers, unimpeded global mobility was then the norm; but with the expansion of popular travel in the middle of the nineteenth century, European governments were under pressure to review and formalize passport procedures. It was usual for the Foreign Secretary to issue passports to persons he was acquainted with or those who came recommended, but this system could not cope with the increased movement of people. It was under these circumstances that the modern pre-printed passport replaced the earlier handwritten document. The document itself, around this time, was a single sheet of paper, headed by a coat of arms and printed with an ornamental script requesting in florid language that the owner be allowed to pass unhindered in the name of the monarch or the state. There was no description of the holder's physiognomy except assertions such as *Gentilhomme Anglais*.

Letters to *The Times* during this period provide ample evidence of the fact that the passport system was generally detested. Even though it took only about twenty-four hours to acquire the document, there was widespread resentment against the bureaucratic process, especially against the undignified idea that the bona fides of an English gentleman could possibly be placed in doubt without the accompanying piece of paper. Though France and Belgium, on the other hand, required passports, Britain generally allowed passportless foreigners to disembark on its shores. The description "British Subject" or "English gentleman traveling with his wife and servants" on a document was sufficient to ensure travel virtually anywhere in the world.

Thus, at the legal level, Britishness was not yet tied to having a national passport. The protocol for issuing passports would change on 19 February 1858, following the defeat in parliament of the Prime Minister Palmerston's Conspiracy to Murder Bill,[5] such that one state could no longer issue a passport that claimed the authority to confer identity on the holder as a national of another state. In other words, an Englishman would no longer be able to travel on a legally issued French passport, something that was common before the defeat of the bill. Napoleon III, the object of Orsini's assassination attempt, commented on the liberty of the individual in Britain:

> In England the first of all liberties, that of going where you please, is never disturbed for there no one is asked for passports. Passports—the oppressive invention of the committee of public safety which are an embarrassment and an obstacle to the peaceable citizen but which are utterly powerless against those who wish to deceive the vigilance of authority. (*Hansard* 23.3.1858)

In fact, the French government had declared on 5 February 1858 that it was discontinuing the practice of issuing passports to British subjects. The British Secretary of State, the Earl of Clarendon, showed enthusiasm for this move and argued for the arrangement to be followed by other nations. A few weeks later, the French government also removed the "no passport" concession for British subjects.

Clarendon's enthusiasm is worth considering, since the loss of an Englishman's right to unimpeded travel on the continent might at face value appear an affront to national pride rather than an expression of it. An insight into the changing perception of the interests of the nation is afforded by a letter to *The Times* of London, published on February 4th of the same year, in which an English reader narrated his experience of international travel from the other side of the Channel:

> Sir,
> The summer before last, while residing with my family at Boulogne, I witnessed on two or three occasions the shipment of batches of Italian refugees on board the Folkestone boat for delivery in England.
> I was particularly struck by one lot who were brought down to the harbor escorted by a large body of police. Judging from the extreme attention shown them by their guardians and the number of those who were linked, in no affectionate bonds, to the wrist of their conductors, I concluded that the party would form a very pretty addition to English society. Two or three of them appeared men of education, and most of them were of the exact type which formed, in Cassius' eyes, the perfect conspirator. Several of them had hunches of black beard in their hands. All of them were buttoned up in rags and half-famished in

appearance. What I learnt of them was, that they had been passed on from police station to police station, and were not wanted in France.
I well remember the insulting gestures and coarse oaths which were flung at the gendarmerie as the boat left the quay and felt satisfied from the violence of one or two of them that had the means been in their hands they would have left with those gentry some more definite token of their opinion of France and its authorities.
Some six weeks afterward I twice met two of these men still buttoned up in their rags, but as erect and defiant as ever, parading in Piccadilly.
Do you think it is possible that this lot may have furnished a band for the rue Lepellier business? ("How we Come to Have Refugees in England" 1858)

Evident in this letter is not only a lack of compassion for people "half-famished in appearance," but a striking confidence in the ability to "know" their true character based on appearance, features which remain central to the discourse around today's refugees and "illegals" arriving on English shores via Calais.

The contemporary discourse on migrants in Britain bears juxtaposition with mobility policies instituted after the abolition of slavery. Mechanisms of state control to monitor the movement of indentured labor (or "free" subjects from India, totaling close to 30 million) were ratified by the British parliament in 1838 (*Parliamentary Papers*, 1837–38, vol. 3). Lack of any legal precedence and objections to this were swept aside on the basis that "it is a distinction common to every metropolis, that their colonies are governed . . . . by special laws, because the elements of society are not the same therein as in Europe" (*Papers Respecting the East India Laborers' Bill* 1836, 56).[6] Curious conditions in the colony, it was argued, allowed differential application of the law, and the very term "British Subject" was "susceptible of important division and modification" (ibid. 56). Despite the theory of liberal equality maintained throughout the empire, the issue of subjecthood and nationality very quickly reveals what Partha Chatterjee has called the "rule of colonial difference" (Chatterjee 1993, 16–22).

Attitudes to nationality and citizenship diverged sharply across the British Empire, divided as it was between the "premier white league" and the others. The Imperial center endorsed the efforts of majority settler populations to set up barriers against the non-white peoples of the empire. The Australian colonies (of New South Wales and Victoria) promulgated policies in the 1850s to obstruct the entry of Asiatics.[7] The racial rather than "national" basis of these policies is apparent in their application not only to non-subjects, such as migrants from China, but also to the Queen's own British subjects from India. The Southern African colony of Natal in the 1890s charted laws against British Indians, with the concession that an education test was undertaken to serve these goals. At the 1897 Imperial Conference, Joseph Chamberlain asked the Australian colonies to "*arrange a form of words* which will avoid hurting the feelings of any of Her majesty's subjects" (emphasis added). He was in unison with the white colonies' desire to shield themselves against the incursion of people "alien in civilization, alien in religion, alien in customs, whose influx, moreover, would seriously interfere with the legitimate rights of the existing labor population" (Hancock 1937: 166). [8]

The contradictions in the imperial claim to universalism are brought into focus in the case of the annexation of Oudh, or Awadh (better known today as the region around Lucknow) between 1856 and 1858, a period which includes the momentous events of the Mutiny and the consequent consolidation of the Crown's stranglehold over India. Alongside the English rhetoric of civilizing (i.e. making citizens of) the decadent residents of Oudh,[9] the annexation saw the disenfranchisement and dislocation of Oudh's first family (apart from its peoples) to the point where they found themselves pleading for a British passport in London in order to travel to France.

The Paradoxes of Imperial Subjecthood

On 7 February 1856, the last King of Awadh, Wajid Ali Shah, was deposed and the territory declared annexed by the East India Company. In the month of June, Malika Kishwar (or Jenabi Auliah Tajara Begum), the king's mother (and Begum of Oudh), led a delegation with Special Envoy Muhammad Maseehud-din, Major R.W. Bird (who resigned his position with the East India Company as Assistant Resident at the court of Awadh) and the king's friend, Brandon, to London to present the case against the annexation to the Queen and Parliament. The party was met by the members of the Court of Directors of the Company and, for the first time, a properly framed series of charges against the king (in a document called *The Oude Blue Book)* for his dereliction of duties were offered as explanation. After the submission of replies from the king (who was then resident in Calcutta), Malika Kishwar was given audience by Queen Victoria in July 1857 in a special court.

By then the Mutiny was well under way and the story of the massacre of Englishmen in Kanpur made headlines in the London newspapers. The deposition of the king was an important factor in the Revolt. Wajid Ali Shah was placed under arrest in the dingy cells of Fort Williams in Calcutta while the king's party in London suffered discord. Malika Kishwar finally left for Paris in January 1858, where she would die. Her son General Hashmat also died in March 1858 in London and his body was taken to Paris to be buried alongside his mother (Khan n.d.: 431–32; also Mohan 1977).

The following correspondence between the king's party and the Foreign Office concerning their travel to France is illuminating. By virtue of the fact that Oudh was now part and parcel of the British Raj in India, it follows that the all people living there *had become British subjects.* With this newly acquired status, members of the deposed royal family would logically have the right to travel with all the protection and privileges accorded to any other British subject. The Foreign Office, however, did not think it was a good idea to grant them traveling documents. It is not clear as to the explanation for this, though in part there must have been anxieties relating to French sympathy and potential support for the dispossessed subjects: Malika Kishwar eventually did go to France but I have been unable to establish, given that she and her party were denied British passports, whether the French authorities waived the requirement in her case.[10] But equally, this reluctance also reveals the contradictions underlying the conflation of nation and empire which for most of the nineteenth century could be kept at a distance.

Addressing Her Majesty's Secretary of State for Foreign Affairs, the Queen Mother's solicitors in London filed an application:[11]

189 Fleet Street,
14th October 1857
My Lord,
We request that your Lordship will authorize the grant of a Passport for traveling on the Continent to Jenabi Auliah Tajara Begum the Queen Mother of Oude; accompanied by Mirza Mohummud Hamid Allies Eldest Son and Heir Apparent of His Majesty the King of Oude; Mirza Mohummud Iowaad Alliesek under Hushmut Bahadoor next Brother of His Majesty the King of Oude, and Moulvee Musieh Ood Deen Khan Bahadoor.
We have the honor to be,
My Lord,
Your most obedient Servants,
Praed Hay
[PRO: FO 612/14]

In a memo dated the same day, the Foreign Office wondered about the citizenship status of the supplicants: "Does the Queen Mother of Oude ask for a Passport as a British Subject?" A copy of the same was forwarded to the India Board the next day. This was crucial to the British government as any acknowledgment on the part of the king's party to have become British subjects implied that they accepted the fact of British absorption of Oudh territories. A letter to the solicitors was issued on the same day:

F.O.
October 14, 1857
Messrs Praed & Co.
Gentlemen

In reply to your letter of this day requesting a Passport for Jenabi Auliah Tajara Begum, the Queen Mother of Oude and her party, I am directed by the Earl of Clarendon to remind you that Passports are issued from this Department only

to British Subjects, and I am to request that you will inform Lord Clarendon whether the Queen applies for a Passport in that character for Herself and Party.
I am the
(signed) [illegible]

The Foreign Office was clearly pushing for an acceptance from the applicants that the occupation of Oudh was not only *de facto* but *de jure* as well, thereby undermining their own argument for independence. The kingdom of Oudh, prior to annexation, was already paying tribute to the Raj. The Queen Mother's new solicitors, in their reply, brought the point to the F.O.'s attention:

Messers Gregory Skirrow and Rowcliffe Solicitors
Oct. 15. 1857
The Queen of Oude and her family requested Passports under the impression that they were entitled to do so, as being under British protection.
Copy to India
Board —Oct. 15/57

To which the F.O. responded curtly by citing the Foreign Secretary, Earl of Clarendon's inability to grant passports:

Foreign Office
October 16. 1857

Gregory Skirrow Rhowcliffe
(Bedford Row)
Gentlemen,
In reply to your letter of yesterday I am directed by the Earl of Clarendon to express to you his regret that it will not be in his power to give Passports to the Queen of Oude and her Suite.
I am
(signed) illegible

The king's party was also in touch with the India House and the Board of Control who referred the matter back to the Foreign Office.[12] After a flurry of letters, and in consultation with the India Board, an opinion was formed against granting passports to the Queen Mother and the Princes of Oudh.

Lord Dalhousie, the governor–general, was largely responsible for setting these events in motion. Colonel William Sleeman was appointed in 1849 as Resident in Oudh and reported on the "depraved" state of affairs there, describing Wajid Ali as "a crazy imbecile in the hands of a few fiddlers, eunuchs, and poetasters" (1858: 382). An anonymous book (regarded as most probably the work of Captain Robert Bird, an ex-assistant to Sleeman and later a supporter of Wajid Ali) disagreed with the Sleeman report in these terms: "He affected to inspect and make a report, but the character of his report was determined for him before he entered Oude. He professed to examine, but he was under orders to sentence; he pretended to try, but he was instructed simply to condemn . . . [he] was the principal source of the charges afterward brought against [the royal family]" (1857: 104). Colonel Outram was sent to Lucknow to file an updated report in 1854, which only reinforced the picture of "deplorable conditions," the "gross misrule" of the sovereign, the oppression of his subjects, and the moral backwardness of the people improvable only by the liberal civilizing norms of Englishness. Inaction was identified with moral error, and legal justifications for intervention abounded. In particular, the moral duties of empire and the virtues of Englishness were invoked. To cite but one example, Outram testifies:

> I have been listening all day to stories . . . any one of which would make the House of Commons quiver with indignation . . . I doubt if Tiberius or Caligula were a bit worse either in cruelty or debauchery, than the Nasir-ud-din; and the present man is as bad, though of a feebler energy . . . "Why is not indigo grown?" Said I. "Well," said he (a man of Lucknow), "it has been tried, two Englishman tried it. One was murdered, and the other had to fly. You see there is no security of life or property here." I heard, too, one little statistical fact, that will give you some idea of the state of morals. There are upward of one hundred houses in Lucknow, all taxed and registered, and inhabited not by women but by men. Was Gomorrah worse? (in Edwardes 1960: 175).

Powered by moral outrage, the court of directors in London and the governor-general's council in Calcutta spurred Dalhousie to offer a new treaty to the king or face removal. With British troops advancing to the borders of Lucknow, Major-General Outram met Wajid Ali Shah on 4 February 1856. The encounter is narrated in an official report: "His majesty turned toward the Resident and said, 'Why have I deserved this? What have I committed?'" On the Resident's explanation of options, the king went into a "passionate burst of grief and exclaimed: 'Treaties are necessary between equals only: who am I, now, that the British government should enter into treaties with?' . . . Uncovering himself, he placed his turban in the hands of Resident, declaring that, now his titles, rank, and position were all gone, it was not for him to sign a treaty, or to enter into any negotiation . . . He touched on the future fate which awaited his heirs and family, and declared his unalterable resolution to seek in Europe for that redress which it was vain to find in India" (*Oude Blue Book* 287–89). Just over a year following confiscation, in May 1857, the whole of northern India broke out in the most violent revolt ever in British India's history, with Oudh at the centre of it and one of the wives of the king leading the uprising along with various landlords and chiefs, and an Islamic cleric.

It has been argued that the toppling of English norms by the mutineers in some ways threatened aspects of the supranational appeal of Britishness entrenched in colonial discourse. Together with the physical intrusion into domestic space, the cultural idealization of Englishness located at "home" (among the colonial administrative community away from home) stood despoiled.[13] "Ultimately," writes Hadfield, "historical, social and moral elements merged in communitarian terms of a threat to the contextuality of Englishness. That which had represented the severest threat to the domestic discourse (embodying both identity and moral legitimacy) necessitated a retaliation of the severest kind. The Mutiny, lodged idealistically in the English consciousness as an attack on the English civilizing discourse of Empire 'fuelled calls for vengeance and brutal retaliation in line with masculine, national, and imperial discourses of honor and prestige'" (2006).[14] The denial of passports to the Queen of Oudh can be read as a reactive demarcation of Englishness against the contest claims of a supranational imperial ideology, as the belated reclamation of the geography of home against the supranational drive of empire. As Ian Baucom has argued, "in creating an empire [which] depended on a continuous traffic between the English here and the imperial there, England rendered its spaces of belonging susceptible to . . . global . . . renegotiatio[n]," for "as [colonial] subjects took their places within the locations of Englishness, they also took partial possession of those places" (Baucom 1999: 38).

The Passport and Exclusion

Framing the incident in these terms, what we run into is a moment where the paradoxes generated by the conflation of nation and empire become visible. While the immediate contradiction appears to be "played on" the Queen Mother's party—whose acceptance of a passport would be construed as acceptance of imperial rule—at a more fundamental level, the contradiction revealed is that between nation and empire, as signaled by the problematic conflation of Englishness and Britishness. As *The Oude Blue Book* demonstrates, imperial expansion was legitimized through appeals to the civilizing and modernizing claims of a Britishness which in turn implied a supranational identity open to all imperial subjects. But as this instance reveals, the closed concept of nation ultimately could not accept the threat of renegotiation, transformation, and translation incumbent on the extended borders of empire, and the issuing of British passports—even though it would have supported imperial policy—so threatened national identity that it could not be countenanced. At the practical level, the problem that arose was how to separate or distinguish between members of the national community and those who remained in English eyes irretrievably foreign without endangering the entire ethic of the empire; that is, to distinguish *between* "British Subjects." My reading of the archival materials suggest that the administrative arms of the liberal nation-state applied strategies of bureaucratic discretion (through caveats in policy) time and again to get around the possible charge of discrimination against other British subjects. In the process, the passport was transformed from a document concerned with making passage secure to a document primarily concerned with designating national inclusion and exclusion.

If, as we have argued in the introduction to this volume, the incompatibility of nation and empire was a fundamental feature of European imperialism, it was not experienced in uniform ways within the different imperial homelands. According to Hannah Arendt, while the French tried to iron out the inconsistencies of nation-based imperialism by seeking to expand the nation territorially with the incorporation of Algeria into France, the British on the contrary sought to keep the poles apart (Arendt [1951] 1973: 130–31). Unwilling to face up to this fundamental contradiction, the British Empire preferred to keep it at bay, "solving" the problem by relying on the very expansionist dynamic of empire. But such a "solution" was of course only a deferral, and it is precisely this contradiction that Britain would come to face in the period of decolonization, when former colonial subjects, now cast adrift in a globalized economy, would demand recognition by, and entry into, what had once proclaimed itself to be the "mother country." The fate of the deposed house of Oudh is particularly redolent, then, because it anticipates the developments that will begin to unfold a century later from the Empire Windrush to Powell to Thatcher.[15] While within the horizon of the nineteenth century, the situation of the royal family of Oudh may look idiosyncratic and unusual, from the vantage point of the twenty-first century it can be recognized as a fate that would be shared by millions.

Notes

1. The space of empire or the links between political identity and territory, Mehta further observes, was neglected by British thinkers of the nineteenth century. The "absence of self-consciousness regarding the empire's own locality foretold its fated terminus in the fate of nationalism, which, . . . insisted on the political credence of drawing boundaries" (1999: 116). He notes an irony in the theoretical disregard of the importance of boundaries to political identity. When they have imagined an ideal polity—like Francis Bacon in New Atlantis and Thomas More in Utopia—they have done so by giving it the geographical form of an island state. With the presumption of such natural boundaries, "they have failed to recognize their more general significance as expressions of distinct political identity" (1999: 146). R.L. Stevenson's Treasure Island, William Golding's The Lord of the Flies, and Shakespeare's "this sceptred Isle" passage from Richard II are noted as better known examples of this.

2. See Paul (1997: 182). The 1971 Act formally divided British subjects into patrials and nonpatrials, placing nonpatrials on virtually the same footing as aliens. Those with ancestors born in the UK tend to be descendants of UK colonists, and patrials

are overwhelmingly white. Nonpatrial subjects tend to have ancestors in the colonized lands and tend to be colored.

3. The "airport people" of sub-continental origin who were thrown out of Kenya and found themselves stuck in Heathrow and Gatwick were not only British subjects but held British passports. Even though they had a lawful claim to residence in Britain, they were nonetheless treated with hostility. The horror of the Wilson Cabinet at the spectacle of these "Kenya Asians with British passports" gaining entry is registered in Richard Crossman's diaries (in Dummett and Nichol 1990: 200).

4. Security needs, the reinstatement of order, strategic deployment of troops, and the need to generate revenues to offset these expenses were cited as reasons for annexation. Oudh was already a major supplier of Indigo, cotton, textiles, and opium.

5. A foreigner had taken exile in Britain and had plotted to commit a crime upon another foreigner, to be perpetrated abroad. This was the famous case of Count Felice Orsini who was found involved in conspiracy, assassination, and false passports. Lord Palmerston, in response, proposed the Bill in the House of Commons: "A conspiracy has been formed, partly in this country for the purposes of committing a most atrocious crime. That conspiracy has led to most disastrous consequences . . . the law in this country—in England—treats a conspiracy to murder simply as a misdemeanor subject to fine and a short period of imprisonment . . . the conspiracy to murder is punishable on the same manner as a conspiracy for any other purpose such as hissing at the theatre" (*Hansard* 8.2.1858).

6. John Locke, widely regarded as the originator of liberal rights theory, also provided moral justification for imperial rule. He argued that although all men were in a natural state of freedom and equality, there were some—lunatics, idiots, children, innocents— who required the tutelage and government of others since they could not be free on their own (1690). John Stuart Mill, likewise, held that "implied obedience to an Akbar" was necessary before colonial subjects could be allowed to become full citizens (1978: 10). Theorists and defenders of liberty thus helped set up an equation between imperial domination and enlightened British absolutism.

7. Australia's own indigenous people were decimated, and those who survived reduced to nothing more than objects. Drawing from a mid-nineteenth century true story, David Malouf writes in *Remembering Babylon* of how a blond English boy, brought up by Aborigines for sixteen years, rejoins colonial society in a white settlement in Queensland. He appears at the edge of the settlement, a spindly scarecrow thing, falling off a fence, shouting: "Do not shoot. I am a B-b-british object."

8. The implications of Indian independence and the British Nationality Act of 1948 on the hyphenated Anglo-Indians or Eurasians are interesting. They were required to prove the British origins of a paternal ancestor. Blunt (2003) argues that ideas of Britain as home were inextricably bound up with ideas of whiteness. Ideas about an Anglo-Indian diaspora long predated decolonization, and their migration under the Act led to a recolonization of Anglo-Indian identity.

9. In the liberal worldview then, "Contemporary European, especially British, culture alone represented civilization . . . . There was no such thing as 'Western' civilization: there existed only 'civilization'" (Metcalf 1995: 34).

10. Competitive metropolitan interests constituted an essential element of the dynamic. Anxiety and fear over French machinations in relation to Indian rulers was never far away. In his troubles with the Company, Tipu Sultan had, after all, set a precedent by approaching the revolutionary government in Paris.

11. I have retained the spellings as they appear in the correspondence.

12. A copy of the correspondence [P.R.O.: F.O. 612/14]:

India Board
October 16th 1857

Sir,

I am desired by the Commissioners of the affairs of India to acknowledge the receipt of your letter of the 15th instant, respecting the application which has been made to the Secretary of State for Foreign Affairs to grant passports to Paris for the members of the King of Oude now residing in this country.

It will be for the Secretary of State to determine whether the British protection which these Royal Personages enjoy constitutes them British Subjects.

The Board observe that Messers Gregory and Co. say: "The Royal Family have brought the India House and the Board of Control acquainted with their wish to go to France"; and they were told, as we are informed, "that there was no objection to their going." What they were told was, "that the most expedient course for them to pursue would be to apply for the passports at the Foreign Office in the usual manner." The Board were not willing to apply for them, as such application might be interpreted as a sanction to their proceedings; and they are of opinion that it would be better that the Oude family should not go to France; but they cannot prevent their taking that step.

I am,
Sir,
Your most obedient servant,
Hammond [signed, illegible]

13. Among the well-known tropes of empire was "the paradox of England claiming exaggerated subjective affiliation overseas . . . far beyond the home shores of geographical England where imagined England was more intensely idealized than 'at home'" (Schwarz 1992: 95).

14. In an attempt to reinscribe the self through "right," overwhelming might was used to suppress other revolts in different parts of the empire: the African Frontier Wars of the Cape Colony, the Morant Bay uprising in Jamaica, the Maori Wars in New Zealand, and the Afghan Wars.

15. Enoch Powell declared: "The West Indian or Indian does not, by being born in England, become an Englishman" (Foot 1969: 119). Margaret Thatcher sought to justify her nationality law on the grounds that the public was afraid "that this country might be rather swamped by people with a different culture" (Messina 1989: 122).

Bibliography

Arendt, Hannah. 1973 [1951]. *The Origins of Totalitarianism.* San Diego: Harcourt Brace.

Blunt, Alison. 2003. "Geographies of Diaspora and Mixed Descent: Anglo-Indians in India and Britain." *International Journal of Population Geography* 9(4): 281–94.

Baucom, Ian. 1999. *Out of Place: Englishness, Empire and the Locations of Identity.* Princeton: Princeton University Press.

Chatterjee, Partha. 1993. *The Nation and its Fragments: Colonial and Postcolonial Histories.* Princeton, NJ: Princeton University Press.

"Commentary." 1991. *The Guardian* (April 17).

Dacoitee in Excelsis: or the Spoilation of Oude by the East India Company. 1857. London: J.R. Taylor.

Dummett, Ann and Andrew Nicol. 1990. *Subjects, Citizens, Aliens and Others: Nationality and Immigration Law*. London: Wiedenfeld and Nicolson.

Edwardes, Michael. 1960. *The Orchid House: Splendours and Miseries of the Kingdom of Oudh, 1827–1857*. London: Cassell.

Foot, Paul. 1969. *The Rise of Enoch Powell*. London: Penguin.

Foster, W. (ed.) 1905. *The Journal of John Jourdain 1608–1617*, Hakluyt Society.

Hadfield, Amelia. "ReOrientation: Ethical Imperatives in the Construction of English Colonial Identity during the 1857 'Indian Mutiny'." [Accessed on 10 February 2006.] <http://www.isanet.org/noarchive/reorientation.html#_ftn74>.

Hancock, W.K. 1937. *Survey of British Commonwealth Affairs*, Vol. 1: *Problems of Nationalism 1918–1936*. London: Oxford University Press.

Hansard 8.2. 1858.

"How we Come to Have Refugees in England." 1858. *The Times* (February 4).

Khan, Mohammad Masih Uddin. not dated. *Safarnama*. Kutub-khana-i-Anwaria Kakoria Manuscript.

Locke, John. 1967 [1690]. *Two Treatises of Government*. P. Laslett (ed.). Cambridge: Cambridge University Press.

Malouf, David. 1993. *Remembering Babylon*. London: Chatto and Windus.

Mehta, Uday Singh. 1999. *Liberalism and Empire*. Delhi: Oxford University Press.

Messina, A. 1989. *Race and Party Competition in Britain*. Oxford: Clarendon Press.

Metcalf, Thomas. 1995. *Ideologies of the Raj: The New Cambridge History of India, III. 4*. Cambridge: Cambridge University Press.

Mill, J.S. 1978 [1859] *On Liberty*. Cambridge and Indianapolis: Hackett.

Mohan, Surendra. 1977. *Awadh under the Nawabs: Politics, Culture and Communal Relations*. New Delhi: Manohar.

Oude Blue Book or *Parliamentary Papers: Papers relating to Oude, presented to both Houses of Parliament by Command of her Majesty*. 1856.

Papers Respecting the East India Labourers' Bill. 1836.

Parliamentary Debates (Commons). 5th series, [1950]. v. 474, c. 1895.

Parliamentary Papers. 1837–38. Vol.3.

Paul, Kathleen. 1997. *Whitewashing Britain*. Ithaca and London: Cornell University Press.

Public Record Office, Kew: FO 612/14 series.

Schwarz, Bill. 1992. "An Englishman Abroad and at Home." *New Formations*. Vol. 17.

Sleeman, W.H. 1858. *A Journey through the Kingdom of Oude 1849–1850*. London: Richard Bentley.

CHAPTER 4

Friends Across the Water

British Orientalists and Middle Eastern Nationalisms

Geoffrey Nash

Affinity and Otherness

I n this essay I shall focus on the identification of English travelers with specific oriental peoples and societies in nineteenth and early twentieth century travel and political writing, and how this might be seen to intersect with considerations of "home."[1] My geographical areas of concern are England and the Middle East, in the nineteenth century polarities in terms of the conventional binaries of developed/undeveloped, modern/primitive, civilized/uncivilized. The connection between them is established in a body of writings by English travelers to the region, including famous names like Burton, Palgrave, Doughty, the Blunts, and Thesiger.

In the field of British travel writing on Arabia, the travelers' search for something beyond their humdrum Victorian lives has long been recognized:

> As the nineteenth century progressed, life became so ordered and secure that certain temperaments began to yearn for the open desert horizons and the free wandering life of the Beduin. Their picture was Utopian but as Europe became ever more bourgeois and materialist, so the Middle East seemed to stand out in starker contrast. For some, unsure of their place in society, to travel became a spiritual quest for different and better values. Arabia was a place where some went to discover themselves: many returned transformed (Bidwell 1976: 19).

In an age in which Britain's imperial control followed the paths of travelers, the imperial idea invariably traveled with them. For some, like the young George Curzon, bent on establishing for himself a career on the back of his eastern expertise, travel to the Orient was travel with a purpose. Despite the aesthetic pleasure he derived from his interaction with the East—"do we ever escape from the fascination of a turban, or the mystery of the shrouded apparitions that pass for women in the dusty alleys?" (1892:

1.13)—there could be no doubt which factor, pride in British imperial sway or enjoyment of the authentic East, figured more highly in his scheme of values.[2] On the other hand, Wilfred Thesiger, who began his career as a servant to the British Empire, desired only to occlude his Englishness in his travels in the Arabian desert. For example, he resented being refused permission to travel to the Jebel al-Akhdar in the late 1940s by a local sheikh because he had no power to arrange with the British government for the sheikh to be an independent ruler of that area of Oman (Thesiger 1964: 324). Early in the nineteenth century, David Urquhart still found it possible both to valorize Britain in relation to the succor it afforded to less advantaged, oriental peoples and societies, and at the same time arraign it for having fallen from the pedestal of this noble mission.

After the appearance of Edward Said's *Orientalism* (1978), a good deal of cultural analysis has been dedicated to theorizations of what *did* motivate European travelers on their journeys east, and how this motivation was constructed into their travel writing. For my purposes in this essay, an additional issue is whether a specific quality of Englishness was brought to these travelers' materials. According to Billie Melman (2002), Said's *Orientalism* "perpetuates stereotypes of the Middle East and Middle-Eastern people that, Said and others have argued, hardly changed over a millennium" (107). Recent revisions and reversals of Said "seek to resist the reduction of cross-cultural encounter to simple relations of domination and subordination" (S. Clark 1999: 3). New perspectives may include a replacement of an Orientalist construction of a stereotyped "other" by a construction of affinity between metropolitan and peripheral societies (Cannadine 2002). This allows for a space appropriate to the kind of identification with the Middle East by the travelers I shall discuss. Ali Behdad (1994) argued for a "desire for the Orient" on the part of "belated" western travelers to the Middle East. His coining of the term "belated" has been especially useful for the discussion of Arabia as a destination, since the great period of its exploration (circa 1870) by English travelers coincided with the era of late colonialism that might be said to have drawn to a close at the same time as the last noted English traveler, Wilfred Thesiger, made his journeys in the 1940s. As a foil to the "spiritual quest" of the English abroad, Robert Young (1995) writes of a sexualized "colonial desire" that was complicit in articulating the discourses of European racism and imperialism. Young demonstrates how the concept of Anglo-Saxon racial identity, in contrast to Teutonic and Gallic conceptualizations, remained proudly hybrid, or "mongrel." In her analysis of the upper class Englishman's love affair with Arabia, Kathryn Tidrick (1989) foregrounded class, in addition to psychological trauma, as formative factors that drove her English subjects east. (The mongrel categorization nevertheless retains a curious relevance in the case of the Arabian explorer W. Gifford Palgrave, who was only half an English gentleman, the other part of his ancestry being Jewish—a factor Tidrick makes a lot of in accounting for her subject's cosmopolitan wanderlust and underdeveloped patriotism). Palgrave is a good example of the proposition that the western sense of cultural superiority and urge to dominate has coexisted, within certain writers and travelers, with a vulnerability that led them to contrast the underpinning materialist ideology of the West with Asiatic values formed around notions of spirituality and community. The desire to regenerate the West by recourse to eastern spirituality was identified by Said (1978) as an aspect of Romantic utopianism.[3] But this indigenous criticism of western norms should not be confined to the Romantics; indeed, it may represent another counterweight to Said's Orientalist theory.

In the case of travelers who went outside the boundaries of their own culture to investigate alien formations, the reports brought back are conditioned in both cognitive and affective terms by modes of apprehension formed within the native culture. Western travelers who "penetrated" the *dar al-Islam* in the nineteenth century may have adopted some extreme strategies to report on the target culture, but they rarely severed the umbilical cord connecting them with their European heritage. Edward Lane for instance, though an admirer and defender of Islam as a sister religion to his own Judeo-Christianity, remained firmly fixed by his evangelical roots.[4] Richard Burton believed primarily in himself as a member of the British imperial caste, and though respectful of Islam, used it for polemical purposes in order to deprecate a Christianity that for reasons of temperament and upbringing he despised. A figure who in certain respects manifests a dissident streak in his alienation from western modernity, who utilized aspects of eastern society to contest his own, was Thomas Carlyle. Compared with Lane and Burton, Carlyle had no direct contact with the world of Islam, but is known for having contributed to a more positive European image of that faith in the nineteenth century. A supporter of Germanic racial theory, and a proponent of the spread of Anglo-Saxon colonization, Carlyle had few links with the British establishment, remaining a lone voice in his own land. Adrift from his childhood nurturing in a strict version of Protestant Christianity, he never reconciled to any of the anchors of western secular humanism. Carlyle knew no Arabic and never traveled further east than the Prussian battlefields of Frederick the Great. Still, he was drawn to the Prophet Muhammad by a deeper spiritual affinity. His native Calvinism and the religious exemplars of his youth inscribed on him a pietistic frame of mind that lasted long after he had relinquished orthodox Christian belief. Lane's presentation of practical manifestations of Islamic faith in his *Manners and Customs of the Modern Egyptians* clearly impressed Carlyle, who evoked the call of *Allah-u-Akbar* by the Cairo watchman in his Lecture "The Hero as Prophet," concluding: "Islam sounds through the souls, the whole daily existence, of [. . .] millions" (1897: 76). With Lane's book in mind, Carlyle was able to deliver his lecture on Islam and its Prophet, thereby making himself a key figure in challenging the bigoted view of the subject that had obtained in the West since the Middle Ages.[5] Granted, Carlyle's portrait of the Prophet of Islam is hardly a scholarly accurate one. Said saw it as "forc[ing] Muhammad to serve a thesis totally overlooking the historical and cultural circumstances of [his] own time and place." But Said wished Carlyle to fit into his own Orientalist thesis, erroneously concluding the British writer's message was "to show us that the Orient need not cause us undue anxiety, so unequal are Oriental to European achievements" (1978: 152).

Dissidence and a "Desire for the Orient"

The sympathy for Islam pioneered by Carlyle also linked a group of dissidents who feature in a survey by A.J.P. Taylor of individuals who engaged in another peculiarly English activity: foreign policy dissent (Taylor 1957). David Urquhart, born a Scot, but like Carlyle English by self-adoption, was one; the gentleman and Arabian explorer, Wilfrid Scawen Blunt, another. Blunt was in turn allied with Cambridge Professor of Oriental Languages, Edward Granville Browne, who tutored a generation of English diplomatists and imperial administrators, including Ronald Storrs, Mark Sykes, and Reader Bullard, all of whom quote him in their travel writings or memoirs.[6] A significant name Taylor omitted was the traveler, novelist, and translator of the Qur'an, Marmaduke Pickthall. Each of these "dissidents" contributed incrementally to the specifically English activity of berating the homeland for dereliction of duty with respect to smaller or weaker nations they deemed it Britain's part to sponsor and protect. Their backgrounds, political allegiances, and protégé eastern peoples were various. Urquhart and Blunt were both of the lesser aristocracy. The youngest son of the second wife of a Scottish laird, Urquhart inherited no land, and vacillated between Toryism and radicalism. Urquhart's favored people were the Turks, but he acquired his ardor for them while fighting on behalf of the Greeks in the Greek war of independence. He was, he wrote afterward, won over by the "personification of stoical firmness and of dignified resignation of the Turks in defeat" (1839: 1. 35); this started him out on a succession of journeys through Ottoman domains in Thessaly and on the frontier between Greece and Albania.

Blunt inherited a Sussex estate on the death of his elder brother, and in spite of a notorious reputation as a political rebel (paralleled in his private love life), continued to think of himself as a Tory. His identification with the East began with the journeys in the 1870s he and his wife Anne, a granddaughter of Byron, conducted in the Syrian and central Arabian deserts. Out of these emerged his key political idea: transference of the Sultanate/Caliphate from Ottoman Turkey to the Sherif of Mecca and/or the Khedive of Egypt. Blunt later bought a desert property in Egypt to which he made annual winter visits for a decade and a half. E.M. Forster wrote of Blunt's division of his life between stints in the East and West: "perhaps only for an Englishman and only in the nineteenth century, was such a career possible" (1967: 308).

Browne adopted the Liberalism of an upper middle class family with manufacturing connections in the North East. His only travel book, *A Year Amongst the Persians* (1893), delineating his journey in search of the Babis of Persia, laid the foundation of his later advocacy of the Iranian Constitutional Revolution of 1905 to 1911. Son of a Tory country clergymen, in the 1890s Pickthall traveled as a young man in Syria and Palestine, where he took to roaming in native dress in the company of Arab locals. Later, he updated Urquhart's Turcophilia according to the immediate pre-First World War scene, traveling to Turkey to be confirmed as a partisan of the Young Turk Revolution. Pickthall rallied to the defense of the Young Turks in "letters from abroad," later published as *With The Turk in Wartime* (1914a).

The distinguishing factor behind all these writers was the urge to explain and defend their chosen eastern nationality, as well as to agitate on its behalf. Thus, an original desire for the East was converted into a political cause that spilled over into the domains of political dissidence and (in the case of Pickthall, who eventually became a *renegado*, a convert to Islam) religious apostasy.[7] Dissent in the writings of Urquhart, Blunt, Browne, and Pickthall takes the form of engagement in debates in which dominant, establishment orthodoxies centered around imperialism and Orientalism were challenged by discourses that argued for the integrity and autonomy of non-European cultures and their resources. In addition, such activity necessarily involved questioning notions of Englishness and empire, and the production of narratives on the subject of imperialism and the politics of Islam that deploy the twin motifs of British patronage over the East and its betrayal of that trust. In Urquhart, earlier Blunt, Browne, and Pickthall, Britain is encoded as a liberal power that should be moved by altruism and imperial self-interest to embrace the aspirations of reforming Islamic nations. This notion stands as a benchmark against which to set later recidivistic backsliding. Deviations are then accounted for in terms of the corrupting effects of imperialism upon the national character (Blunt, Browne), or the defection of the country's rulers from their ancestors' standards of international behavior (Urquhart, Pickthall).

Orientalist and Counter-Orientalist Discourse

Dissidence may also be discussed in terms of its incorporation within discourse(s) that might be called pro-Islamic, or counter-Orientalist. Such discourse(s) imply identification with a non-European cultural formation as a concomitant and expression of the writer's primary desire for the Orient. But we may ask whether this kind of discourse is merely an unstable form within the Orientalist terrain, which Lisa Lowe (1991) insists occurs when other discourses "such as those of gender, race and class" converge upon or diverge from discourses of Orientalism (1991: 20). Alternatively, it may be considered to function as a discrete entity contesting Orientalist discourses.

In analyzing discourses that develop out of identification with eastern social and cultural practice, Behdad does not allow himself to speak of a stable counter-Orientalist discourse. Where the desire for the East took the form of immersion in the native culture and the production of a discourse identifying with native practice, he shows that these discourses were invariably recuperated within the hegemonic discourses of Orientalism. Indeed, in their engagement with the East, each of the travelers/writers I discuss worked within Orientalist structures and in fact contributed to the process Behdad delineates. In *Spirit of the East* (1839), the early travelogue of his Ottoman journeys, David Urquhart argues persuasively for the discrete authenticity of Ottoman culture, proposing its superiority to European norms in certain aspects of its social etiquette, political order, and economic activity. In several instances, though, he also appears to propose the absorption of these within a superior, albeit protective British framework that could, without much straining, be construed as proto-imperialist. The desire to align the self with an exotic and "authentic" other cannot resist the urge to recuperate that other within the imperial scheme. According to Francis Palgrave, his brother had an abiding interest in "things often unknown and inexplicable to Western civilization," and Gifford admitted hearing communal recitation in the mosque "never without a thrill at the deep, united, concentrated belief it implies" (Allen 1972: 270, 216). But Palgrave's writings on the East rarely escape the context of the European drive to absorb that east within its own structures, and Palgrave's life displays a succession of failed attempts at career advancement through the medium of his oriental "expertise." In *The Future of Islam* (1882), Blunt argued for an Islamic revival under British tutelage, involving the dissolution of the Ottoman empire and the transfer of the caliphate from Constantinople to Mecca. The idea was taken up a generation and a half after its pronouncement and fashioned into the facade of the Arab Revolt by establishment figures like Sir Mark Sykes in London and Lord Kitchener in Cairo. Browne's construction of a narrative of two millennia of Persian spiritual and cultural achievement was of use in his campaign for Iranian self-determination. But after his death, the western-controlled Pahlavi rulers of Iran incorporated the work of Browne and other western Orientalists into a narrative of dynastic nationalism (see Boroujerdi 1996).

In spite of having their ideas co-opted into such hegemonic formations, these dissident Orientalists managed in their time to further anti-imperialist causes by mobilizing or attempting to mobilize a domestic constituency in opposition to the British establishment. Blunt conducted a one-man campaign over the British occupation of Egypt in 1882, inscribing a counter-narrative to the official histories of the likes of Lords Cromer and Milner. In his battle with Edward Grey over the Anglo-Russian Convention of 1907, which allowed Russia scope to intervene in Iran's Constitutional Revolution, E.G. Browne made use of alliances with Liberal anti-imperialists and Tory imperialists such as Lord Curzon.[8] In the process of his mediation of the Iranian revolution to an English audience, Browne first presented to the West Pan-Islamic ideas that would arguably influence later twentieth century Islamic nationalisms, while his personal hatred of Iranian monarchy allied his legacy to the later anti-Pahlavi revolutionaries. Of the English dissidents who favored eastern nationalisms, none was more idiosyncratic than Marmaduke Pickthall. Praised by E.M. Forster for his treatment of oriental subjects in Edwardian novels such as *Said the Fisherman* (1903) and *Children of the Nile* (1908) (Forster 1967), Pickthall turned from being a Tory supporter of the British empire in India and Egypt, to mounting a persistent wartime propaganda in the radical *New Age* journal in favor of Turkey. These cross-currents ensure Pickthall's novels and articles very much present a split discourse in terms of the debate with Orientalism. On the one hand he wrote in favor of Lord Cromer's handling of the notorious Denshawai incident of 1906, employing the imperialist vocabulary of the lazy native to denigrate the cause of Egyptian national self-determination (Pickthall 1914b). Yet on the other, his passionate espousal of the Young Turk revolution later led him to originate a discourse of revolutionary Islamic modernism in which western supports fall away and the British government is accused of double-dealing and betrayal.

The instability of Orientalist/imperialist discourses with respect to possibilities of their fracture into counter-Orientalist/anti-imperialist ones had implications for travelers' representations of Englishness. For Curzon, the anxiety of Russian expansion into frontline competition with Britain's empire in the East caused him to modulate his Orientalist representations of Central Asia with a view to persuading a British readership of the imminent danger a state like Persia presented to British interests. Curzon's *Persia and the Persian Question* (1892) offers a repertoire of Orientalism—a despotic oriental ruler, and an effeminate and ignorant populous oppressed by a debilitating Islamic fanaticism, functioning within a landscape of extremes. Added to this is a strategic assessment of Russian economic and military penetration. English patriotism is aroused by the disadvantaged conditions upon which Britain's exports compete with Russia's, and Russia's inauspicious display of consular representation. Far away Persia is made to rub a raw English nerve and ask the type of unpleasant questions that stirred John Bull's manhood. Blunt's *Secret History of the English Occupation of Egypt* (1907) incorporates the diary of a traveler of means, embarked upon an exploration of the East, which involves him in schemes for its political and religious renewal. It confirms Melman's balancing of the "travelers individual quests and their particular searches for personal redemption in the desert" with the "political vision" that emerged from their journeys (1907: 114). *Secret History* retraces and summarizes Blunt's earlier journeys in North Africa, Anatolia, and the Arabian deserts in order to situate the new venture: a concentrated interface with Egypt, now no longer represented in Orientalist terms of distance and exoticism, but in direct, immediate connection with home. As a traveler, he intensified his questioning of Middle Eastern culture under pressure of its invasion and violent destabilization by English intervention. Starting out a believer in her "pacific, unaggressive" diplomacy of the mid-Victorian period, Blunt had faith in England's "providential mission in the East" being prosecuted "for honest beneficial reasons" (1907: 2, 10). A visit to India in 1879 sowed the first seeds of doubt; after firsthand involvement in the ending of Egyptian national sovereignty, the Orientalist discourse splits. The result is an articulation of a self-fueled Islamic nationalism and a condemnation of an Englishness corrupted from its former paths of glory by the materialism and racism of late imperialism: "We fail because we are no longer honest, no longer just, no longer gentlemen. Our Government is a mob [. . .] For a hundred years we did some good in the world; for a hundred we shall have done evil, and then the world will hear of us no more" (1907: 70).

Polarities of Englishness

In his revisionary account of Britain's imperial relations with its subject peoples, David Cannadine has argued that social ranking was as important if not more important than "color of skin" (2002: 6). The British Empire was "a mechanism for the export, projection and analogization of domestic social structures and social perceptions" (2002: 10). I would like to reformulate this argument according to the proposition that English imperialists and travelers alike carried with themselves a model or models of England's "ideal of social hierarchy" that incorporated radical as well as conservative formulations. For E.G. Browne, it was the liberal idea of national self-determination and individual freedoms that must be exported to the East. The resultant process of filiation generated an idea of responsibility that also had ramifications for English society at home. Browne's politics thus became an export value that were embodied in his former students such as the members of the British embassy in Tehran who furnished him with ideas and information that he in turn built into his history, *The Persian Revolution, 1905-10*. His liberality also returned in the form of the Iranian exiles who found succor during the revolution in Browne's house in Cambridge. (Similar acknowledgment should be made for the Egyptian and Indian nationalists who benefited from Blunt's moral and material support).

In default of the export of the system of British education to the Middle East (which Cromer consciously blocked in Egypt), the presence of liberal Englishmen in Ottoman Turkey and Qajar Iran at least represented a symbolic opposition to the imperialist/Orientalist codifications that drove conservative administrators of the stamp of Cromer, Curzon, Milner, and their epigones. Browne's campaign on behalf of Iranian independence made use of the moral voices of Englishmen abroad who could challenge the reactionary Orientalism that infused popular ideas of the "Persian character" and were especially pedaled by the likes of Valentine Chirol and David Fraser of *The Times* of London, in order to denigrate any hope of the revolution's success.[9] "One Englishman said to me," wrote one of Browne's pro-revolution correspondents from Persia, "'could not the *Times* be stirred up to write the truth on the state of affairs in Persia' [. . .] There is no question of difference of opinion between Englishmen who *know* the Persians. Cannot public opinion at home be roused, or is England so obsessed by the fear of Germany she must stoop to bargain with so horrible a Government as the Russian?" (Browne 1910: 343).[10]

Both Browne and Marmaduke Pickthall were members of the Anglo-Ottoman Society; one might say that contact with the East brought former travelers such as they together, where politics might have previously divided them. Pickthall's construction of Englishness, though it derives from Urquartian and romantic Tory Disraelian notions of affinity and protection for the Muslims of the Ottoman empire, converges almost simultaneously with Browne's writings on behalf of Persia between 1909 to 1914. The title of a pamphlet Browne published in 1912 is telling: "The Reign of Terror at Tabriz: Britain's Responsibilities." That same year Pickthall brought out a group of articles previously published in *The New Age* journal, with the title of "The Black Crusade" in which he denounced Liberal support for the Balkan League in their war against Turkey. "When one hears (as I did lately) in an English church, the Turks compared to Satan, the Bulgarian advance to that of Christian souls assailing Paradise, one can only gasp. Are we really in the twentieth century?" (1912: n. p.). The next year, Pickthall was arraigning Britain for reneging on her responsibilities to support the cause of progressive Turkey. Britain, once the exemplar for universal toleration and for a nationality that should be independent of religious differences, had largely inspired the eastern awakening. Now, with the rest of Europe, the nation shrank back in horror as Frankenstein before his monster (Pickthall: 1914a, ix).

The quality I would like to mark out in dissident writing on Britain's involvement in the Middle East during the high tide of imperialism is not just hostile criticism of Britain's behavior in deviating from its moral or political responsibilities. These writings also incorporate a genuine attempt to create discourses embodying voices from the colonized or those in process of struggling against imperialist encroachment. In giving an opportunity for such voices to be heard, the creator of the new discourse is conscious of his own oppositional stance toward a discourse of British imperial hegemony joined to an Orientalism that disabled Middle Eastern peoples and their religion. This process can be observed in texts such as Blunt's *Secret History*, Browne's *The Persian Revolution*, and Pickthall's novel on the Young Turk Revolution, *The Early Hours* (1921). Each of these writings is constructed out of the writers' personal experience and knowledge of the languages and cultures they seek to represent, incorporating the idioms, ideals and beliefs of Egyptians, Persians, and Turks. For example, in Pickthall's novel, there is a message of Islamic modernism that no longer depends on any provenance other than its own:

> Here, or elsewhere among Muslim peoples it will triumph, and in triumph flourish and become a blessing to the world-if Allah wills! Not all the might of all the Christian powers can extinguish it. What matter then though we suffer, though we die a cruel death, so long as we are servants of the Heavenly will against the Powers of Evil which must pass away. (1921: 270)

Blunt's more rational articulation of the Islamic modernist ideas of the Cairo Azhar University reformers was characterized by Hourani as "an exposition of the Islamic community and the way to reform it, [that] is perhaps [. . .] a true report of what was thought at the time in [Jamal al-Din] Afghani's circle" (Hourani 1963: 155). Browne's whole approach to the Persian Revolution and its import for the resurgence of an Iranian national identity is summed up in the sentence he quotes from the Iranian Press: "Persians have reached years of discretion and need no tutor" (Browne 1910: 187).

English Ventriloquists and Nativist Orientalism?

The matter of the existence of a counter-discourse to Orientalism, embedded in notions of native self-representation and resistance to imperialism, but articulated by Englishmen in the English language, still requires problematizing. Is this a form of what postmodernist thought would call ventriloquism *avant la lettre*? The question is not so much "how and at what points is a counter discourse recuperated by the dominant discourses?" (Behdad 1994: 135). Rather, it concerns the extent to which such discourses intersect with the discourses of western Orientalists on the one hand, and feed into emergent native nationalisms, on the other. Nationalism is, after all, a European construction in the phase of modernity that was exported to the East along with imperialism and the scientific/technological revolution. Oriental nationalities no more "awoke" to generic national identity than did western nations. A process of construction of eastern nationalist identity occurred first, and it was aided by western discourses of both imperialist and anti-imperialist complexions.[11]

In delineating a kind of nativist Orientalism, Mehdi Boroujerdi (1996) points out that:

> Iranian (or oriental) intellectuals try to alleviate present inferiority complex vis-à-vis the West through an uncritical glorification of their ancient past and culture. Ironically enough, however, Orientalists have inadvertently boosted this nativist sentiment and have provided its proponents with ready-made arguments through their scholarly findings. (1996: 143)[12]

In Browne's case especially—since he was the only professional academic Orientalist among the figures I have been discussing—there is a conscious attempt to build a counter-Orientalist discourse underpinning a narrative of an eastern awakening. Significantly, this awakening is represented as self-nurtured, and the influence of European antecedents is underplayed. Browne is either unconscious of or unwilling to acknowledge the degree to which the Persian "awakening" is itself formed by and according to European notions about studying and pronouncing on a nation's history and racial identity.

Blunt's first attempt to originate an eastern national identity around his discovery of an ideal bedouin desert kingdom in central Arabia was deeply involved in dubious Orientalist pronouncements on "pure" and "authentic" Arab racial identity (see Kedourie 1956; Tidrick 1989). Even his second and longer lasting project of valorizing an Islamic modernism that would revive the Islamic *umma* was not unshaped by his own occidental ego—indeed, some of Blunt's statements in his private diaries do come very close to ventriloquism of a hardline Islamic discourse. Of the figures I have been discussing, arguably only Pickthall was able to blend his European belief in progress and modernity with an eastern absorption in Islamic belief. This gained him a niche and acceptance in the East (India), and continuing suspicion and even obloquy at home, as an Englishman who by defecting to the West's historical enemy had gone too far.

Conclusion

In this essay I have attempted to build on the travel theory of academics such as Ali Behdad and Lisa Lowe and interrogate the orientation of a specific group of English travelers to the Orient. I have endeavored to enlarge on A.J.P. Taylor's notion of dissidence from English foreign policy by emphasizing the identification of each of these travelers with eastern nations and nationalisms, to the extent that they attempted to give voice to their respective national causes. My original question as to whether a specific quality of Englishness was brought to these travelers' positionings requires further work and inquiry. The issue of travelers' adoption of disguise, which I have not discussed here because the figures I have written about seemed to have passed beyond that, already introduce the matter of cultural and religious ambiguity. Rumors about the conversion to Islam of figures such as John Lewis Burkhardt and Gifford Palgrave were persistent enough to at least require the Palgrave family's rebuttal. I am satisfied that Blunt and Pickthall should not be accounted guilty of orientalist parasitism, as Behdad labelled Isabelle Eberhardt for her cross-cultural cross-dressing activities. As for Browne, he was, as Hourani pointed out, not the only Orientalist to reject his government's imperial policies (1991: 58).[13] At the very least, then, allowing for the ambiguities I have sketched out, these English travelers resist the usual stereotypical categorizations reserved for travelers to the Orient.

Notes

1. For a fuller exposition of the argument proposed in this essay see my study Nash (2005).
2. See Nash (2001).
3. Said wrote of a "Romantic Orientalist project," instancing Schlegel and Novalis' plan for "the regeneration of Europe by Asia" (1978:115).
4. On Lane, see Leila Ahmed (1978). For a critique of Said's interpretation of Lane, see Rodenbeck (1998).
5. Carlyle's fascination with Islam and Islamic culture has to my knowledge, not been fully studied yet. For the Calvinist equivalences, see Harrold (1936). Evidence from his letters and notebooks show German Romantic Orientalism mediated Carlyle's interest in the East, especially Goethe and the Schlegels. He also read De Sacy; see ApRoberts (1988).
6. See Storrs, *Orientations*, Reader Bullard, *The Camels Must Go*, and Shane Leslie, *Mark Sykes: His Life and Letters*.

7. The only full-length biography of Urquhart, Robinson (1920), is unsatisfactory. On Blunt, see Longford (1980). On Browne, see Wickens and Browne (1990). Peter Clark has written the very useful *Marmaduke Pickthall, British Muslim* (1986).
8. On Browne's campaigns during the Persian Revolution, see Bonakdarian (1993)
9. Chirol's and Fraser's Orientalism are reproduced in their books on the Persian Revolution: *The Middle East Problem* (1902), and *Persia and Turkey in Revolt*, respectively.
10. On the identity of Browne's informants, see Bonakdarian's "Select Correspondents of E.G. Browne . . . " in Browne (1995).
11. This can be seen in the career of Mrak Sykes, the English half of the notorious Sykes-Picot agreement that carved the Arab areas of the Middle East into British and French zones of influence, while endorsing the establishment of Arab, Armenian, and Zionist national entities. See Elie Kedourie (1956).
12. Boroujerdi goes on to quote the Iranian political scientist, Hamid Enayat: "The discovery by Western Iranologists of many elements of our pre-Islamic cultural heritage has been responsible for the growth in Iran of a nationalistic urge for the exaltation of pre-Islamic civilization" (1996: 143). Although he emphasizes the importance of Iran's Islamic heritage, Browne did help to essentialize a Persian nationality within an unbroken narrative of achievement going back up to three millennia.
13. Other examples given by Hourani were the Frenchman, Louis Massignon, and the Dutch orientalist, Snouck Hurgronje.

Bibliography

Ahmed, Leila. 1978. *Edward Lane*. London: Longman.

Allen, Mea. 1972. *Palgrave of Arabia, The Life of William Gifford Palgrave*. London: Macmillan

ApRoberts, Ruth. 1988. *The Ancient Dialect: Carlyle and the Comparative Religion*. Berkeley and Los Angeles: University of California Press.

Behdad, Ali. 1994. *Belated Travelers, Orientalism in the Age of Colonial Dissolution*. Durham: NC.: Duke University Press.

Bidwell, Robin. 1976. *Travellers in Arabia*. London: Hamlyn.

Blunt, Wilfrid [1907] 1922. *Secret History of the English Occupation of Egypt, Being a Personal Narrative of Events*. New York: Knopf.

Bonakdarian, M. 1993. "Edward Granville Browne and The Iranian Constitutional Struggle: form Academic Orientalist to Political Activism." *Iranian Studies*, 26: 7–32.

Browne, Edward Granville. 1910. *The Persian Revolution, 1905–1910*. Cambridge: University Press. Republished 1995. Washington, DC: Mage Publishers.

Boroujerdi, Mehdi. 1996. *Iranian Intellectuals and the West, The Tormented Triumph Of Nativism*. New York: University of Syracuse Press.

Cannadine, David. 2002. *Ornamentalism*. London: Penguin.

Carlyle, Thomas. 1897. "The Hero as Prophet." In *On Heroes, Hero-Worship and the Heroic in History*: 42–77. London: Chapman and Hall.

Clark, Steve. 1999. Introduction to Steve Clark, ed. *Travel Writing and Empire: Postcolonial Theory in Transit*: 1–28. London: Zed.

Clark, Peter. 1986. *Marmaduke Pickthall, British Muslim*. London: Quartet.

Curzon, George Nathaniel. 1892. *Persia and the Persian Question*, 2 vols. London: Longman Green.

Forster, E.M. 1967. *Abinger Harvest*. Harmondsworth: Penguin.

Harrold, C.F. 1936. "The Nature of Carlyle's Calvinism." *Studies in Philology*, 33: 459–75.

Hourani, Albert. 1963. *Arabic Thought in The Liberal Age, 1798–1939*. Cambridge: University Press.

———. 1991. *Islam in European Thought*. Cambridge: University Press.

Kedourie, Elie. 1956. *England and The Middle East: The Destruction of the Ottoman Empire*. London: Bowes & Bowes.

Longford, Elizabeth. 1980. *A Pilgrimage of Passion: The Life of Wilfred Scawen Blunt*. New York: Alfred Knopf.

Lowe, Lisa. 1991. *Critical Terrains, French and British Orientalism*. Ithaca: Cornell University Press.

Melman, Billie. 2002. "The Middle East/Arabia: the 'cradle of Islam'," in Peter Hulme and Tim Youngs (eds.) *The Cambridge Companion to Travel Writing*. Cambridge: University Press.

Nash, Geoffrey. 2001. "Travel as Imperial Strategy: George Nathaniel Curzon Goes East, 1887–1894." *Journeys*, vol. 2, no.1, 24–44.

———. 2005. From Empire to Orient: *Travellers to the Middle East*. London: I.B. Tauris.

New Age. 1912.

Pickthall, Marmaduke. 1914a. *With The Turk in Wartime*. London: J. M. Dent.

———. 1914b. "Concerning Denshawai." *New Age* (26 February).

———. 1921. *The Early Hours*. London: W. Collins.

Robinson, Gertrude. 1920. *David Urquhart: Some Chapters in the Life of a Victorian Knight-Errant of Justice and Liberty*. Oxford: Blackwell.

Rodenbeck, John. 1998. "Edward Said and Edward William Lane." In Paul Starkey and Janet Starkey (eds.) *Travellers in Egypt*. London: I. B. Tauris.

Said, Edward. 1979. *Orientalism, Western Conceptions of the Orient*. London: RKP.

Taylor, A.J.P. 1957. *The Troublemakers: Dissent over Foreign Policy, 1792–1939*. London: Hamish Hamilton.

Thesiger, Wilfred. 1964. *Arabian Sands*. Harmondsworth: Penguin.

Tidrick, Kathryn. 1989. *Heart Beguiling Araby: The English Romance with Arabia*. 2nd ed. London: I.B.Tauris.

Urquhart, David. 1839. *The Spirit of the East*. 2 vols. London: Henry Colburn.

Wickens G. and Edward G. Browne. 1990. "Browne's Life and Academic Career." In Yershalter Ehsan (ed.) *Encyclopedia Iranica*. London: Routledge.

Young, Robert. 1995. *Colonial Desire, Hybridity in Theory, Culture and Race*. London: Routledge.

CHAPTER 5

Under English Eyes
The Disappearance of Irishness in Conrad's *The Secret Agent*

Graham MacPhee

Nations it may be have fashioned their Governments, but the Governments
have paid them back in the same coin. It is unthinkable that any young
Englishman should find himself in Razumov's situation. This being so it would
be a vain enterprise to imagine what he would think. The only safe surmise to
make is that …[h]e would not have an hereditary and personal knowledge of
the means by which historical autocracy represses ideas, guards its power,
and defends its existence.
—Joseph Conrad, *Under Western Eyes* (1911)

Criticism and the Space of the Political

In recent years, Joseph Conrad's fiction has been credited with extraordinary insight into the cultural and intellectual implications of European colonialism, a capacity often tied to the author's status as a Polish exile standing at one remove from the British Empire and its dominant ethos of "Englishness." Recent interest in Conrad's *The Secret Agent* ([1907] 1983), a novel that revolves around an anarchist bomb attack on the Greenwich Observatory in London, suggests that Conrad may assume a similar role for critics and commentators attempting to map the broader cultural significance of the attacks on the Pentagon and the World Trade Center on 11 September 2001.[1] However, if Conrad's awareness of the brutality of colonialism might suggest that he is well placed to offer insights into the political violence of the metropolis, before transferring his critical credentials from colonial periphery to imperial center, we might take this opportunity to reassess Conrad's triangulation of politics, violence, and colonialism. For although the impact of colonial violence is explicitly pursued across Conrad's fiction at the level of the psychological, the existential, the epistemological, and the ethical, it is only in *The Secret Agent* that his engagement with its consequences for modern politics becomes more than implicit.[2]

A sense of why *The Secret Agent* may prove suggestive for our critical present is indicated by Alex Houen's *Terrorism and Modern Literature*, which sees the novel's presentation of political violence as moving beyond the oppositions that are said to structure modern discourses of emancipation, equality, and social justice. In contrast to such discourses, Houen's reading pursues a conception of modern politics as "bureaucratic Being," wherein "the state's law . . . comes to incorporate everything" (2002: 51–52). According to Houen, "Conrad . . . sketches a landscape of critique in showing that the creation of zones of ambiguity and double-agency bolsters the functioning of the system," since the novel reveals that "the possibility of 'political crime' is essential for the state's law" (2002: 52). Yet at the same time, Houen argues that Conrad's text keeps open a space for "counter" action in terms that resemble Deleuze and Guattari's notion of "micropolitics" or "molecularity" (2002: 53). In this way, Houen claims to identify a way of responding to contemporary events that avoids falling in step with the rhetoric of the "war on terror," while nonetheless retaining a critical perspective on "terrorism and its mediation" (Houen 2002: 20).[3]

Implicit in Houen's reading of Conrad is the wager that such a conception of modern politics will be compatible with a sensitivity to the particularity of historical context and location. Houen affirms the political urgency of this sensitivity by recalling Edward Said's warning some three months after the attack on the World Trade Center, that already:

> Osama bin Laden's name and face have become so numbingly familiar to Americans as in effect to obliterate any history he and his shadowy followers might have had (e.g. as useful conscripts in the jihad raised twenty years ago by the US against the Soviet Union in Afghanistan) before they became stock symbols of everything loathsome and hateful to the collective imagination. (Said 2001)[4]

Given the role of the United States in arming and funding *muhajadeen* groups in the later years of the Cold War (Cooley 2002), Said's observation about the need for a recognition of the hidden histories which configure the present is clearly fundamental to any analysis of the representation of "terrorism." But by invoking Said's warning, Houen raises a question that is becoming increasingly significant for both Conrad's text and for the impulse within contemporary criticism to rule out any externality to power, the commodity, or the violence of law: namely, whether such attempts to refigure the political are able to retain a sensitivity to the histories of coercion and emancipation which they claim have been erased.

This essay returns to the figuring of political violence in *The Secret Agent* in order to examine how far Conrad's conception of the political is able to recognize the histories that configure the space of politics. But in doing so, it also asks to what extent Conrad's text is able to register the historicity of its *own location* within the historical consolidation of European imperialism. For although *The Secret Agent* is ostensibly based on a historical incident— the detonation of a bomb by the anarchist Martial Bourdin in Greenwich in 1894—as Seamus Deane has noted, in fact it offers an "expert conflation of the Fenian and Russian anarchist stereotypes" of the day, a conflation that gives a "national" inflection to the political questions we have raised (Deane 1986: 39). In this respect, Conrad's Englishness is not *so* eccentric, but joins the powerful tendency within nineteenth and twentieth-century British culture in submerging Irish political violence—which emerged within the political and economic contexts of British colonial rule—under the banner of an abstract and irrational assault on "civilization." [5]

The Logic of "Terrorism"

Despite its broader ambitions, Conrad's novel deploys a relatively straight-forward plot and a limited cast of characters. The central event, the dyna-mite attack on the Greenwich Observatory, is organized by an unlikely agent provocateur, Verloc, who has infiltrated the ranks of London's anar-chists; but the attack is instigated by the embassy of a foreign power, which, although unnamed in the novel, is clearly that of Imperial Russia. Verloc chooses his malleable brother-in-law Stevie—who suffers learning difficul-ties and is uninvolved in anarchism—to carry out the attack. Stevie's pointless and pathetic death causes his sister, Winnie, to kill her husband and commit suicide. This central chain of events is refracted through two additional groups of characters, who provide the background or "sur-roundings" against which the central event is to be understood and judged (Conrad 1983: xxxvii). First, there are the anarchists, who embody a series of modern types or stock figures: Michealis, the corpulent armchair revo-lutionary; Yundt, the sham man of action who goads others into violence; Ossipon, the self-regarding freeloader with intellectual pretensions; and the Professor, the quintessential nobody convinced of his own historical im-portance and genius. Ranged against them are the forces of the law: the dogged but unimaginative functionary, Chief Inspector Heat; the Assistant Commissioner, a frustrated colonial adventurer now deskbound; and Sir Ethelred, the British Home Secretary whose Olympian perspective encodes the indifference of bureaucracy.

Although Verloc, working undercover for a foreign embassy, is the literal secret agent of Conrad's tale, Houen's reading prefers to focus on a more diffuse "secret agency" or "entropolitics" that joins anarchists and police, law and violence within an overarching structure of "bureaucratic Being" modeled on the closed systems of thermodynamics (Houen 2002: 51, 53ff).

Conrad's "Author's Note" appears to support this decision, since according to Conrad, what crystallized the story were not the details of the bombing nor the tragedy of the bomber's sister, but his chancing upon the memoirs of Sir Robert Anderson, a former Assistant Commissioner of the Metropolitan Police, who is described as "an obviously able man with a strong religious strain." The incident that prompted the novel, Conrad recounts, is the complaint made by the policeman's political superior, Liberal Home Secretary Sir William Harcourt, that Anderson's "idea of secrecy . . . seems to consist in keeping the Home Secretary in the dark" (Conrad 1983: xxxv).[6]

According to Houen, the novel figures the obscurity of modern bureaucracy as an all-encompassing thermodynamics of entropy, where ostensible social oppositions are incorporated, dissipated, and neutralized within the invisible interconnectedness of the system (Houen 2002: 50). The all-encompassing nature of this system is articulated in the novel from its opposing sides, by Chief Inspector Heat—who complains that the anarchists break the established rules of the game between police and "ordinary" criminals, both of whom are "products of the same machine"—and the Professor, who complains on the contrary that the anarchists fail to do so (Conrad 1983: 92, 73). At the level of meaning, the system's capacity to incorporate political opposition is figured by the popular press, whose entropic absorption of daily events provides the semantic conditions for political violence. This logic is articulated by the foreign spymaster Vladimir, who demands an act that will confound the "ready made phrases" which are deployed "in every newspaper . . . to explain . . . away" conventional protest. The thermodynamics of obscurity give rise, then, to a logic of terrorism, since for "a bomb outrage to have any influence on public opinion now," as Vladimir explains, it "must go beyond the intention of vengeance or terrorism. It must be purely destructive. It must be that, and only that, beyond the faintest suspicion of any other object" (Conrad 1983: 32).

While Vladimir is the first to articulate the novel's hyperbolic logic of terrorism, this logic is embodied in the figure of the Professor, significantly the only anarchist who actively pursues his professed end. The Professor's commitment is not to an ideology, cause, or program of any kind, but to destruction itself. Whereas the other anarchists "plan the future" and so "lose [themselves] in reveries of economical systems derived from what is," the Professor demands a total break with the past, a "clean sweep": "that sort of future," he explains, "will take care of itself if you will only make room for it." What is needed, then, are not steps to create a new world, but the demolition of this one, and so he declares that the most productive political act would be "to shovel" dynamite "in heaps at the corners of streets" (Conrad 1983: 73). Crucially, the Professor's association with dynamite, and therefore destruction, is not just talk: he remains at liberty because he has dynamite strapped around his body, which he can detonate within twenty seconds. As a potential suicide bomber, the Professor is placed outside of the existing social order, which as he explains "depends on life, which . . . is a historical fact surrounded by all sorts of restraints and considerations, a complex, organized fact open to attack at every point," while he "depends on death, which knows no restraint and cannot be attacked" (1983: 68).

According to Houen, the Professor not only embodies but also reveals the limits of this ultimatist logic, since his claim to stand outside the social order is undone by his reliance upon the fear he induces within it, and he is as much part of "the system" as anyone else. And it is here that Houen identifies the space for an alternative or "counter" action, a "micropolitics" of feeling or affect that is of another order to the "macropolitics" of opposition between legality and anarchy, domination and emancipation. This micropolitics is figured by the temporal deferral of the Professor's detonator, which despite his best efforts cannot be made instantaneous, but takes twenty seconds. For Houen, such an irreducible deferral suggests a different temporality than that implied by the polarity of full presence or absolute absence demanded by the Professor's "clean sweep." However, for all its claims to revelation and exposure, Houen's deconstructive logic itself involves a significant elision: for while it wagers its politics on what it sees as irreducible moments of deferral and difference, such moments are in fact articulated in the novel as implying an experiential immediacy that is in important ways blinding.

Houen envisages this other temporality as a return of the past in a moment of primordial violence that undoes the macropolitics of law, morality, and meaning, a violent return which he identifies with the death of Stevie and Winnie's murder of her husband, Verloc (Houen 2002: 44–45). In the case of Stevie's death, the temporality of return is articulated by Chief Inspector Heat, who, when staring at the bloody remains of the hapless bomber, "rose by the force of sympathy . . . above the vulgar conception of time":

> Instantaneous! He remembered all he had ever read in popular publications of long and terrifying dreams dreamed in the instant of waking; of the whole past life lived with frightful intensity by a drowning man as his doomed head bobs up . . . for the last time. The inextricable mysteries of conscious existence beset Chief Inspector Heat till he evolved the horrible notion that ages of atrocious pain and mental torture could be contained within two successive winks of an eye. (Conrad 1983: 88)

And in the case of Winnie's fatal stabbing of Verloc, it is the narrative voice whose superior perspective loads the act with an uncommon significance:

> Into that plunging blow, delivered over the side of the couch, Mrs. Verloc had put all the inheritance of her immemorial and obscure descent, the simple ferocity of the age of caverns, and the unbalanced nervous fury of the age of barrooms. (Conrad 1983: 263)

Houen describes this violent return as "a political unconscious," and claims that it marks the involvement of "terror and violence" within "a wider social field" (2002: 47). But such a claim disregards the fact that this return is clearly marked as a resurgence of chthonic forces—"the simple ferocity of the age of caverns" now manifested as "the unbalanced nervous fury of bar-rooms"—forces which are not only outside of history and politics, but are ahistorical and anti-political. Indeed, as Houen concedes, both Winnie and Verloc become "virtual automota," "possessed by the past at the same time as embodying it" (2002: 48). There is no place within such a primeval return for the political interplay of determination and decision, and politics is thereby subordinated to the unfolding of a mythic fate.

Houen's uncritical attitude to the political implications of the novel's "logic of terrorism" suggests something more than a failure of close-reading: namely, a certain blindness resulting from the affinity between his own conception of the political—as the absolute violence of the state's law— and Conrad's presentation of politics in terms of an all-encompassing bureaucracy. What Houen's reading therefore occludes is the propensity of such all-encompassing systems or logics to reduce politics to an abstract formalism, however finely they detail the mechanisms and processes of assimilation and incorporation. For if the differential demands of politics are always incorporated within the unity of "the system" — whether conceived in terms of "law," "bureaucracy," "power," "commodification," the "spectacle," "identity thinking," or simply "reason" — then the alternative to this unity cannot be found in the potentiality of historical differences, but in an abstract "difference" that holds itself apart from historical actuality.

Ironically enough, Houen's own survey of the term "terrorism" suggests ways of engaging with the historical locatedness of Conrad's text which exceed the logic of its equation of politics and bureaucracy. For as Houen rightly points out, while the word was famously used by Edmund Burke to describe the French revolutionary regime of 1793 to 1794, it gained its current sense in the second half of the nineteenth century in response to acts of political violence by both Russian Anarchists *and* Irish Republicans, or Fenians (2002: 19–30; see also Laqueur 2001: 6–11). Although Conrad's novel is ostensibly only concerned with the first of these, as a number of critics have pointed out, it draws on the English experience of Fenian political violence in important ways. To gain a sense of the historical location of *The Secret Agent* therefore means uncovering the hidden history of Fenian political violence within the novel.

From Dynamite to the Politics of Parnell

Although notoriously indefinable, the contemporary sense of the term "terrorism" usually seeks to identify violence that is not primarily directed to the immediate military imperatives of insurrection or the achievement of state power, but which is orientated instead to producing an effect on the morale of civilian populations, and thereby on their political leaderships. Consequently, targets are often symbolic or involve a highly visible or "spectacular" use of violence, designed both to embolden sympathetic audiences and to undermine the feeling of safety enjoyed by civilian populations removed from the immediate arena of political dispute. The emergence of such spectacular violence in the second half of the nineteenth century was fueled by three major factors: the invention of dynamite by Alfred Nobel in 1863; the extension of popular literacy and the growth of the popular press; and the frustration of the democratic or nationalist aspirations of significant popular constituencies by existing political arrangements (Houen 2002: 20; Laqueur 2001: 11).

The commitment of Irish republican groups—principally the Irish Republican Brotherhood (IRB, initially known as the Irish Revolutionary Brotherhood), an offshoot known as the Invincibles, and the Irish-American Clan na Gael—to spectacular political violence grew from the unexpectedly strong response produced by more "traditional" deployments of force, in particular the attacks in 1867 on a police van in Manchester and on Clerkenwell prison which were both aimed at freeing captured republicans. While the attacks themselves were directed to immediate aims, they also generated a level of panic among a previously indifferent British public, while the subsequent execution of one of those involved in the Clerkenwell bombing and three of the attackers of the police van—who came to be known as the "Manchester Martyrs"—gave rise to a significant outcry in Ireland and America. While the best remembered act of Fenian political violence is the assassination of Lord Frederick Cavendish, the British Chief Secretary for Ireland, and his aide in Phoenix Park in 1882, the decade also saw a sustained campaign of dynamite attacks on symbolic locations and buildings, including Victoria station, Nelson's Column, the Houses of Parliament and the Tower of London (Townshend 1993: 138ff.). However, the dynamite campaign was discontinued in 1887, when the IRB shifted support away from violent action and toward political negotiation in the light of the growing success of the Home Rule movement under the leadership of Charles Stuart Parnell (Foster 1988: 400–430; Houen 2002: 30). As such, the Fenian dynamite campaign did not occur in isolation, but was one of a number of violent and nonviolent responses to British colonial rule in the wake of the Famine of 1845 to 1849, ranging from the mass civil disobedience of the Land League and the rural insurgency of the "land war," to Parnell's parliamentary bargaining for Home Rule (Foster 1988: 373–99).

That the Fenian bombings of the 1880s remained a significant reference point in popular consciousness in 1907, when *The Secret Agent* was published, is attested to by the novel's Home Secretary, Sir Ethelred, whose first reaction to the news of the attack is to ask "if this is the beginning of another dynamite campaign"(Conrad 1983: 136).[7] Indeed, as Norman Sherry recounts in painstaking detail, Conrad drew extensively on events and figures associated with Fenian political violence. The attack on the police van in Manchester is incorporated into the history of the anarchist Michealis, whose subsequent release on license—or "ticket-of-leave" as it was known—is modeled on the fate of a prominent nationalist figure, Michael Davitt (Sherry 1971: 260–9; see Conrad 1983: 106–7). Equally, according to Sherry, the figure of the Professor, the potential suicide-bomber and incarnation of destruction, draws on the historical figure of Luke Dillon, nicknamed "Dynamite Dillon," who was involved in the bombing of the Junior Carlton Club and the House of Commons, but remained uncaught. Dillon reportedly wore dynamite strapped around his body with a protruding fuse, which he planned to light with the cigar he habitually smoked (Sherry 1971: 283–5).

However, as Sherry points out, although Conrad was well informed about both anarchist and Fenian political violence, in fictionalizing events and individuals he consistently "chooses those aspects which deny sympathetic response in the reader, and which lead to the presentation of an extreme type" (Sherry 1971: 285). For example, although originally sentenced for procuring weapons, on his release in 1877 Michael Davitt did not return to political violence, but launched a strategic policy shift or "new departure" which sought to align the Fenian movement with the parliamentary activity of the Home Rulers and the popular agitation surrounding land issues (Moody 1981: 236–64). Indeed, as a leading figure in the Land League, which united parliamentary nationalism under Parnell with a mass popular movement for land reform, Davitt condemned the assassination of Cavendish in 1882 (Moody 1981: 536). And unlike Michaelis, who enjoys uninterrupted liberty, Davitt was re-imprisoned alongside Parnell and other Home Rule MPs as part of the failed attempt by Gladstone's government to break the will of the Land League, at the heart of which lay the notorious Coercion Act of 1880 that allowed for indefinite detention without trial.

The point here is not to complain that Conrad's fiction fails to present the "facts" as they "really were," a demand that is both nonsensical and naïve. Rather, an awareness of the historical context within which the novel was written helps to open up critical perspectives on the political paradigm that it implies, particularly in light of the affinity we have identified between the novel's conception of politics and that informing its current critical reception. Thus, while the public sympathy enjoyed by Michealis in the novel evidences the entropic tendency of the press and public opinion—which erase the suffering produced by political violence by incorporating this figure within lazy stereotypes of the prophet or seer—a different relationship between publicity and politics is suggested by the fate of Michael Davitt. Davitt's re-arrest was unsupported by evidence of criminality and was patently extra-legal, forming part of a panoply of "emergency" security measures designed to undermine political mobilization in Ireland (Moody 1981: 462–3). Conversely, Devitt's election as MP for Meath while in prison indicates that popular support was explicitly political and tied to an informed constituency, itself directly engaged in the political conflict (Moody 1981: 500). What Davitt's case reveals, then, is both the political nature of violence in the colonial context of Ireland and the corrosive effects on the British state of its pursuit of colonial pacification. The overall effect of Conrad's decision to figure political violence in terms of anarchism rather than in terms of the Fenian response to the British rule in Ireland is to *abstract violence from politics* and present it, in the words of ambassador Vladimir, as "purely destructive ... and only that."[8]

If it is tempting to think that this process of abstraction nonetheless makes Conrad's political vision less tied to parochial circumstance and thus more universally applicable, it is important to remember the role of Vladimir and the unnamed foreign embassy, an element of the novel which Houen's reading neglects. Vladimir orders the anarchist bombing not to engender a state of conflict between the British Empire and his own state, but precisely to bring "England . . . into line," since "England lags" behind the rest of Europe with its "absurd" and "sentimental regard for individual liberty" (Conrad 1983: 29). As he complains to Verloc, "the general leniency of the judicial procedure here, and the utter absence of all repressive measures, are a scandal to Europe" (1983: 17). This viewpoint is mirrored by the response of the English police and politicians in the novel. On learning of the role of the foreign embassy and its use of a secret agent among the anarchists, Sir Ethelred demands to know "What they mean by importing their methods of Crim-Tartary here?," adding that "A Turk would have more decency!" (Conrad 1983: 138). The same sentiments, albeit shorn of any explicit racial inflection, are articulated by the Assistant Commissioner, who insists that the whole affair "makes . . . an excellent starting-point for a piece of work which I've felt must be taken in hand—that is, clearing out of this country of all the foreign political spies, police, and that sort of—of—dogs. In my opinion they are a ghastly nuisance. . . . The only way is to make their employment unpleasant to their employers" (Conrad 1983: 226). While Houen claims the novel demonstrates that both state and opposition are functions of the same totalizing "game" (2002: 51), in fact, the novel very clearly implies that some national—or racial—versions of the game are preferable to others.

The Empire Game

Significantly, Houen's reading ignores the fact that Conrad's nihilism has a decidedly national inflection, maintaining a high regard for what it views as an open and tolerant English liberalism while at the same time insisting on its lack of rational necessity or metaphysical foundation. If the novel implies, in Houen's words, that "the possibility of 'political crime' is essential for the state's law," this does not mean that it asks us to view them as equally desirable or as morally equivalent (2002: 52). Against the arbitrary arrangements of social structure and political ideology, the novel directs sympathy toward the hapless and innocent Stevie, who figures the plight of the individual caught up in political machinations it does not understand. The moment of pathos experienced by Chief Inspector Heat on viewing Stevie's disintegrated remains marks a crucial point in the moral cartography of the novel, opposing the existential experience of human pain to the abstract and idealized ideology of anarchism. Ironically, the novel invests the moment of Stevie's suffering with a cosmic significance through the prosaic consciousness of the secret policeman: "The inextricable mysteries of conscious existence beset Chief Inspector Heat till he evolved the horrible notion that ages of atrocious pain and mental torture could be contained within two successive winks of an eye" (Conrad 1983: 88). If political structures are arbitrary and ungrounded, the novel implies, then at least let us have arbitrary structures that do not crush the confused and lonely individual, abandoned by God in a universe without direction or meaning. Or in other words, let us have English liberalism, with its "absurd" and "sentimental regard for individual liberty" (Conrad 1983: 29).

Given this failure to address the national commitments of Conrad's nihilism, it is perhaps not so surprising that Houen fails to observe that the central moment of identification and empathy in the novel—between Heat and Stevie, but also of course between the ideal reader and Heat—centers on a senior member of the secret police. Indeed, other than Stevie, Winnie, and their mother—characters who are defined by their exclusion from the realm of the political—Heat is the only character who evinces such conventionally human qualities. What this suggests is that Houen's enthusiasm for Conrad's equation of bureaucracy and politics not only blinds him to the role of a certain version of Englishness in the novel, but also to the implications for the relationship between politics, visibility, and the police generated by empire.

Nonetheless, the impact of empire on the domestic space of the nation is evident in the figure of another secret policeman, the Assistant Commissioner. For if Chief Inspector Heat illustrates the "sentimental" side of liberal individualism, its existential or "absurd" conception of freedom is figured by the Assistant Commissioner, head of the Special Crimes Department of the Metropolitan Police. The Assistant Commissioner "had begun [his career] in a tropical colony," where "he had been very successful in tracking and breaking up certain nefarious secret societies amongst the natives." We learn that "He liked the work there" because it "was police work" pure and simple, rather than the impersonal, fragmented, and isolated operations of bureaucracy (Conrad 1983: 99). However, due to the demands of marriage, he now finds himself chained to a desk far away from the adventure of the colonies, where the individual confronts a hostile existence without institutional support or the metaphysical illusions of civilization. Yet there is one way that the Assistant Commissioner can nonetheless leave behind his status as administrator and relive the freedom of colonial adventure—by shedding his official identity and entering the world of covert action. Adopting disguise, the Assistant Commissioner leaves his office and travels unseen around nighttime London, transporting himself from the administered world of the metropolis to the primeval jungle, and transforming himself at a stroke from somber bureaucrat to "lighthearted" adventurer:

> The adventurous head of the Special Crimes Department . . . . felt lighthearted, as though he had been ambushed all alone in a jungle many thousands of miles away from departmental desks and office inkstands. This joyousness and dispersion of thought before a task of some importance seems to prove that this world of ours is not such a very serious affair after all. For the Assistant Commissioner was not constitutionally inclined to levity. (Conrad 1983: 150)

While the world of the anarchist revolutionaries is hypocritical and inauthentic, the role of the secret policeman is the sole locus in the novel where the individual is exposed to existential risk and so granted insight into the ineffable lightness of being.

However, if the Assistant Commissioner's release from "departmental desks and office inkstands" appears as freedom from the perspective of *The Secret Agent's* existentialism, it looks rather different from the perspective of a historical assessment of the relationship between imperialism, bureaucracy, and modern politics. As Hannah Arendt argues in the second part of *The Origins of Totalitarianism*, it is precisely imperialism's subordination of human life to the "aimless process" of accumulation and expansion that makes abstract, individual life appear as the absolute value: "since life itself ultimately has to be lived for its own sake," Arendt writes, "adventure and love of the game for its own sake easily appear to be the most intensely human symbol of life" (Arendt 1973: 216–17). More ominously, Arendt points out, this sense of the ineffable lightness of being provides the perfect subjective disposition for the functioning of bureaucracy, which is defined *in its difference to politics* as "a form of government" whose "inherent" dynamic is the "replacement of law with temporary and changing decree."

And far from providing refuge from bureaucracy, as Arendt observes, "the two key figures" of imperialism "are the bureaucrat on the one side and the secret agent on the other" (Arendt 1973: 216).

While the novel construes the freedom of action enjoyed by the colonial policeman "in tracking and breaking up certain nefarious secret societies amongst the natives" as existential freedom (Conrad 1983: 99), following Arendt it can be better understood in terms of the "aloofness [that] became the new attitude of all members of the British [Imperial] services." In Arendt's view this aloofness "was a more dangerous form of governing than despotism and arbitrariness [since] it did not even tolerate that last link between despot and his subjects, which is formed by bribery and gifts," but implied instead "an absolute division of interests to the point where they were not even permitted to conflict" (1973: 212).

English Liberalism and the Secret Police

It may seem anachronistic and unreasonable to complain about the novel's attempt to figure freedom through the unrestrained field of action enjoyed by the colonial security-police; after all, Conrad's vision was shaped by his own time and he was not privy to the hindsight we now enjoy. But there was ample evidence available to Conrad at the time of writing that might have suggested this equation was decidedly implausible. Indeed, a very different picture of the relationship between police and politics can be found much closer to home than the far-flung edges of empire—in the very book that Conrad identifies as having inspired his novel, Sir Robert Anderson's *Sidelights on the Home Rule Movement* (1906).

Like the novel's Chief Inspector Heat, Sir Robert Anderson claims in his memoirs to have had the Fenian bombing groups "practically 'in my pocket'" throughout the dynamite campaign of the 1880s (Anderson 1906: 125), and as Norman Sherry points out, Conrad draws extensively on Anderson's recollections in his portrayal of Heat, the Assistant Commissioner, and Sir Ethelred (Sherry 1971: 303).[9] But Anderson's book is not a police procedural concerned with reliving the drama of criminal detection, but a strategic intervention in the politics of the day, which witnessed the return of Home Rule to the political agenda after the hiatus that accompanied the fall of Parnell. Its central concern is not so much with the dynamite attacks themselves as with reviving the already discredited project of connecting the now-dead Parnell with them; or, in Anderson's words, of convincing British public opinion "that the miscreants of the principal dynamite outrages in this country were the paid emissaries of the movement which, on its public side, owned Mr. Parnell as its 'esteemed and honored leader'" (1906: 134).

Anderson himself played an important role in advising on the British state's response to Irish political demands, both as a security consultant for the British colonial administration in Dublin Castle—where he advised on the timing of Davitt's original arrest in 1870—and then as the head of the Imperial capital's security police. According to his memoirs, Anderson is nothing if not consistent, applauding the re-arrest of Davitt in 1881 and the suspension of "ordinary law" which enabled mass arrests of Land League officials under the Coercion Act, but fiercely critical of judicial attempts to subordinate police action to legality (Anderson 1906: 92–93). Such oversight is envisaged as the predicament where "the rules of the prize ring are held to apply to the struggle between the law and those breaking the law," a situation that prompts Anderson to call for the withdrawal of police action from all scrutiny and publicity: "For a mine can only be reached by a counter-mine," he maintains. Indeed, Anderson demands the exemption of police operations from *all moral strictures*, since the administration of security lies "outside the sphere of morals," and any negotiation between the two is deemed "a phase of folly that leads not only individuals but Governments into trouble" (Anderson 1906: 136).

However, Anderson's involvement in British attempts to suppress the political campaign for Home Rule was not only philosophical, as he details in his memoirs. He played an important role in what would today be called a "Psy Ops" or "black propaganda" conspiracy, the notorious "Pigott forgeries" which sought to discredit the Home Rule leadership through the publication of forged letters in *The Times* of London in 1887: the letters purported to express Parnell's support for the assassination of Cavendish and his desire for a new bombing campaign.[10] The publication of the letters caused a political crisis for the Home Rule movement and Parnell, who sought in vain to have the allegations investigated by a Parliamentary committee, but was granted instead a Special Commission which many saw as weighted in favor of the British establishment. Nonetheless, the plot collapsed even under this limited scrutiny, and although the conspiracy was not pursued, it became difficult to ignore the collusion of the government of the day with the premier organ of the English press and the covert security apparatus in an extralegal operation that involved forged documents, paid informers, and double agents.[11] A large part of Anderson's memoirs are taken up with defending his own role in the plot itself and in the subsequent cover up: in particular, he is concerned with justifying his refusal to face cross-examination at the Special Commission and his reluctance thereafter to answer questions about the infiltration of Irish groups by informers and agent provocateurs under his direction.

If *The Secret Agent* envisages a systematic thermodynamics of obscurity—in which all significance is submerged in the entropy of the popular press and "public opinion," and all opposition is incorporated in a political realm reduced to bureaucracy—a different set of relationships between politics, publicity, and bureaucracy is implied by Anderson's memoirs. Rather than simply equating politics and bureaucracy, so casting the political as that "bureaucratic Being" wherein "the state's law . . . comes to incorporate everything" (Houen 2002: 51-52), in fact Anderson recognizes the potential for their *non-identity* in the prospect of the political success of the Home Rule movement over and against the will of the British security apparatus. Characteristically, this recognition prompts a call for the restrictive policing of the bounds of the political, since as Anderson remarks, "the Home Rule vote depends entirely upon the lower strata of the electorate, of whom, in three of the four provinces [of Ireland], the vast majority are Roman Catholics." His proposal for a "political settlement" in Ireland is, therefore, to exert administrative control over the space of the political by raising "the franchise [qualification] . . . to a level which would exclude the ignorant masses," with the result that "the Home Rule majority would disappear" (Anderson 1906: 173).[12]

That politics and bureaucracy do not coincide absolutely implies that publicity is not to be conceived of simply in terms of "entropy" or the inevitable dissipation of significance. And indeed, Anderson's conception of publicity is much more differentiated and nuanced than that presented by *The Secret Agent*. In the novel, it is the anarchists who try (unsuccessfully) to affect public consciousness, while the forces of the state work to keep it undisturbed. But for Anderson, publicity works in a number of different ways for each actor: for example, it may enable judicial and political oversight of the security apparatus, but it may equally be utilized by the police bureaucracy to spread misinformation or propaganda that furthers its own ends. And, of course, this awareness is demonstrated not only by the conspiracy to discredit Parnell, but also by Anderson's memoirs themselves, which seek to continue via mass-market publishing the project previously pursued through covert operations.

The novel's failure to learn the lessons taught by Anderson's memoirs is signaled most graphically by the transformation of the incident which Conrad tells us inspired the novel. In *Sidelights on the Home Rule Movement*, it is the political figure of the Home Secretary, Sir William Harcourt, who complains that "Anderson's idea of secrecy is not to tell the Secretary of State" (1906: 89); but in *The Secret Agent*, it is the Assistant Commissioner, the novel's senior secret policeman, who complains of his subordinate Chief Inspector Heat that "Your idea of secrecy seems to consist in keeping the chief of your department in the dark" (Conrad 1983: 132). In Conrad's novel, then, the issue is not the opacity of the police bureaucracy to politics, but to *itself*, for in *The Secret Agent* the political is reduced absolutely to the bureaucracy without excess or remainder. In disregarding the possibility of an externality to the administrative apparatus, the novel abstracts violence from politics and so restricts the potentiality of the political by insisting on its absolute identity with bureaucracy. And in so doing, it occludes the role of imperialism in eroding the constitutional and legal dimension of the political realm of the nation-state.

To recall *The Secret Agent's* commitment to a certain version of English-ness implied by the "disappearance" of Irish politics in the novel is to question the equation of politics and bureaucracy enabled by this elision. And in turn, this suggests the need to reassess contemporary attempts to recast the political through the refusal of any externality to power, the commodity, or the violence of the law. For in dispensing with modern discourses of emancipation and social justice, these critical perspectives are in danger of forgetting, like Conrad's novel, the complex triangulation of politics, bureaucracy, and visibility that underlies the postimperial articulation of violence and civility.

Notes

1. For an example of the way on which Conrad's novel was quickly enlisted to interpret the 9/11 attacks, see Kaplan (2001). The assessment of Conrad's relationship to the dominant imperial culture has been read in very different terms within postcolonial criticism; for two very famous but very different assessments, see Achebe (1990) and Said (1993: 19–31).

2. By this I mean that *The Secret Agent* is the only novel by Conrad wholly set within a polity that exemplifies the modern political condition of formal freedom, characterized by representative democracy and equality before the law.

3. For Houen's sense of the contemporary significance of his reading, see (2002: 1–17).

4. In this piece Said also links the attack on the World Trade Center with Conrad's novel: "With astonishing prescience in 1907, Joseph Conrad drew the portrait of the archetypal terrorist, whom he calls laconically 'the Professor' in his novel *The Secret Agent*; this is a man whose sole concern is to perfect a detonator that will work under any circumstances and whose handiwork results in a bomb exploded by a poor boy sent, unknowingly, to destroy the Greenwich Observatory as a strike against 'pure science'" (Said, 2001).

5. According to Deane, "the language of politics in Ireland and England … is still dominated by the putative division between barbarism and civilization" (1986: 39). The same structure of opposition has returned in current claims for the "clash of civilizations" mobilized in defense of the ongoing "war on terror."

6. For the original account of the incident, see Anderson (1906: 89).

7. The question of Irish Home Rule effectively returned to the political

agenda with the election of a Liberal government in 1906, although a new Home Rule Bill was not formally tabled in the Commons until 1912.

8.   Conrad (1983: 32). As Charles Townshend observes, in fact Fenian political violence "did not manifest the 'irrationality' . . . which underlay the beliefs of the *narodovl'tsy*" (1993: 160).

9.   In Anderson's case, the claim appears particularly implausible given the continuation of the dynamite campaign over a period of years.

10.   See chapters 12–14 of Lyons (1977). Significantly, the publication of the letters was designed to coincide with the voting on a new and permanent Irish Coercion Bill, which would no longer require annual parliamentary review. The Bill became law in July 1887.

11.   According to Lyons, "there were good grounds for suspecting a substantial amount of collusion" between the British government and *The Times* of London. He also notes the "widespread contemporary view that the government had succumbed to the temptation to use its parliamentary majority to create a Commission which, despite the veneer of legality conferred by the appointment of judges to preside over it, would in effect be what Randolph Churchill called it, 'a revolutionary tribunal for the trial of political opponents'" (Lyons 1977: 393, 395).

12.   While Anderson's proposal for an administrative reshaping of the political was not put into practice on an all-Ireland basis, its logic underpins Partition, where the boundaries of the political are restricted *territorially* rather than *economically*.

Bibliography

Achebe, Chinua. 1990. "An Image of Africa." In R.D. Hamner (ed.), *Joseph Conrad: Third World Perspectives*. Washington D.C.: Three Continents.

Anderson, Robert. 1906. *Sidelights on the Home Rule Movement*. London: Murray.

Arendt, Hannah. 1973. *The Origins of Totalitarianism*. San Diego: Harcourt Brace.

Conrad, Joseph. [1907] 1983. *The Secret Agent*. Oxford: Oxford University Press.

Cooley, John. 2002. *Unholy Wars. Afghanistan, America and International Terrorism*. London: Pluto.

Deane, Seamus. 1986. "Civilians and Barbarians." In Seamus Deane et al., *Ireland's Field Day*. Notre Dame: Notre Dame University Press.

Foster, R.F. 1988. *Modern Ireland 1600–1972*. Harmondsworth: Penguin.

Houen, Alex. 2002. *Terrorism and Modern Literature: From Joseph Conrad to Ciaran Carson*. Oxford: Oxford University Press.

Kaplan, Robert D. 2001. "US Foreign Policy Brought Back Home." *Washington Post* (September 23): B5.

Laqueur, Walter. 2001. *A History of Terrorism*. New Brunswick: Transaction.

Lyons, F.S.L. 1977. *Charles Stuart Parnell*. New York: Oxford University Press.

Moody, T.W. 1981. *Davitt and the Irish Revolution 1846–82*. Oxford: Clarendon.

Said, Edward. 1993. *Culture and Imperialism*. New York: Knopf.

———. 2001. "Collective Passion." [Accessed 18 May 2004 at Arab Media Internet Network] <http://www.amin.org/eng/edward_said/2001/20sept2001.html>.

Sherry, Norman. 1971. *Conrad's Western World*. Cambridge: Cambridge University Press.

Townshend, Charles. 1993. *Political Violence in Ireland*. Oxford: Clarendon.

PART II

Postcolonial Legacies

CHAPTER 6

Brit Bomber

The Fundamentalist Trope in Hanif Kureishi's *The Black Album*
and "My Son the Fanatic"

Sheila Ghose

A CNN segment commenting on the 7 July 2005 London terrorist attacks juxtaposes images of three bearded, swarthy men, identified by a reporter's voice as terrorists: "shoe bombers" Richard Reid and Sajid Badat, and Ahmed Omar Saeed Sheikh, killer of reporter Daniel Pearl in Pakistan. The voice then states, "What do these men have in common? A British passport." A large image of such a passport fills the screen, covering and replacing the men's faces.[1] The segment ends by emphasizing the "risk of home-grown terrorism"; the London terror acts were not only executed but also possibly thought up "at home." "Home" has thus been rendered unsafe by a specific group: British Muslims. While briefly considering the disenfranchisement caused by disproportionately high unemployment among young Muslim British men, the segment stresses their extranational identification with Muslims in Iraq and Palestine as an explanation. Such extranational loyalty would override the national loyalty demanded by the document of a British national belonging featured—a passport, that is recognizable also as an EU standard passport, and thus as a signifier of Britishness within a larger Europe in transformation.[2]

By representing these terrorists' acts as perverting the idea of home, the segment thus draws attention to the instability of Britishness. It thereby also touches on questions about the ability of Britishness to solve the problems of race and ethnicity coded within Englishness. Since the 1990s, Britishness has increasingly come to denote a more inclusive national identity in contrast to Englishness, which has historically been used to assert a hegemonic, racially determined—white—domestic identity in imperial and in post-second world war constructions of national identity. Yasmin Alibhai-Brown articulates this emerging sense of Britishness in a manifesto-like tone:

> Instead of "ethnic minorities" I prefer to use descriptions such as "British black," "British Asian," "Chinese British," because I feel that the British identity is now an umbrella term which gathers under it a large number of bi-racial and combined ethnicity people, as well as all kinds of ethnic and religious

---

groups including the English, Scottish, Welsh, Irish, Polish, Turkish, Jewish, Chinese, and a host of other people. One day soon it will be commonplace (I hope) to use "English British" or "Scots British" too which would finally make us all equal at least in name. (Alibhai-Brown 2000: ix–x)

By positioning Englishness as one ethnicity among others, Alibhai-Brown attempts to separate Britishness from its historical identification with Englishness and direct a challenge to the exclusionary discourses of Englishness that arose after 1948 as a reaction to Commonwealth immigration.[3] Such a project is thrown into doubt, however, by sentiments like those expressed in the CNN segment, in which Britishness is associated with loss of domestic security; the passport evokes confusion and fear of loss of control. The document symbolizes an ambivalent and unstable sense of belonging. A contested national discourse is conjured that can be claimed by a diverse number of people with perhaps multiple allegiances that in some cases, the reporter suggests, compromises the idea of home. The ability of Britishness to signify a multicultural society is questioned; the idea of diasporic belonging, associated with terror and violence, haunts the domestic space.

This essay will focus primarily on the deployment of the Asian British radical "fundamentalist" or "fanatic" as a trope in two texts negotiating Asian British belonging: Hanif Kureishi's novel *The Black Album* (1995) and short story "My Son the Fanatic" (1994). *The Black Album* seems to set up a binary between Muslim fundamentalism and Western liberal discourse. However, we can perceive ambivalence and critique of both discourses in this novel if we resist rehearsing the oppositional mode it sets up. The book, I argue, denaturalizes belonging by emphasizing the work that belonging entails for everyone. However, because its Asian British protagonist is already threatened by marginalization, the text is troubled by this denaturalization. This resistance and confusion causes some critics to repeat the binary opposition that the text seemingly cannot avoid; they see the text as falling into "the trap of specularity" (Ranasinha 2002: 82), pandering to a white mainstream liberal discourse of professed tolerance and multiculturalism. If we concentrate on the contradictions and gaps opened up by the text's confusions, it can provide a useful starting point for a discussion of the precariousness of securing a place in a national imaginary, specifically, of a European nation like Britain.

The ambiguities opened up by its aesthetic strategies—particularly the tensions occasioned by the text's deployment of the fundamentalist trope and by Kureishi's choice of the *Bildungsroman* form, with its drive toward integration and its teleological progress narrative—allow us to perceive some of the difficulties involved in imagining and writing diasporic belonging. Ultimately, the fundamentalist's refusal of a recognizable kind of liberal Britishness problematizes the project of imagining diasporic, or hyphenated, multiple belongings. If this trope is admitted as formative of a kind of

Asian British mode of belonging, the (absent) hyphen in "Asian British" seems endangered, as an either/or logic imposes itself on the text: multiple belongings risk being associated with espionage, double agents, undercover activities, betrayal or, most extremely, terrorism. The text seems to be struggling with mainstream society's fears and paranoias, rehearsing them but also ambivalently resisting them. In the end, *The Black Album* cannot resolve its dilemmas; the protagonist, Shahid, rejects what Arundhati Roy terms the politics of "the big," the large structures and discourses demanding his allegiance and commitment. Instead, he restarts with politics of "the small," on an individual level (for which the book has been accused of being apolitical): for the first time in his life he begins provisionally to trust and to commit to something or someone, his lover Deedee. As he explains, "[h]e'd take what she offered; he'd give her what he could. He had never relied on anyone before" (Kureishi 1995: 275).

"Brit Bomber"

The alliterative headline of the 13 July 2005 edition of the British tabloid *The Sun*, "The Brit Bomber," ironically and horrifically connects two entities that, it implies, should be incompatible. The headline points to the bomber's Britishness but also foregrounds the fact that the bomber bombed Brits. He is an insider who has rendered himself an outsider, the headline suggests, a traitor who has negated his British belonging by turning on what is supposed to be his own nation, a nation that has increasingly come to regard itself as multicultural. Britishness can no longer be easily conflated with whiteness; the fact that the young man in question, Shahzad Tanweer, was clearly a member of a "visible community"—we can see this in the photograph of him juxtaposed with the headline—does not mark him automatically as an outsider. Instead, his image could signify a kind of syncretic belonging, the emerging "new" Britain. However, what looms behind such headlines as *The Sun's* is the purported binary between a liberal, secular, even multicultural mainstream Britishness versus an intolerant, un-British version of Islam, a binary fortified by, among other things, the *Satanic Verses* controversy in Britain.[4] An Orientalist discourse which others Muslims resurfaces, one that has been thriving in particular since 9/11 and the beginning of the "war on terrorism."[5] "Brit" invokes democracy and openness, and "Bomber" encompasses fundamentalist and radical foreignness.

Here we must note that there are accepted "Brit Bombers," that is, British soldiers who have bombed other places in the world—some of them predominantly Muslim—sanctioned by a British national context and therefore obviously not foreign or other. Even against innocent people, violence is thus not incompatible with Britishness. To point this out does not mean to lift the blame off any bombers' shoulders, but rather to lay bare the effects of the binary proposed by the tabloid. The coupling of Britishness and such frightening and saddening violence evokes not only the incompatibility of the terms but also their intimacy. The violence purportedly foreign or exterior could in fact be inherent in the word "Brit" also: there is potential violence in the act of constructing national belonging, of drawing boundaries that sanction national belonging against foreignness, and the violence that can ensue when such boundaries are transgressed. There is also the violence of Britain's worldwide involvement in nation-building (and destroying) efforts in the nation's colonial past and in the present. I am not interested here in defining terrorism, or in questioning whether we can speak of state-sanctioned terrorism, or who has the power to define terrorism, etc. Rather, my preliminary suggestions provide a framework for my exploration of the complex, sometimes failed work undertaken in my chosen literary texts of confronting the binary of liberal British multiculturalism versus intolerant, non-Western Muslim fundamentalism. My attempt at unraveling the "Brit Bomber" coupling initiates a dialogue with the texts' negotiations of Asian British belonging to which the figure of the Muslim "fundamentalist" or "fanatic" seems to pose a challenge. Particularly, I theorize "Asian British" here in terms of diasporic belonging, which makes possible multiple allegiances and their attendant dangers. The Muslim fundamentalist appears in Kureishi's texts as a threat or obstacle to such a diasporic state by virtue of his refusal of multiple interpretations.

As we have seen, this dialogue is largely prompted by extraliterary concerns that form another text to be carefully scrutinized, but that can also actualize certain questions about my chosen texts' formal characteristics as well as place them in a specific historical, post-9/11 context. My investigation can, of course, only offer partial and unfinished suggestions about the larger implications of the constructions of Britishness and diasporic belonging taking place in these texts, for no critic can completely know the ideological and historical context forming her or him. Gayatri Spivak formulates an idea of ethical pedagogy, as well as reading practice, that would "constantly seek to undo the opposition between the verbal and the social at the same time as it knows its own inability to know its own ideological provenance fully" (Spivak 1988: 98). This insight seems especially important to keep in mind when theorizing a phenomenon like diaspora, where the recognition of gaps in understanding would be requisite to perceiving the multi-faceted strategies employed to handle the fears and possibilities opened up by diasporic multiple belonging. Spivak thus proposes a reading practice that brings out the provisional nature—one that accepts the possibility of failures in our reading practice—of our understanding of larger political issues, but also of our interpretations, our attempts at formulating ideas that may or may not respect the inherent instability of literary as well as historical (i.e., "real") texts. With her idea in mind, it is important for me to be sensitive to my chosen literary texts' openly stated desires to also stress provisionality and fluidity. As politically minded critics, we are tempted to read texts in the light of a particular set of political goals, to champion their efforts, and chide them for their failure in following through on such projects. In this context, the monologic fundamentalist seems radically incongruous and downright threatening. What work does he perform in these texts?[6] What resistances does he put up? How do Kureishi's texts negotiate the seemingly intractable binary of liberal, multicultural tolerance versus dogmatism—a binary that could as well be formulated in temporal terms (modernity vs. medieval feudalism), or geographical ones (West vs. "Oriental")?

Again, to focus on the fundamentalist as a trope does not entail an exclusively textualizing approach. What is of interest is the tricky project of understanding the continuum of the extraliterary and the aesthetic.[7] The fraught relationship between aesthetic and "extraliterary" concerns is concretized by the difficult negotiations of the fundamentalist trope, which clearly signals these texts' interest in drawing on their immediate historical context of a Britain in transformation. They are also active agents in this process of change. Mark Stein, among others, warns of the dangers of assigning texts like these testimonial value or the burden of representation, which would severely restrict the range of interpretations one could elicit from them (Stein 2004: 53–54). Such a reductive move would bypass the fruitful and difficult negotiations of aesthetic and political concerns by relegating the aesthetic to a secondary position. My discussion instead attempts to locate the gaps and fissures in the literary texts and their implication in the extraliterary by practicing the kind of Spivakian self-reflection outlined above. Taking into consideration my inability to completely grasp my own "ideological provenance" forces reflection on the fact that my investigation contains such gaps. Such reflection necessitates respecting the texts' instabilities and ambiguities, working with what Hayden White describes as the "inexpungeable relativity" of representations of historical phenomena: their inescapably aesthetic dimension, which problematizes the activity of historiography and "truthful" representation (White 1992: 37). I want to emphasize the word problematize here; like White, I am not advocating a complete negation or relativization of the idea of historical "truth." Rather, the idea is to underline the impossibility of escaping the aesthetic, and therefore inherently unstable, dimension of representations of history: every such representation is subject to generic and linguistic limitations that frame our perception of events.

The Black Album: Double Agent of Transformation

The Black Album is composed around the powerful challenge to literature posed by a ritual book burning—a revisiting of the Bradford burning of Rushdie's *The Satanic Verses*. The novel explores the central questions about the role of literature raised by this incident: wrenching debates about censorship, freedom of speech, and the question of "literature" versus the "sacred." Its protagonist, Shahid, moves from his Pakistani immigrant parents' wealthy home in a leafy Kent suburb into central London to attend a derelict university college. He is soon torn between a hedonistic affair with his Literature and Cultural Studies professor Deedee Osgood and a group of young Muslim "fundamentalists" who seem to him in some way to represent "his" people. This binary becomes increasingly fortified throughout the book, and toward the end of his *Bildung* process, Shahid predictably chooses to ally himself with Deedee while the text dispenses with the violence and intolerance with which the "fundamentalist" group is associated. In the end, he formulates a purpose for literature and for writing:

> [H]e found a fountain pen with a decent nib, and began to write with concentrated excitement. He had to find some sense in his recent experiences; he wanted to know and understand. How could anyone confine themselves to one system or creed? Why should they feel they had to? There was no fixed self; surely our several selves melted and mutated daily? There had to be innumerable ways of being in the world. He would spread himself out, in his work and in love, following his curiosity. (Kureishi 1995: 274)

Identities are fluid, a fact that literature helps us understand. Shahid sits down to write with a sense of urgency to record this insight gained from his experiences, feeling he would otherwise be "missing something important" (1995: 274). He formulates, finally, a sense of selfhood as one that will always be provisional, feeling that he is liberated from the dogmatic constraints of the sacred. And according to *The Black Album's* teleological *Bildungsroman* logic, as Shahid arrives at this understanding, so should the reader. The novel should thereby embody its insights, but it has difficulties doing so because of its difficulties in dealing with the straw persons it shoots down: the fundamentalists. In the process, it burrows into the undergrowth of the tangled discourses of belonging that restrain Shahid and render him vulnerable as a so-called second-generation immigrant and British Muslim, bringing to light the complexities of securing a place of belonging in the face of contradictory histories of racism, colonialism, and even liberal multiculturalism.

The novel's troubles with this project are noticeable in the tension caused by Kureishi's choice to center it around the powerful but unspoken presence of Rushdie's book. This confusion is indicated not least by the formal differences between *The Black Album* and *The Satanic Verses*. Rushdie's text—never explicitly named—uses postmodern techniques to draw on the idea of the "satanic" difficulties of committing to any one mode of belonging, mingling hallucinatory states with realistic ones. In contrast, Kureishi's texts are, as Bart Moore-Gilbert points out, "strongly linear. Indeed, prolepsis and analepsis are extremely rare in comparison to Rushdie's work" (Moore-Gilbert 2001: 109). Kureishi's choice to use such a linear *Bildungsroman* to build a defense of literature around Rushdie's text seems almost willful. Moore-Gilbert points to a self-reflexive passage in *The Black Album* where Shahid comments on his difficulties reading *Midnight's Children*, which he takes to show Kureishi's explicit stylistic positioning against Rushdie's:

> "I found the book difficult initially. Its rhythms aren't Western. It dashes all over the place. Then I saw the author on television attacking racism, informing the people how it all arose. I tell you, I wanted to cheer. But it made me feel worse, because I was finally recognizing something. I began to get terrible feelings in my head." (Kureishi 1995: 9)

Moore-Gilbert asserts that Kureishi, while expressing appreciation of Rushdie, primarily affiliates himself with social realism (Moore-Gilbert 2001:109). Yet, importantly, Shahid states that he found the book difficult only "initially": some kind of understanding is hinted at, though never explicitly explained. And this understanding seems connected with a political realization about the nature of racism; Shahid proceeds to recount the racist persecution and resulting interiorized racism he experienced as an adolescent. Rushdie's literary text is thus awkwardly juxtaposed in this passage with Shahid's political awakening. "Then I saw the author on television": what does the "then" indicate here? "Then" seems to point to a connection between Shahid's political awakening and his experience of the text. But *post hoc ergo procter hoc*: "then" could function merely as a temporal marker, illustrating a random occurrence—after having read a book he did not quite understand, he happened to see the author make a political speech. The "then" must bridge the separation of Rushdie's postmodern style and his political engagement. What disturbs this separation is the unfinished line of thought opened up by Shahid's indeterminate "initially": the difficult, incomprehensible, non-Western book seems to help him recognize his racist oppression and his perverted complicity in it. This political realization is intimately bound up with Shahid's aesthetic experience of Rushdie's "rhythms," prompting him to understand how he has "picked up the vibe" (Kureishi 1995: 12), as his friend Chad expresses it, of the hegemony of racism in Britain and to find a way to purge himself of this influence. Rushdie's style and politics thus seem to be a driving force in Kureishi's politico-aesthetic project in The Black Album, though their connection is articulated in an elliptical manner.

This intertextual dialogue points toward a central confusion in Kureishi's novel regarding the role of literature: its difficulties in squaring its own strong adherence to a realist, Bildungsroman form with Rushdie's postmodern experiment that utilizes a fragmenting technique to embody migrant realities. Due to The Black Album's difficulties articulating its aesthetic vision, it is not easy to pronounce straightforward judgments about its political effects.

The Bildungsroman form is no arbitrary choice for writers who, like Kureishi, attempt to make visible or write a "new" or different kind of subjectivity into being: the genre has served as an aesthetic model for human identity since its beginnings in the late eighteenth century, initially for European bourgeois masculinity.[8] As the paradigmatic genre of bourgeois faith in the aesthetic's ability to educate the emerging self into subjecthood, the Bildungsroman is a, if not the, medium through which a liberal humanist idea of subjectivity has been and is imagined. Pointing to the central role that aesthetics—an eighteenth-century invention—is accorded in bourgeois mythology, Marc Redfield explains that aesthetics "realizes its ideological potential when the artwork becomes the model for human identity, the state, and, most generally, the historical and phenomenal realization of the Subject" (1996: 63). The Bildungsroman is the genre in which such a realization can take place most fully, providing a narrative of the subject's formation as an integrated member of society, one who can partake in its upkeep or, in the spirit of liberal humanist debate, scrutinize and critique it.

Especially since the twentieth century, the genre has increasingly become appropriated and redefined by marginalized groups—women, postcolonial subjects, gay people, and ethnic minorities—who have seized on its politico-pedagogical function. Through the reader's identification with the protagonist's development and eventual integration into a society, a subject can be written into being. The Bildungsroman takes on an exemplary role, narrating the process whereby "the anomalous individual learns to be reconciled with society and its projects, whether, as mostly for men, through labor or, as mostly for women, through love and marriage" (Lloyd 1993: 134). Kureishi's book ends on a somewhat irresolute note, indicating that this process might not be so straightforward. Nevertheless, it conforms to the genre's basic framework for writing "new" subjectivities, of creating what David Lloyd refers to as "ethical identity," the identity formed as the reader moves through the progress narrative of Bildung, undergoing a "civilizing process": the individual story of self-formation is "subsumed in the larger narrative of . . . the passage from savagery to civility, which is the master narrative of modernity" (1993: 134). The aesthetic, in effect, takes on a regulative function:

Ethical identity is thus the end of the novel in a double sense. On the one hand, it narrates the passage of an individual or a people-nation from contingent particularity to universal value, their history becoming representative exactly insofar as it reproduces the general form of universal human history. On the other, it seeks to produce ethical identity as an intrinsic element of its aesthetic effect: the mechanisms of identification, or in nineteenth-century terms, "sympathy," are crucial to the pedagogical claims of the novel as means to induce in the reader an ethical disposition. The process of reading ideally repeats the learning process undergone by the novel's protagonist. (1993: 134)

As stated earlier, this learning and identification process threatens to be interrupted by the different political understanding infusing *The Black Album* through its muddled dialogue with Rushdie's text: the unfinished work of relating to the politics of racism and the "not Western"—or postmodern and postcolonial-aesthetic strategies. And through this muddle, we can perceive the novel's unease with its difficulties of aesthetically incorporating the Muslim fundamentalists, of rendering them even two-dimensional.

Resisting the Migrant Aesthetic

In sum, *The Black Album* constructs a version of Asian British subjectivity largely through the gaps opened up by its troubled intertextual interlacing with *The Satanic Verses*. With reference to his novel, Rushdie claims his ambition is to "create a literary language and literary forms in which the experience of formerly colonized, still disadvantaged peoples might find full expression," and his multiplicity of styles as determined by "the experience of uprooting, disjuncture, and metamorphosis . . . that is the migrant condition" (Rushdie 1992: 394). Stating his intention to create a migrant aesthetic expressed through his fragmented and playful styles, Rushdie creates a manifesto that clearly announces the connection between his aesthetic choices and his political concerns, emphasizing the painful history of colonization that haunts, for instance, Asian British diasporic belonging. *The Black Album's* engagement with the effects of this history is evident in, for example, its descriptions of the derelict London housing estates where immigrants are persecuted, and of Shahid's subjection to racist bullying in high school. However, a term like "migrant" throws a spanner in the works; Shahid is intensely aware of "racial" and class-determined inequalities, but shies away from the term's perpetuation of outsiderness, its stress on fluid belonging. This hesitation would seem to contradict his final realization that identities are provisional; yet it also highlights his precarious status as a non-white Briton. His Britishness and national belonging is questioned openly and aggressively by racist thugs but also, in more implicit ways, by the liberal discourse represented in the text by, e.g., his conflicted relationship with the education he receives in his crumbling college and by the caricatured Labour council representative Rudder, who cynically partakes in the ludicrous worship of a divinely inscribed eggplant to curry favor with the local Asian community.[9]

A power relationship is ambiguously evoked by Rushdie's term "migrant," which offers the possibility of diasporic forms of being, but which can also gloss over local power constellations. In the case of *The Black Album*, Shahid, and thereby the text, struggles with the logic of the term "second generation" immigrant, which reinforces a power relationship that privileges the native belonging of the British—meaning "white" in more than a symbolic sense—over the kind of belonging that will apparently always be extraneous, extended into "third," "fourth" generation immigrants, and so on. What does it mean for such perpetual "outsiders within" to forge a "British way of life"?[10] Rushdie's style and term work as political-aesthetic driving forces in *The Black Album*, but largely through the lacunae opened up by the texts' differences. The possibility of political engagement through the creation and maintenance of diasporic "bifocal commitment" (Desai 2000: 23)—or indeed multifocal commitment—is opened up by Shahid's defense of *The Satanic Verses* (or, since it is unnamed, any text like it). But as noted above, this engagement is recognized in a moment of confusion. Shahid's *Bildung* challenge is to forge an Asian British identity and secure a place in the British imaginary on his own terms. He recognizes the political aspect of this process through his identification with the "formerly colonized peoples" to whose experiences Rushdie wants to give voice, and with whom Shahid's "fundamentalist" friends align themselves. They are, however, portrayed as more or less voluntary outsiders in Britain. For example, in a discussion with Shahid, the leader of the Muslim group, Riaz, asks,

> "Do you think someone should abandon the others to whom he belongs?"
> "This matter of belonging, brother. I wish I understood it. Do you, for instance, like living in England?"
> Riaz blinked and looked around; it was as if he'd never considered the question before.
> "This will never be my home," he said. "I will never entirely understand it. And you?"
> "It suits me. There's nowhere else I will feel more comfortable." (Kureishi 1995: 175)

"England" seems to mean different things to the speakers. Riaz, clearly, cannot relate to it; speaking of Shahid as his "fellow countryman" (1995: 2), he defines them both as Pakistani by virtue of their looks—when Shahid protests, he states, "Oh, yes, you are, I have observed you" (1995: 2), inducting him into a racial and ethnic community by insisting on this identity. Englishness is an alien racial category to him; "Britain," as a multicultural signifier means little. Shahid, characteristically, does not use the word "home," and admits to not understanding commitment. But England is, in spite of racism, the place he can provisionally inhabit as less uncomfortable than others. It is more than an idea to him: it is a space he inhabits (and possibly changes while so doing). Embracing this provisional state of being requires struggle throughout the whole book, however, as the text is haunted by the specter of its implication in colonial history, and yet its assertion of difference in relation to this history.

One of the clearest instances of *The Black Album's* negotiation of this ambivalent sense of belonging is that of the character Chad, who tries in vain to suppress the role of literature—and indeed art in general—in his self-formation, and is consequently destroyed. "Chad" is the short name for Muhammad Shahabuddin Ali-Shah, formerly Trevor Buss, of Pakistani extraction but adopted by a white English couple. Formerly a huge Prince fan and lover of stylish clothes and drugs, Chad has been "saved" by "his" people and is now a driving force in the local fundamentalist group to which Shahid finds himself temporarily attracted. Toward the end of the novel Chad, is badly burnt in an attack on a bookshop as the Molotov cocktail that he intends to throw at the shop window blows up in his face. Having taken up a quest to destroy literature, the crowning moment of which is his orchestration of the burning of the unnamed "heretic" book that insults Muslims the world over, he is finally shown to be participating in the destruction of himself. Chad is clearly Shahid's double, the Shahid-that-could-have-been that the narrative must rid itself of; Chad is the parodic version of a subject courting his own annihilation by his attempts to properly belong.

Chad and Shahid part in a violent showdown over their different conceptions of literature that illustrates the novel's strong belief in art as a survival strategy for the Asian British character, as well as its desire for, but difference from, what Rushdie's text encapsulates. Like *The Satanic Verses'* Salman, who transcribes the verses dictated to him by Mahound, God's messenger, Shahid must rewrite a supposedly sacred text. Shahid has been assigned to transcribe Riaz's dogmatic poetry—poems with titles like "The Heretical Artist"—but finds himself physically unable to copy it verbatim, especially after returning from lovemaking with his literature lecturer Deedee Osgood. He infuses the poems with sensuality to the point where his renderings give him erections "which just wouldn't go away" (1995: 76). But unlike Salman, Shahid is not saddened by his act of rewriting; rather, he takes pleasure in it. Salman is horrified to discover that Mahound does not seem to notice changes in the words that are supposedly delivered straight from God, whereas Shahid enjoys and is empowered by his act in which phallus and pen are rather neatly conflated. For him, rewriting is a

necessity: he cannot simply transcribe poetry that rejects the nature of poetry but must transform it into his own version, which forces him to flee for
his life, the enraged fundamentalist group chasing after him.

Most enraged of the group members is of course Chad, who has after all
given up his own powers to rewrite the script governing his life. Whereas
Shahid starts parodying religious fundamentalist discourse, Chad fetishizes
it, regards it as, finally, home, a static point of reference. He has found a
community that can legitimize him; he has acquired a sense of belonging.
What Chad does not realize, the narrative suggests, is that in his search for
authenticity he perpetuates his racist oppressors' logic, which reduces language to the point where poetry is impossible. There is only one way to be
authentic, according to racist discourse, and the religious fundamentalist
mindset holds the same opinion. Chad trades one single-truth discourse for
another, one that arrests the chain of signification and reifies or deifies one
set of ideas. Parody can of course not be tolerated, by its very nature introducing the idea of a multi-layered discourse.

Chad rejects the potentially liberating force of invention and thereby
gives up agency. And as we have seen, giving up his rights to authorship
seals his destiny: he negates the possible trajectory of *Bildung*. It is no acci-
dent that he is burnt, deformed, bereft of what has caused his alienation
and his desperate attempts to stabilize meaning: his brown skin. Chad has
grown up with what Deedee Osgood refers to as the "Orwellian idea of
England," a place where he "would hear church bells. He would see English country cottages and ordinary English people who were secure, who effortlessly belonged" (1995: 106). Chad's burns dissolve the boundaries
between his physical self and the larger forces in which he has let his body
and psyche become trapped. He succumbs to the exclusionary impulse that
makes people "effortlessly" belong; Deedee Osgood, again, observes that
the Orwellian England's "sense of exclusion practically drove him mad"
(1995: 107). *The Black Album* suggests that Chad's physical deformation is
the only condition of existence available to him in such an exclusionary
schema unless he decides to resist its stagnating effects.

Superfunkycalifragisexy[11]

Accepting (literary) ambiguity is thus a life and death matter in the novel.
Recurrent self-reflexive passages show Shahid defending it against the fundamentalists—in particular Chad—who lose their individual traits in such
discussions and appear as mouthpieces for an authoritarian ideology. There
is little room for contradiction in the text's ventriloquism of fundamentalist talk; the monolithic idea of the religious "fanatic" tends to be recycled
and reiterated. It seems the trajectory of *Bildung* traced by the novel can be

completed only when these characters are written out. The text thereby risks falling prey to the absolutist mode with which it struggles.

Again, Chad functions as a figure of negotiation. He suppresses ambiguity at great cost: he must, after all, fight his addiction to Prince, after whose notorious album Kureishi has named his novel. The prime protean figure whose spirit imbues the novel more than Rushdie's, Prince, is seen as a mix of "half black and half white, half man, half woman, half size, feminine but macho, too" (1995: 25). The troubled aura surrounding Prince's album also functions as a self-reflexive ironic comment on the novel itself: a dark and mysterious, sex and violence-filled experiment held in ambivalent regard by its creator.[12] Prince used an alter ego, Camille, to comment on and provide the album's point of view, a move that allows Prince the distance to comment on his creation. We might note that Kureishi's *The Black Album* also uses a distancing third-person narrator in contrast to his previous novel, *The Buddha of Suburbia*, whose protagonist, Karim, bears similarities to Shahid.

Nevertheless, the fact remains that the novel's depiction of the Muslim fundamentalist group risks playing into a discourse that has difficulties coping with difference: liberalism. According to Ruvani Ranasinha, this discourse is characterized by "intolerance of any intolerance itself" (Ranasinha 2002: 84), a contradiction, she asserts, that Kureishi unreflectively rehearses:

> Despite his sympathy regarding the conditions that heighten Islamic fundamentalism, Kureishi never questions the assumptions and biases of liberal ideology nor the limits of liberalism in accommodating minorities in pluralistic societies. He does not engage with the possibility of a rethinking of liberal ideology. (Ranasinha 2002:83)

The Black Album's form indeed provides such a liberal humanist framework for its investigation; the *Bildungsroman's* conventionality weighs heavily here. The weight of tradition lends Kureishi's text ostensible stability by veiling the instability inherent in all genres and classifications of all kinds. Through this mystification the *Bildungsroman* can provide a strategy for naturalizing the minority subject and insert it into a mainstream discourse. But this strategy risks conferring visibility on majoritarian terms. "New ethnicity" writing might thus be subjected to the liberal multiculturalist machinery that has trouble handling the idea of radical difference, something particularly evidenced by the "war on terror." The figure of the Muslim—"fundamentalist" or not—can swiftly render "home" strange, as indicated by the media coverage of the kind described above. *The Black Album* cannot quite handle this threat of estrangement, to the point where it deflects Chad's bomb onto himself; Chad is set up as the text's ambiguous nemesis. And here we detect the violence at work that underpins the binary opposition the text risks upholding. Violence is not only perpetrated by the fundamentalist characters but clearly by this *Bildungsroman*, too, in its rejection of Chad and the group.

Ranasinha's observations thus carry weight in pinpointing *The Black Album*'s adherence to liberal ideology. They also lead her to condemn the novel, accusing it of muslimophobia. However, the text's fears seem less irrational than the word "phobia" would suggest, in the face of the violence infusing the discourses of belonging it draws on and that threatens to lock its protagonist into an either/or logic. To fend off this threat, the novel provisionally forwards "home" as a mobile, tentative and local state — "home" is, after all, constantly threatened by destabilization through discursive violence in *The Black Album*, and thereby always already rendered unsafe. At the end of the novel, Shahid and Deedee decide — significantly, while traveling on a train—to explore the world together "until it stops being fun" (Kureishi 1995: 276). This hedonistic emphasis might seem frivolous; yet, it quite logically encapsulates the mood of the album Prince released as a substitute for *The Black Album*: the light-hearted, positive *Lovesexy*. In a rather classical *Bildungsroman* fashion, the ending thus signals a new beginning.

I want to end with a Kureishi text that consciously foregrounds aesthetic instability in its attempts to engage with the Muslim "fanatic," "My Son the Fanatic" (Kureishi 1997). This short story makes an attempt to question a presumed Western reader and thereby also perform a kind of self-interrogation. It displays a sympathetic kind of bewilderment with the figure of the Asian British Muslim "fundamentalist," which it posits as a cipher of almost incomprehensible radical otherness. This figure is all the more puzzling for having been "home-grown." A reader holding so-called Western values of liberalism and freedom of choice is invited to identify with a main character, the Pakistani immigrant taxi driver Parvez, who asserts his right to such values, and through him, view his son's upsetting development into a Muslim "fanatic."[13]

From the beginning, the story presents the son's behavior as a mystery to be investigated. We enter the text with Parvez entering his son's bedroom stealthily:

> Surreptitiously the father began going into his son's bedroom. He would sit there for hours, rousing himself only to seek clues. What bewildered him was that Ali was getting tidier. Instead of the usual tangle of clothes, books, cricket bats, video games, the room was becoming neat and ordered; spaces began appearing where before there had been only mess. (1997: 119)

Parvez experiences his son's sudden change of behavior as "mysterious," as an "eccentricity" (1997: 119). Initially, he suspects drug addiction, continuing his inspections of his son's room by "looking under the carpet, in his drawers, behind the empty wardrobe, sniffing, inspecting, probing" (1997:

122). But he finds nothing, merely empty "spaces," until he one day, while spying, observes his son praying. However, this discovery leads to more non-communication and confusion, as it becomes evident to Parvez that his son will not engage in dialogue with him any more; instead Ali prefers to spout dogma, sounding to Parvez as if "he'd swallowed someone else's voice" (1997: 126). Ali seems uncanny to Parvez in his "watchful" (1997: 122) refusal to communicate, and to the reader, too, Ali appears ghost-like and somewhat frightening. We never get to know him; the story is wholly told from Parvez's point of view, this integrated immigrant ("I love England," he exclaims [1997: 126]) who has struggled to create a good life for his son in this in country of his: Parvez, caring for the lonely prostitute Bettina, and enjoying the odd bacon-buttie or a few glasses of whisky after working ten-hour shifts. Kureishi represents Parvez as a man who appreciates the freedoms he has found in England, since "[t]hey let you do *almost* anything here" (1997: 126; emphasis added). Ali gets the last word, however. Parvez is driven to fury by his son's behavior and resorts to violence:

> Parvez kicked him over. Then he dragged the boy up by the shirt and hit him. The boy fell back. Parvez hit him again. The boy's face was bloody. Parvez was panting. He knew the boy was unreachable, but he struck him nonetheless. The boy neither covered himself nor retaliated; there was no fear in his eyes. He only said, through his split lip: "So who's the fanatic now?" (1997: 131)

In the end, Parvez and the reader sympathetic to his integrationist drive are confronted by this figure challenging the liberal values purportedly underpinning British/European society. In the story, Ali poses a frightening, seemingly insoluble problem. The story, initially published seven years before 9/11 and eleven years before 7/7, brings out the potential violence that the defense of this discourse can engender, a violence that seems endemic to it, and which is globally in evidence at present in, e.g., the undermining of universal human rights by liberal democracy itself.[14] Pure in his beliefs, and "unreachable," the figure of the fundamentalist Asian Briton is posed as a challenge and threat to liberal discourse. Yet the story does not quite fully appropriate and domesticate this radical other, as it ends on an ambiguous note. It is unclear whether the story demonizes him or respects his alterity as a necessity for posing a crucial question that throws into relief the possible contradictions of liberal discourse and points to its limits. Does the text keep a fearful or respectful distance to this entity that threatens to undermine the liberal humanist framework within which to write a "new" kind of European/British subjectivity, one that allows for negotiations of multiculturalism and competing versions of communitarian and individual identities?

The story, thus, invites the reader into the project of cultural identity construction in a different manner than the *Bildungsroman* form of The *Black Album*. "My Son the Fanatic" explicitly thematizes its incomprehension of the fundamentalist. Gaps in understanding are foregrounded. Ali is caricatured and clichéd, but the text self-reflexively questions the extent to which the reader is also active in thus constructing him. This story, in fact, engages with the "work" of belonging discussed above. Through Ali, the question of cultural identity construction is made visible, denaturalized. Ali's transformation from a recognizably normal teenager into a fundamentalist is mostly hinted at; however, we understand that, as with Chad, there is a history of racist abuse and pain involved in his efforts to negotiate Britishness. Kureishi, it seems, taps into incomprehension and knowledge gaps to promote self-reflection, pointing to the possibility of a "politics of ethnicity predicated on difference and diversity" (Hall 1995: 25). Emphasizing its failure to explain, the story also centers on a generational conflict, the so-called second generation character refusing his affiliation, his ancestral heritage, demanding his right to construct his kind of ethnicity. He is Shahid's and Karim's antithesis, but like them he must create his own subcontinental identity if he wants one. Lack or refusal of history functions as much for Ali as for Shahid and Karim to invent identity. The short story resists Ali's reification of his creation, however; Kureishi's story remains apprehensive, distanced, questioning. And, perhaps most importantly, it explicitly involves its reader in the creative work of understanding and questioning, and thereby constructing, Asian British cultural identities.

Notes

1. Charles Hodson, 9 July 2005, CNN International.
2. A Europe that must contend with about 14 million Muslims already living in Europe and possible Turkish membership, which forces Europeans to confront its self-image as secular or, if religious, mainly Christian.
3. The most infamous spokesman for this kind of Englishness is Enoch Powell; nevertheless, his images of flooding and swamping of the UK by non-white former colonial subjects, and of the ensuing corruption of "home," were not exclusively his. For investigations of such post-1948 public discourse imagery, see for example Ian Baucom, *Out of Place: Englishness, Empire and the Locations of Identity* (1999), and Wendy Webster, *Englishness and Empire 1939–1965* (2005).
4. A caveat: I do not wish to conflate British Muslims' reactions to *The Satanic Verses* with the terrorism that occurred in London, but point to the generalizing and polarizing ideas about Islam and Muslims as a group that were activated in mainstream debates.

5. For instance, as Said pointed out in *Covering Islam* long before 9/11, Muslims are the one group onto which the Western public imagination projects its fears and desires in a way not possible to do with other religious or ethnic communities: "Malicious generalizations about Islam have become the last acceptable form of denigration of foreign culture in the West; what is said about the Muslim mind, or character, or religion, or culture as a whole cannot now be said in mainstream discussion about African, Jews, other Orientals, or Asians" (Said 1997: xii).

6. The fundamentalist characters are predominantly male in Kureishi's short story and novel.

7. While emphasizing the continuum of the aesthetic and the political, I also want to maintain the crucial difference between texts with a documentary or journalistic ambition, or even the texts we read as "reality," and fictional texts. The instability of the aesthetic works in different ways in them; fictional texts, however, explicitly engage with the risky and unpredictable effects of the aesthetic.

8. As Marc Redfield rightly points out, the genre is notoriously difficult to define, to the point of being a "phantom formation." I do not aim to work with specific generical criteria, but discuss the general ideological machinery mobilized by it, which seems particularly important as *The Black Album* fits into an aesthetico-political trend: the *Bildungroman* has been a popular genre for writing Asian British subjectivities. Besides Kureishi's novels, we find Atima Srivastava's *Transmission* (1992), Meera Syal's *Anita and Me* (1996), and Shyama Perera's *Haven't Stopped Dancing Yet* (1999). A well-known film with a Bildung plot would be Gurinder Chadha's *Bend It Like Beckham* (2002). Mark Stein, in his detailed study of the *Black British* "novel of transformation," argues that the *Bildungroman* is in fact "a dominant form in Black British literature" (Stein 2004: xiii).

9. Lack of faith in a liberal arts education is for instance expressed in the depiction of his college—"[i]t was said that college reunions were held in Wandsworth Prison" (1995: 24)—and through his irritation at being taught pop culture as if it were more "his" culture (1995: 135), of being ghettoised. Through his adulation of canonical (male) authors, he does however seem to also admire liberal humanist traditions; these references also align *The Black Album* with such a canon. Shahid ambivalently hankers to be admitted to a mainstream discourse.

10. The expression is used by Prime Minister Tony Blair as a defiant marker of what is to be defended (against the threat of terrorism) and what anyone living in Britain must be loyal to.

11. Prince, *The Black Album*, track 6.

12. Prince's album is surrounded by legend: just before its release onto the market in 1987, Prince, for unclear reasons, withdrew all copies, leaving a few hundred in circulation that became valuable bootlegs (Shahid has in fact acquired one of them). It was officially released in 1994. Full of "dirtybassfunk" (Ford 2005), it has been described as "sexually aggressive, almost gangster-like" (Ford 2005). In an obscure statement, Prince comments, as "Camille," on the album: Camille claims to have succumbed to his evil side, "Spooky Electric," that prompted him to furiously defy his detractors through violence and hate. The album plays with different personae, sometimes distorting Prince's voice, like in the disturbing track featuring the pimp Bob George. Camille supposedly realized his mistake, creating instead the lighter and happier Lovesexy album. The history of Kureishi's intertext, the dark, extreme experiment *The Black Album*, is thus characterized by role-play, self-commentary and irony (after the album's fade-out, Prince can be heard saying, "What kind of fuck ending was that?").

13. Though there are disturbing clues to the fact that Parvez denies his wife such a choice.

14. "My Son the Fanatic" was first published in 1994 in *The New Yorker.*

Bibliography

Alibhai-Brown, Yasmin. 2000. *Who Do We Think We Are: Imagining the New Britain*. London: Allen Lane.

Baucom, Ian. 1999. *Out of Place: Englishness, Empire, and the Locations of Identity*. Princeton: Princeton University Press.

Desai, Jigna. 2000. *Beyond Bollywood: The Cultural Politics of South Asian Diasporic Film*. Durham: Duke University Press.

Ford, Adam. 2005. "Prince: *The Black Album*." *The Scam* (14 August). [Downloaded 15 August 2005]. <http://www.renewal.org.au/scam/princeblackalbum.html>.

Hall, Stuart.1995. "New Ethnicites" in James Donald and Ali Rattansi, Eds. *"Race," Culture and Difference*. London: Sage.

Kureishi, Hanif. 1995. *The Black Album*. London: Faber and Faber.

———. 1997. "My Son the Fanatic." In *Love in a Blue Time*. London: Faber and Faber.

Lloyd, David. 1993. *Anomalous States: Irish Writing and the Post-Colonial Movement*. Dublin: Lilliput.

Moore-Gilbert, Bart. 2001. Hanif Kureishi. Manchester: Manchester University Press.

Perera, Shyama. 1999. *Haven't Stopped Dancing Yet*. London: Sceptre.

Ranasinha, Ruvani. 2002. *Hanif Kureishi*. Tavistock: Northcote House/The British Council.

Redfield, Marc. 1996. *Phantom Formations: Aesthetic Ideology and the Bildungsroman*. Ithaca, NY: Cornell University Press.

Rushdie, Salman. 1992. "In Good Faith." In *Imaginary Homelands: Essays and Criticism 1981–1991*. London: Granta.

Said, Edward. 1997. *Covering Islam: How the Media and the Experts Determine How We See the Rest of the World*. New York: Vintage.

Spivak, Gayatri Chakravorty. 1988. "Reading the World: Literary Studies in the Eighties." In *In Other Worlds: Essays in Cultural Politics*. New York: Routledge.

Srivastava, Atima. 1992. *Transmission*. New Delhi: Penguin.

Stein, Mark. 2004. *Black British Literature: Novels of Transformation*. Columbus: Ohio State University Press.

Sullivan, Mike. 2005. "The Brit Bomber; 7/7." *The Sun* (13 July).

Syal, Meera. 1997. *Anita and Me*. London: Flamingo.

Webster, Wendy. 2005. *Englishness and Empire 1939–1965*. Oxford: Oxford University Press.

White, Hayden.1992. "Historical Emplotment and the Problem of Truth." In *Probing the Limits of Representation: Nazism and the "Final Solution."* Saul Friedlander (ed.). Cambridge, MA: Harvard University Press.

CHAPTER 7

Crisis of Identity?

Englishness, Britishness and Whiteness

Bridget Byrne

Introduction

In 1998, the Runnymede Trust set up a Commission on the "Future of Multi-Ethnic Britain" which set out to produce a review of the current state of multi-ethnic Britain. After two years of extensive consultation and discussion, the Commission produced a report which argues that Britain in the year 2000 was at a turning point or crossroads with different potential roads ahead:

> Will it try to turn the clock back, digging in, defending old values and ancient hierarchies, relying on a narrow English-dominated, backward-looking definition of the nation? Or will it seize the opportunity to create a more flexible, inclusive, cosmopolitan image of itself? (Parekh 2000: 14–15)

The report argues for a "purposeful process of change" rather than "multicultural drift" (2000: 2). Part of this process is, the report argues, a re-imagining of British national identity and its history. An important obstacle to Britain's transformation into an inclusive, pluralist society is that "Britishness, as much as Englishness, has systematic, largely unspoken, racial connotations" (2000: 38). The report further argues that "Unless these deep-rooted antagonisms to racial and cultural difference can be defeated in practice, as well as symbolically written out of the national story, the idea of a multicultural post-nation remains an empty promise" (2000: 38).

The report received widespread attention, particularly in the print media, and drew an emotional and largely hostile response that centered on the question of re-imagining Britishness. What I am interested in here is the distinction drawn between a "narrow" Englishness and a more "inclusive" Britishness. In this chapter, I will examine the often distinct racialization involved in these two identities of English and British and reflect on how national identity is one modality through which British people, and particularly white English people, talk about race. This chapter is based on

Notes for this section begin on page 155.

research conducted for a larger project that sought to examine white lives as racialized (see Byrne 2006). Qualitative interviews were conducted[1] with mothers of young children living in Clapham and Camberwell on a range of issues concerning their everyday practices and experiences. They also covered more abstract questions of identity, including the participants' sense of national identity. While the majority of the interviewees were white, the following quotation comes from a woman interviewed in the pilot stage of the fieldwork. Dawn is a black woman, born in England and whose parents came from the Caribbean. She clearly sets out the enduring racialized politics surrounding national identity in Britain and England:

> I see myself as British, um because, even though I was born here, society has shown me, has led me to believe that I'm British. Not that I'm *English*, that I'm British. The way that I look at it, just because of what I've seen, just through working, going to school and working in, you know, in England, you *are* British, you're not English. English people are white, that's how we see English people, they're white. (Interview 3; emphasis in original)[2]

It should not be seen as inevitable that Englishness is generally seen as a white identity and Britishness has more possibility for being open or inclusive, but it can only be understood in the context of empire and postcoloniality. As Bill Schwarz argues:

> That elusive, displaced notion of Englishness, apparently so insular and self-contained, cannot be grasped without seeing its intimate and complex connections to the wider imperial world . . . . The historic connection between England and its colonial empire—and the separate but overlapping relations between white English men and women and their ethnic and racial Others—ineluctably lies at the very heart of the matter even, or perhaps especially, when it remains unspoken. (Schwarz 1996: 1)

The end of empire has resulted in a crisis of identity for the white English and British, a crisis which is, to a certain extent, lived through race. Englishness and Britishness have an ongoing confusion as to their relationship to themselves—where does Englishness stop and Britishness begin? In addition, these identities have lost their former moorings in empire and have to reposition themselves in terms of evolving relations with Europe and with the national identities of the Irish, Welsh, and Scottish as well as with changing postcolonial relations. As Krishnan Kumar argues: "In whichever direction they look, the English find themselves called upon to reflect upon their identity and to re-think their position in the world. The protective walls that shielded them from these questions are all coming down" (Kumar 2003: 16). There are different levels at which the question of national identity and its changing nature and formation can be addressed. National identity is the product of state intervention in terms of politico-legal definitions of borders, citizenship, and belonging. But it also exists at the level of what Michael Billig describes as "banal nationalism"—the language and repetition of nationalism in the everyday (Billig 1995; see also Bhabha 1990). This national identity, the sense of belonging to an "imagined community" (Anderson 1991) is a lived experience involving everyday rituals and practices and acts of identification (and sometimes disidentification).

Of course, the crisis of national identity is not restricted to England and reflects a general crisis in the nation-state. Arjun Appadurai argues that we "need to think ourselves beyond the nation" (1996: 158). This injunction comes about largely because of the inadequacy of nations to deal with the challenges of a globalized world. Nation-states are, according to Appadurai, "poorly equipped to deal with the interlinked diasporas of people and images that mark the here and now. Nation-states, as units in a complex interactive system, are not very likely to be the long-term arbiters of the relationship between globality and modernity" (1996: 19). Nonetheless, national identity holds a powerful pull on the imagination of self. For Perry Anderson, nationality or nation-ness and nationalism are "cultural artifacts of a particular kind," created in the eighteenth century and now universal: "in the modern world everyone can, should, will 'have' a nationality, as he or she 'has' a gender" (1991: 4–5).

For those living in the "English" part of the British Isles, this raises the question of which nationality they have, to what imagined community do they belong? As Bernard Crick points out: "I am a citizen of a country with no agreed colloquial name" (1991: 90). This suggests at least some confusions or ambiguities in the imagination and narration of nation (Bhabha 1990). Since the 1980s, there has been a flood of both popular and academic books on the origins of Britain and/or England and the nature of English and/or British national identities.[3] This has also been mirrored by a seemingly constant debate in the British print media, and to a lesser extent, broadcast media on the state of the nation. This debate hovers uneasily around questions of race, racism and colonial history, and inheritances. Paul Gilroy argues that "a refusal to think about racism as something that structures the life of the postimperial polity is associated with what has become a morbid fixation with the fluctuating substance of national culture and identity" (2004: 13).

"Once upon a time the English knew who they were," begins Jeremy Paxman in his "portrait of a people" (1998: 1) and, after several pages of charting the changes (decline) in England, notes that "apart from at a few football and cricket matches, England scarcely exists as a nation: nationalism was, and remains a *British* thing." Krishnan Kumar argues that the English did not work on developing ideas of who they were, as projects of both imperialism without and unification within Britain were best served by emphasizing an imperial, or at best British, identity rather than English one: "The English did not so much celebrate themselves as identify with the projects—the 'mission'—they were, as it were providentially, called upon to carry out in the world . . . . the English could not see themselves as just another nation in a world of nations" (Kumar 2003: x; see also Crick 1991: 92).

These projects, and particularly the imperial one, while they may not have been served by emphasizing Englishness, did foster notions, not just of superiority, but racialized superiority in particular, which played a central notion in the construction of both Britishness and Englishness (see Young 1995; McClintock 1995; Cohen 1994). As several feminist texts have explored,[4] the empire was a gendered as well as a classed and raced enterprise. Anne McClintock argues that "controlling women's sexuality, exalting maternity and breeding a virile race of empire-builders were widely perceived as the paramount means for controlling the health and wealth of the male imperial body politic, so that, by the end of the century, sexual purity emerged as a controlling metaphor for racial, economic and political power" (1995: 47). Catherine Hall also argues that middle class white women played a central role in articulating national-imperial identity (1992: 207). As McClintock shows through examination of advertising, the empire was intimately related to the domestic with imperial bric-a-brac cluttering up domestic spaces in Britain and the domestic playing a key role in the civilizing mission of empire. Through the importation and marketing of soap, the imperial powers were spreading a particular version of the domestic to colonial subjects, in a similar way that it was also promoted to the working classes (1995; see also Bonnett 2000: chapter 3). In this process, Englishness and Britishness involved the imagination of both racialized and classed others, with a particular relationship to notions of "home" and the domestic.

Given the end of colonization, the expanded immigration of postcolonial subjects ("we're here because you were there") as well as the repositioning of Britain within an expanded and consolidated Europe, the question remains as to what extent the imagination of Englishness and Britishness has adjusted to this new context. Jonathon Rutherford explores the work of Enoch Powell who, he argues, expressed the "irreconcilable loss of Empire, of identity, of belonging" in his politics and writing (Rutherford 1997: 106). The enduring racialization of Englishness in particular can be read from the seeming dissonance of the phrase Black English[5] as opposed to the politically struggled-for-identity of Black British. In the context of racial exclusions to nationhood in Britain, there have been artists, film-makers, and writers who responded by staking their claims as Black British (see Owusu 2000). Yet others have argued that Black British as a political identity has excluded and/or marginalized those non-white identities which are not African-Caribbean. Tariq Modood, for example stresses the need to understand Britain as "multi-racist," particularly in the context of increasing Islamophobia (Modood 1997: 160; see also Parekh 2000). As minority identities within the national space become increasingly complex, but also explicitly narrativized, the question remains as to what happens to "majority" identities. Anoop Nayak argues that there has been a de-racialization of the white English, while visible minorities are now correspondingly over-racialized: "A pressing question for ethnic scholars may now centre on the identities of the hither to under-researched white Anglo majority—who they are and who they may yet 'become'" (Nayak 2003: 139; see also Bonnett 2000).

This chapter is concerned with the construction of nationhood or belonging and the ways in which this is lived and talked about by white women living in London. It seeks to address this question by examining the response of a small sample of interviewees to questions around their own national identities. This chapter explores some of the relationships, rites, and symbols out of which national identity is stitched (Bourke 1994: 170). The interest in national identity is to explore the extent to which it is in crisis, and remains racialized, as well as the ways in which it is experienced as gendered. However, this is not to say that the nation should be taken as the most important framework out of which identities are constructed (see Burton 2000). While Anderson may be right that everyone is required to have a nationality just as they have a gender, the extent to which this features in an individual consciousness will vary considerably both between individuals and in different contexts. Indeed, the ways in which individuals *evade* identifying with the nation, in different times and spaces, may be much more significant than the embracing of national identity and nationhood.

Nostalgia and Longing: "Deep England"

For Gilroy, the narrative of Britain involves "obsessive repetition of key themes—invasion, war, contamination, loss of identity—and the resulting mixture suggests that an anxious, melancholic mood has become part of the cultural infrastructure of the place, an immovable ontological counterpart to the nation-defining ramparts of the white cliffs of Dover" (2004: 15). Here he is largely referring to debates at the level of policy makers and representations in the public arena. These themes were to a certain extent reiterated in the interview material, but it is important to be aware of the gendered nature of some of the articulations. In particular, narratives of invasion and war are likely to be presented differently, and with differing levels of attachment, by men and women.

Apart from gender, one thing the interviewees all shared in common, at least at the time of the interviews, was place. All were living in London, which has a specific place in the imaginative map of nation. London is not merely the capital city but is also often imagined as a cosmopolitan or multicultural space, at least in part as a legacy of being an imperial metropolis. The different ways in which London is imagined by the interviewees will be returned to later, but it is important to note the particular nature of the rural in the imagination of Englishness (perhaps more so than in the imagination of Britishness). Patrick Wright (1985) has been influential in understanding the nature and place of the rural in the English imagination. He stresses the role of nostalgia, in particular in relations to ideas of "heritage." Wright stresses the potency, for some, of England as a place of rural heritage and idyll:

> Deep England can indeed be deeply moving to those whose particular experience is most directly in line with its privileged imagination. [However] just about anyone who, in the developing turmoil of modern society, has ever had cause to look back and wonder about old forms of security will surely be able to find meaning in Deep England. (1985: 86)

For those interviewees with an attachment to "Deep England," living in London could involve an added sense of loss. This suggests that the loss felt was not solely a loss of identity, but also a loss of particular modes of living, which was associated not only with place (in terms of rural/urban), but also class and lifestyle.

For example, for Emma (a woman in her late twenties living in Peckham), Englishness was about myths of history, civility, and honor. Her England was rooted in the past and, in particular, in class and gender relations. She realized that the place in which she lived, and the way she lived, was very different from her imagined England. This was associated with a sense of loss. To a certain extent, the loss she felt about the perceived changes in Englishness was mirrored by a loss in her own class position. She came from an upper-class provincial family and her loss of social status came with a marriage to a man who was perceived as working-class by both herself and her family, despite his professional status. She also lived in what she regarded as an undesirable area. Thus, diagnosis of the state of the nation provided a route for articulating personal experiences and concerns. Her summoning up of the rural idyll of Englishness functioned to explain the alienation she felt living in a racially mixed area. In the following extract, the street scenes in the area of London where she lived are presented as "alien" and "foreign," to be contrasted to the "quaintness" of a village shop. This juxtaposition underlines the ways in which national identity was negotiated in the interviews through the domestic with food being a recurring theme. How can Emma reproduce Englishness not only in an urban setting but also among shops that serve food that she is unused to and "smells funny"? Here is Gilroy's theme of contamination brought to the level of the domestic:

> Living in London is much more about culture, about different cultures. And it's really, (it's) very stimulating. I guess, I mean I would like to live in New York and I would like that kind of thing, but I'd never want to destroy England and its grassy plains [laugh] . . . . I mean, there are not many parts of Peckham that I'd live in. ... and we live here because this house was very cheap. And it's a nice road, vaguely . . . . lots of light . . . um. But I wouldn't go shopping in some of the shops. Have you walked round here at all? . . . [I]f you go round the back there are some, in the marketplace you get all this halal meat and all sorts of stuff. I wouldn't touch that with a barge pole. Not because it's different, or because of anything. But just because I think it smells funny. They're not, they're probably not very educated black people. Because otherwise they would have got out. Because everyone's trying to get out really. Everyone's trying to move on. It's not like having a little village shop in the country, it's not as quaint as that. I don't think people want necessarily to be doing it. (Interview 16)

For Emma, Englishness was represented by upper middleclass manners and traditions: "Well, I sort of consider English and things sort of like *Howard's End* and that kind of thing. And I think there's something, I mean I know it's 200 years ago or whatever, but I think there's something wonderful about all that." Emma was aware that her idealization was based on a fictionalized account. She emphasized this by exaggerating how long ago the books were written. Nonetheless, at one time it almost had a lived reality for her. For Emma, Englishness was a romantic and nostalgic vision that was located in the past in two senses. Firstly, because it was based on a representation from a novel, a fictional world rather than a reality. It is, for instance, interesting that this picture of the past she painted made no mention of imperialism or the basis on which the wealth was built. And secondly, because, in terms of her own life, it represented something that was in the past, set in her childhood. Emma described her childhood, particularly at boarding school as having fitted in with this proposed idyll of manners and civility:

> And perhaps I'm being swept away on a story, and perhaps it's because I spent seven years of my life in a church, all girls' boarding school. And spent my time singing hymns and going to church and it's very special thing to be patriotic. And you know, going to balls and always being treated very nicely by boys. Who actually on the one hand weren't treating you very nicely, but they'd always hold the door open for you and always pay for your taxi. So it's kind of weird really. But there's something that I'd hate to lose over that. And I think, for me, because where I come from that's about being English. (Interview 16)

"All Change": Modern Living and Identity

Other interviewees also had rural childhoods on which to reflect. They also expressed the changes involved both in living in London, but also the loss of particular rhythms and routines (or "forms of living" (Bhabha 1990: 292)) which tied them back into national identity. This is illustrated for Rosalind who lived in Clapham, but had grown up in Shropshire. She was less concerned about Englishness than Emma in the way she talked, but still suggested a sense of loss or at least emptiness:

> So, in a sense there's . . . you know, the English bit is always a bit lacking. The kind of English is still the kind of majority way, so I suppose it's something we never have to think about. But I'm not sure what kind of amount of culture we do pass on. Cos I don't feel any great tradition to pass on to Emily and Harry really. (Interview 20)

Rosalind could not send her children to the village Sunday School and nor did she sit down with them to Sunday lunch. The seemingly immovable routines of eating were no longer possible: "the whole time I was at home we had, you know, tea at 5 or half past 5 every day, and you'd think it was very odd if you didn't all sit down and eat together. So that's gone." Now, her children ate what she saw as more "cosmopolitan" food such as pizza and pasta, rather than the traditional "meat and two veg" and ate separately from their parents who came home after they had finished. All of these changes left Rosalind struggling to think what English represented, particularly in contrast to the more "interesting" cultures that surrounded them in London: "in a lot of circumstances, it's always the English who haven't got a kind of interesting cultural thing to [do]."

This evocation of ritualized Sunday lunches was repeated by other interviewees in very similar terms, such as, for instance, the following extract from Helen who lived in Camberwell, but had grown up in a remote area of Northumberland:

> We always ate round a table, we always had Sunday lunch. You know I think in the last 20 years since that was the case for me, I think England has changed a lot, but that was very English then, very sort of middle of the road, ordinary, probably no longer is. So I suppose, yes, I think I probably did, and it probably came from things like diet, . . . and just routines, rituals that are very English, like Sunday lunch, the way we ate. (Interview 12)

Helen suggested that her sense of Englishness, or at least the ways in which it shaped her "form of living" was different from the experience of her parents. For Helen, these changes were connected to class and locational changes as well as altered relationships with Europe. Talking of ways of living identity, of changes in domestic attitudes and arrangement became, for Helen, a way of marking her separation from her parents. Her parents "became middleclass when their parents were workingclass." They stayed in the village in the North of England where they had been born and aspired to regular habits and traditions: "if we didn't have Sunday lunch at lunch time when I was a child it was *odd*, not having a lunch, you were either having a family crisis, you were on your way to somewhere, you had to have a reason for it" (Interview 12). In contrast, Helen became "more" middleclass having gone to university and having a career (unlike her mother). She moved to London and created new modes of living for her children in a "more homogenized Europe-wide" context. It was also in a much more racially mixed context compared to the village in which she grew up:

> It's all about travel isn't it. People have more money, it's easier to go abroad, you pick up different customs and ways of living that you like and then you sort of make a patchwork quilt of what appeals to you, you just sort of make it up as you go along, do your own thing, so, And anyway, how can you be, how can Englishness survive, say in this area where you're surrounded by, people have brought with them all sorts of . . . um customs from, gosh a *huge* variety of places. And we have a lot of mixed marriages around here as well, so you've got the mix of the two. (Interview 12)

In the face of these new ways of being—what "English" people have brought from abroad and what has been brought by those who have moved to England, Englishness will not survive. This statement shows a sense of Englishness that was closed, fixed, and white. It could not include new things and move on to other modes of being, but was faced with extinction. Englishness could not survive in the face of "mixed marriages." Here, Englishness was constructed less as a nationality than as an ethnicity or cultural identity that was bound to be disrupted cultural influence.

Certainly for Helen, and perhaps also for Rosalind, London represented at least in part a welcome escape from living in remote rural areas. For other interviewees as well, the typical Englishness represented by rural life was not necessarily something to be celebrated or looked on with nostalgia. For instance, Sally came to look back at the place where she grew up as a narrow and even racist environment, a place to escape from:

> I was brought up in a tiny village in Norfolk and that's where I spent all my childhood. So apart from the fact that everyone in the village was white anyway, I think without exception. [. . .] I think I was brought up *really* looking at things through white eyes. I think it was quite, in some ways it was quite a racist kind of up bringing. There was a *lot of* suspicion, a lot of, in a way, yeah, there was kind of outright derogatory remarks. And it was very much seen as

something which was *totally* alien to us. We were really *white* English, you know in terms of our food and everything I think. (Interview 22)

Here Sally is coming close to suggesting that Englishness, and white Englishness in particular, could be regarded as an ethnicity, as argued by Catherine Hall (1992). However, apart from a sense of Englishness as characterized by racism, it is difficult for Sally to identify what might mark something as English or white English.

> Umm, I don't know if I can say what distinguished it. I think for me there was just this feeling that there wasn't really anything else. I don't think we were particularly patriotic, if you see what I mean, in our family. But I don't think there was any kind of open-mindedness. Or *any* questioning of the fact that people had really racist views. Or any questioning of the fact that the media might present people in a certain way. There was none of that. So in a way, I suppose what I'm saying is that I feel that I grew up until the age of 18 in this vacuum of "it just was what it was." There wasn't any sort of . . . it was more ignorance rather than sort of an aggressive racism. But in terms of the whole British thing, I suppose I just wasn't aware that there was anything else. I was, that's just how we were. Do you know what I mean? I mean I know probably there are some families who get into this real patriotic thing, we certainly didn't have any of that either. It was almost like a bit of a vacuum like that. (Interview 22)

Sally conveys a sense of insularity of her childhood in a small village where homogeneity is apparently so overpowering that it becomes almost indiscernible. This echoes the literature around whiteness that suggests that power is retained for whiteness partly through its "invisibility"[6] and lack of content and specificity. As Richard Dyer argues: "defining whiteness through negation and absence is fundamental to understanding it as a symbol" (1997: 74).

Quintessentially British?

Englishness was not characterized by absence for all the interviewees. Heather was an interviewee who, while she used English and British almost interchangeably, at the same time felt a different depth of feeling for Englishness, rather than Britishness:

> [I would put "British" on a form] probably because I am trying to be politically correct. I would say I am absolutely English. You know, I am not Scottish or Irish. They are very different. Very different. There is no point in pretending that I am other than Southern English. I am quintessentially English in a lot of those things but I would be British because I would feel that that was a politically correct thing to do. (Interview 15)

Thus, Englishness is something that it is not "politically correct" with which to identify. But at the same time, Britishness does not have the same purchase on Heather's emotions or identity. One could not be "quintessentially" British. This had no meaning for her as an identity. Nonetheless, in the interview, Heather referred to things English and British interchangeably and generally meant "English." She had a strong sense of her British/English identity which, like Emma, involved harking back to distant and not so distant pasts and was also illustrated by contrasting it to cultural and racial others. Heather was interested in what she called "earlier British history" of the Middle Ages and the Tudors and Stuarts. She was less interested in "getting into Victoria and the Empire." This may have been a means of sidestepping some of the more difficult and contentious aspects of British/English history. Being British was rooted in the domestic and everyday, for example in drinking tea. Heather joked: "My mother always says, you know, that she is sure I cannot really be British because I don't like tea." Britishness was also represented by:

> Classic British costume drama series, things like that as well as things like . . . *The Good Life* that when I was young, was on telly [TV] and I used to really enjoy, and was quintessentially British and, you know, and *Monty Python* again could never have come from another country. It is very British humor. (Interview 15)

Heather's reference to the *Good Life* as being "quintessentially British" is a good example of how "British" used to mean "English." This situation comedy was based on the cultural clash produced in the encounters between suburban neighbors living two different forms of middleclass white Englishness. It is hard to think of a more characteristically white, English, and middleclass program. Heather contrasted this British humor to that of black adolescents and Germans who she said have very different senses of humor. Thus, "foreignness" and blackness provided boundaries or points of demarcation to Britishness/Englishness.

Emma also had quite an elaborated notion of the distinction between Englishness and Britishness. Her demarcation between the two was a means for dealing with the idea of contamination that threatened national identity through the threats of postcolonial immigration, devolution, and integration in to Europe:

> Emma: But where I suppose British means what we are now with all our multicultural mix, with all our, Ireland and Scotland and all of that kind of stuff. And I mean, there's been so many things that have happened to try and destroy England. All the problems with the monarchy and all of that kind of stuff and it's all kind of sour, or it feels sour. I'd put that under the bracket of British [big laugh].

BB: Which under the bracket of British?
Emma: All that nastiness [laugh].
BB: That's your dumping ground!
Emma: The dumping ground.
(Interview 16)

When I asked Emma whether she would call herself English or British, her response had been clear. Furthermore, Englishness could not be imagined without immediately summoning up the abject racialized other—those excluded from the category who at once threatened Englishness:

English. Yes, it's about being English rather than being British I think . . . . But I'm actually very proud of being English. It's interesting though, because you know this thing about the gypsies.[7] That's been a point of conversation with lots of people really. And, you know that thing of them coming into, it feels like an invasion to some people, and it's mostly to do with money. They're thinking, you know, all this money is being spent when there's not enough, you know they're not giving students enough money, they're not giving the NHS enough money. My purse was stolen from my workplace last week and the woman who stole it was on police bail and she's now in Holloway [women's prison]. And for her to be in Holloway for a year is the same as sending someone to Eton for a year. And she wasn't English, she was Portuguese. But I guess because of this new European thing, you don't just push her back to Portugal. But I don't know really how it works. I was sort of saying to my husband, you know "what about the money and everything" and he was saying "yes but they're people and they've been harassed, they've been maltreated." So it's very difficult, but I think that when you're struggling, when the nation is struggling, it sort of gets annoying when people that you might consider as foreign, when perhaps it's not politically correct to call them foreign. (Interview 16)

Here we can see the ways in which, for some at least, Englishness is racialized in a way that is different from Britishness. Englishness is retained as a purer and whiter category to protect it from the polluting influences of change and diversity. Emma was the interviewee who expressed this perception with the most clarity and force, but the sense of Englishness as something narrower and less inclusive than Britishness was present in most of the interviews. This can perhaps be detected in Teresa's over-protestation about her sense of comfort with Englishness. She was a middleclass woman living in Clapham who in all external appearances (particularly accent) came over as English. But she came from a Catholic family with Irish ancestry, and this worked to undermine her confidence in her own Englishness. Her repeated assertions of her Englishness suggest that she felt some discomfort with the identification:

Well, no, I *do* feel English. Yes, I do, I very *much* feel English. But I'm aware of the roots as well. So, I think I do feel English actually. I wouldn't say I felt Irish although there's bits of me, you know, I know I look Irish, and I am very *proud* of, very proud of that, but I guess it . . . it's difficult, I often describe, I mean I would always describe the family as, you know, "I'm an Irish Catholic," that's how I was brought up and I'm not a practicing Catholic at all, and so it's a mix . . . I don't know really. I'm probably being a bit waffley here because I'm very proud of that, you know, . . . ancestry, . . . but I don't feel this burning need to be waving it around, if you see what I mean. (Interview 18)

Equally, for Helen, regional geography colored a sense of national identity:

Ah well, at this point we have to start talking about the North/South divide because I think, obviously coming from Northumberland and so there was always this great sense of north and south, and Scotland seemed very near and almost not like another country really, because it was so close. And England, as in the South of England felt a million miles away, it really did. There were school trips to London, and if . . . ever anyone came to the school that was from the South and had a different accent, endless teasing, terrible really. Yeah . . . but there was definitely a North/South thing very strong [. . .] for me at the time, we thought we were right and they were wrong and we thought we were English. But I'd say that now, as an adult, an adult that lives in the South, probably Englishness that is perceived by the outside world is embodied by the South of England. (Interview 12)

Some of the interviewees resisted the sense of exclusiveness that they felt attached itself to Englishness or Britishness: "I don't feel white British is okay. I'm very open to more and different, I think people are different. In fact, I think white British is pretty awful in some respects . . . mostly because of history. And also I feel currently our country . . . I think that there's quite a bit of complacency attached to it. Which I don't think is a good thing at any stage in life."

British or English Shame and London Pride

For those interviewees who were less attached to ideas of national identity, Britishness and Englishness could be associated with feelings of shame or national guilt. There were ready available negative images of British xenophobia and violent patriotism, suggested by European battles over beef exports and football hooliganism, and antiquated adherence to tradition and hierarchy possibly represented by the royal family, as for example articulated by Madeleine:

I've no really kind of national identity. I'm quite ashamed of, you know, whenever I see the Union Jack, I don't personally have any feeling of great pride, I have associations of it with, you know, I associate it with football hooligans, British beef and the royal family, really. None of whom I have any particular desire to be associated with [half laugh] really, so, you know. (Interview 17)

These reservations included both past history and present politics. As Madeleine also suggests, awareness comes from a particular relationship to "others":

> I've been interested in other cultures and had close friends from other cultures and been interested in the history of other cultures. And every time you read the history of anybody else, there are the British, do you know what I mean? Enslaving people and shooting people [laugh] and it just gets to the point where you think I can't *bear* it, it's just hideous. It feels like, sometimes it feels like a weight that you carry around with you. And I know times when I've been traveling. I was in East Africa, when I was about 19 and it was when the Americans bombed Libya and they'd refueled here. And I'd been having a really nice, I was traveling on my own and everyone had been *really* friendly. And suddenly people would stop you and say "Are you English" or "Are you American" and I'd have to go [putting on accent] "No Dutch" [laugh]. Yeah because suddenly it was actually quite, I felt quite threatened, you know because people were genuinely very angry about it. (Interview 44)

One way of evading or dealing with a sense of shame or negativity around national identity was to attach more significance to alternative forms of identification. A geographically based identity that could play this role was that of London. It had the advantage of being available to all who lived there (London), including those who had not been born there, as Helen described:

> It's about friends, it's about feeling comfortable in a place, and I mean, I moan about London, who doesn't? But then I guess you'd moan about wherever you were. If I lived in a small village, I'd moan about it being boring. I live in London, I moan about it being big and dirty and not having enough space, but, you know, that's just human nature. At the end of the day, this is where my root has grown. (Interview 12)

In contrast to ideas of British and English identities as narrow, traditional, and xenophobic, constructions of London involved imagination of openness, cosmopolitanism, and vibrancy, providing an attractive alternative. Identification with London also appeared to give the interviewees the chance to participate in a more multicultural, even exotic cultural experience. This contrasted with the feeling that Englishness and Britishness were "empty" or lacking in culture:

> Madeleine: 'um . . . Well, I suppose I've always, I see myself as much more of a *Londoner* than *English* perhaps so I suppose I have that kind of identity.
> BB: And that's a more positive one?
> Madeleine: Yeah. In lots of ways definitely.
> BB: Because?

Madeleine: Because, um, because although, you know London has lots of . . . downsides to it, its also, I don't know, it's lively, it's very very multicultural and you can just be part of . . . . I went to live in Wales for a little while and it was just like [horrified expression], it wasn't even *Welsh*, do you know what I mean, there wasn't even any *Welsh* culture there at all. Whereas I think in London people are very vocal about their cultures and what they're doing. And I'm sure people like, even more so in some of the Northern cities, you know because at heart even us Londoners are quite repressed and don't like to talk to each other. . . . I like, I really like the mix of people here and I like the fact that there's different things, there's different colors and cultures and, you know, I like the fact that there's different, you know you can go and sit in Kensington gardens and then come back to Peckham. You have access to all sorts of different places, which is nice.
(Interview 44)

While the suggestion of London as a place of multicultural harmony may be largely fantastical, its place in the imagination of Britishness is nonetheless important. This was clear in the final stages of the recent (2005) competition for the right to host the 2012 Olympics, where it was frequently suggested that London won because of its ability to sell itself as a cosmopolitan and multicultural capital of the world which could "welcome all." Jane M. Jacobs argues that London cannot truly be seen as postcolonial or postimperial:

Formal decolonization and postwar migration and settlement have brought an embodied edge of empire into the heart, while the demise of empire has meant that Britain now has different global and regional affiliations. These changes have not marked the end of empire—a pure postcolonialism—but established the conditions for revised imperial articulations. (Jacobs 1996: 159)

She also argues that older forms of imperialism have been replaced by new regimes of desire: "Otherness is no longer a repressed negativity in the constitution of the Self, but a required positivity which brings the Self closer to, say, a multicultural present or an ecological future. Contemporary spaces of consumption seek out otherness" (Jacobs 1996: 160).

This consumption of otherness can be read to a certain extent in Madeleine's account. What London offers her is "different colors and cultures." She does not reflect on the ways in which her experience of the city is mediated through race. It is her whiteness that enables her to move easily between Peckham, an area associated with innercity multiculturalism, and Kensington Gardens, which is in the heart of one of the most expensive areas of London and at the time of her speaking was particularly associated with Princess Diana.

Conclusion

The crisis of identity facing Englishness and Britishness at the end of empire is likely to be most deeply felt by white people; yet, as Nayak argues:

> The striking contradiction is that we now seem to know far less about the racialized identities of the ethnic majority (notably English whites) and who they are in the present post-imperial moment. The "burden of representation" endured by visible minorities has unwittingly implied that they have an ethnicity or a culture whilst others, in particular the white English have not. This has led to an over-racialization of visible minorities at the expense of a de-racialization of ethnic majorities. (2003: 139)

White people in Britain are much less likely to be asked by their compatriots, "where do you come from." This chapter has sought to reverse some of that burden of representation and questioning and examine white experience of national identity. Examination of the interview material has illuminated shown some of the different ways in which England and Britain are imagined and the way national identities are felt and lived by white women living in London. One result of living the gap between what Homi Bhabha (1990) calls the pedagogical and performative—between the nationalist construction of a continuous and seamless connection with the past and the recursive demands of living nation-ness in everyday life—is an uncertainty about what Englishness contains. A theme, which emerged through the interviews, was a sense of narrowness and/or emptiness in Englishness. Classic renditions of England as a "green and pleasant land" populated by historical figures and perhaps even John Major's spinsters cycling to church around village greens are clearly raced and build upon a racialized discourse of national and imperial superiority in which white women play a particular, protected, role. In the interviews, there were clear echoes of this discourse in the juxtapositions between England and others, where Englishness was white, middleclass, rural, and clean as opposed to the threat posed by dirty others (such as gypsies or Muslims selling halal meat). The interviews also showed the insecure basis of imaginings of Englishness. They were disrupted by urban life, by the presence of differently raced subjects, and by the individuals' own sense of a loss of class position. Thus, there is an inflexibility in the formal narration of Englishness that made it impossible to sustain it in the everyday. Some of this tension was expressed in the difference between the image of a nostalgic "Deep England," and multicultural and multiracial Britain.

For other interviewees, the everyday, and in particular the domestic as a space and practice, did not necessarily provide a sense of difference demanded by the nationalist rhetoric. So Englishness and also perhaps

Britishness was experienced by some as an empty or unmarked norm, which appeared to lack content in the face of what was seen as the cultural richness of other identities and forms of living. Its very whiteness and normalcy made it invisible. For example, some did not feel that they or their children lived Englishness through consumption of food or in the rituals of life, in the way that they did in their childhoods. Although it was in the domestic, one interviewee suggested, that culture might have real meaning, through which "roots" are established. Englishness, characterized by an inflexibility toward difference, was likely to disappear in the face of other cultural practices and identities that were more visible and felt to have more meaning.

For yet others, Englishness was to be actively evaded or escaped. There was nothing to be salvaged from an identity associated with class and "race" prejudice. In this response to collective identity, all national identities were seen as potentially negative, particularly if "deep-rooted," but Britain's imperial history made it particularly unattractive and sometimes oppressive. What we see emerging in some interviews, and in particular Madeleine's account, is a rejection of pedagogical accounts of nationhood and a turn to more fluid and temporary identifications, for example as "Londoners." This enabled difference to be embraced as a positive and integral part of a collective identity, rather than as a threat. Yet there remains some uncertainty as to how this is to be achieved outside the kinds of explicit attachments that characterize certain young people's cultural practices. Madeleine's critique and then evasion of an English or British identity based on whiteness and class exclusion was relatively exceptional within this research. Given the ongoing anxieties about race and national culture, especially those as expressed through current debates around immigration, it would seem that her rethinking of national identity remains a minority position.

Notes

1. The interviews took place from 1997 to 1998.
2. All names have been changed.
3. See for example, Kumar (2003); Cohen (1994); Colley (1992); Colls (1986); Crick (1991); Jones (1998); Kearney (1991); Nairn (1981); Paxman (1998); Wright (1985).
4. See in particular McClintock (1995); Ware (1992); Hall (1992).
5. Except in the instance of linguistics where Black English or 'Blinglish' is a more familiar concept.
6. It is important to note that this supposed invisibility will vary according the

perspective from which it is viewed. Whiteness is likely to be invisible only to white people; see hooks (1997) and Byrne (2006).
7. This reference to 'the gypsies' was prompted by reports in the newspapers in the week of the interview about Roma asylum seekers fleeing discrimination in Eastern Europe—or coming as "economic migrants" and seeking benefit payments, depending on which interpretation was followed.

Bibliography

Anderson, Benedict. 1991. *Imagined Communities. Reflections on the Origin and Spread of Nationalism*. London: Verso.

Appadurai, Arjun. 1996. *Modernity at Large. Cultural Dimensions of Globalisation*. Minneapolis, MN: University of Minnesota Press.

Bhabha, Homi. 1990. "DissemiNation: time, narrative and the margins of the modern Nation." In Homi Bhabha (ed.) *Nation and Narration*. London: Routledge.

Billig, Michael. 1995. *Banal Nationalism*. London: Sage Publications.

Bonnett, Alistair. 2000. *Anti-Racism*. London: Routledge.

Bourke, Jenny. 1994. *Working-class Cultures in Britain 1890–1960. Gender, class and ethnicity*. London: Routledge.

Burton, Antoinette. 2000. "Who Needs the Nation? Interrogating British History." In Catherine Hall (ed.) *Cultures of Empire. A Reader. Colonizers in Britain and the Empire in the Nineteenth and Twentieth Centuries*. Manchester: Manchester University Press: 137–153.

Byrne, Bridget. 2003. "Reciting the Self." *Feminist Theory*, Vol. 4: 29–49.

———. 2006. *White Lives: Gender, "Race" and Class in Contemporary London*. London: Routledge.

Cohen, Robin. 1994. *Frontiers of Identity. The British and the Others*. London: Longman.

Colley, Linda. 1992."Britishness and Otherness: An Argument" *Journal of British Studies*, Vol 31: 309–329.

Colls, Robert and Philip Dodd, (eds.) 1986. *Englishness. Politics and Culture 1880–1920*. Kent: Croom Helm.

Crick, Bernard. 1991. "The English and the British." In B. Crick (ed.), *National Identities. The Constitution of the United Kingdom*. Oxford: Blackwell: 90–105.

Dyer, Richard. 1997. *White*. London: Routledge.

Gilroy, Paul. 2004. *After Empire. Melancholia or Convivial Culture?* London: Routledge.

Hall, Catherine. 1992. *White, Male and Middle-class. Explorations in Feminism and History*. Cambridge: Polity Press.

hooks, bell. 1997. "Representing Whiteness in the Black Imagination." In *Displacing Whiteness. Essays in Social and Cultural Criticism*. Ruth Frankenberg (ed.) Durham, NC: Duke University Press.

Interviews with London Women 1–44. 1997–8.

Jacobs, Jane M. 1996. *Edge of Empire. Postcolonialism and the City.* London: Routledge.

Jones, E. 1998. *The English Nation The Great Myth.* Stroud: Sutton Publishing.

Kearney, Hugh. 1991. "Four nations or one?" In B. Crick (ed.). *National Identities. The Constitution of the United Kingdom.* Oxford: Blackwell: 1–6.

Kumar, Krishnan. 2003. *The Making of English Identity.* Cambridge: Cambridge University Press.

McClintock, Anne. 1995. *Imperial Leather: Race, Gender and Sexuality in the Colonial Context.* New York: Routledge.

Modood, Tariq. 1997. "'Difference', Cultural Racism and Anti-Racism." In Pnina Werbner and Tariq Modood. *Debating Cultural Hybridity. Multi-cultural Identities and the Politics of Anti-Racism.* London & New Jersey: Zed Books: 154–172.

Nairn, Tom. 1981. *The Break-up of Britain.* London: Verso.

Nayak, Anoop. 2003. *Race, Place and Globalization. Youth cultures in a changing world.* Oxford: Berg.

Owusu, Kwesi. 2000. "Introduction: charting the genealogy of Black British cultural Studies." In Owusu, K, Ed. *Black British Culture and Society. A Text Reader.* London: Routledge.

Parekh, Bhikhu. 2000. *The Future of Multi-Ethnic Britain.* London: Profile Books.

Paxman, Jeremy. 1998. *The English. A Portrait of a People.* Harmonsworth: Penguin.

Rutherford, John. 1997. *Forever England. Reflections on Masculinity and Empire.* London: Lawrence and Wishhart.

Schwarz, Bill. 1996. *The Expansion of England. Race, Ethnicity and Cultural History.* London: Routledge.

Wright, Paul. 1985. *On Living in an Old Country: the National Past in Contemporary Britain.* London: Verso.

Young, Robert J.C. 1995. *Colonial Desire. Hybridity in Theory, Culture and Race.* London: Routledge.

Ware, Vron. 1992. *Beyond the Pale. White Women, Racism and History.* London: Verso.

CHAPTER 8.

Conserving Purity, Labouring the Past

A Tropological Evolution of Englishness

Colin Wright

Colonial and postcolonial theorists alike have frequently referred to the "rhetoric of Nationalism," yet they have rarely considered the application of rhetorical analyses to discourses of nationalism, English or otherwise. The phrase "rhetoric of Nationalism" thus tends to carry simplistically pejorative resonances, tapping into both a traditional philosophical distrust of rhetoric (dating back to Plato) and a liberal critique of nationalism (allying it with right-wing extremism). In contrast, if rhetoric is conceived of more generously—in its full disciplinary complexity as a theory and site of symbolic negotiation—national identity becomes thinkable not only as a violent grand narrative, but also as an aspect of the politics of identity in general. That is to say, rhetoric enables us to rethink the intimate relationship between "who we are" and "where we come from" as both an ever contestable, because ever-essentializing mythology, and as a potently persuasive discourse whose pragmatics it *remains* the role of theory to analyze.

In what follows, I undertake a rhetorical examination of the changing fortunes of a certain trope of "Englishness" in terms of its relationship to the ideal of cosmopolitanism. This is undertaken in order, firstly, to sketch the very particular pragmatics of "Englishness," and secondly, to gesture toward the role of rhetoric in the construction of nationalisms in general. I will confine my analysis to two political speeches: first, the infamous "Rivers of Blood" speech by the former Conservative minister Enoch Powell delivered on 20 April 1968 (Utley 1968); and second, the more recent but also controversial "Chicken Tikka Masala" speech delivered on 19 April 2001 by former Labour Foreign Secretary, and now late, Robin Cook (Cook 2001). Many other speeches could have been chosen, particularly from the Thatcher years when English nationalism was more *visible*: yet, that her era has been bracketed by my examples arguably implicates its centrality all the more. For while these two speeches alone cannot define a specifically Conservative or Labour tropology of Englishness, it is nonetheless hoped that by their juxtaposition—tonally, but also temporally (they are separated by a thirty-three year gap)—they will imply the trajectory of an evolving Englishness, across and through Thatcherism. To repeat: it is *not* my aim to formulate a reductive theoretical grid with which to divide the complex play of national tropes of "Englishness" into blue and red zones. Rather, it is to discern firstly the extent to which political speeches in general reflect, but also reconstitute, the symbolic particularity of nation and nationhood for their intended audiences, and secondly, the increasing rhetic force attaching to the concept of cosmopolitanism in this reflective-reconstitutive process.

Insofar as they employ epideictic language in a performance with persuasion as its aim, I contend that such speeches remain analyzable within the criteria which classical rhetoric established under the term "oratory." While rejecting the formalism of classical rhetoric—which would reduce these speeches to merely empty schemata—I will nonetheless retain Aristotle's dictum that "the political orator is concerned with the future [and] aims at establishing the expediency or the harmfulness of a proposed course of action" (Aristotle 1991: s.1358b). What passes as expedient or harmful is of course contingent upon the persuasive forces brought to bear upon the manner of presentation. Hence, I will augment Aristotle's theory of oratorical motivation with Kenneth Burke's *Rhetoric of Motives* (1969). In this work, Burke outlines the aspect of Aristotelian rhetoric which operates by identification: "You persuade a man only insofar as you can talk his language by speech, gesture, tonality, order, image, attitude, idea, *identifying* your ways with his" (1969: 55). One of the main theses of this paper will therefore be that the politician-rhetor must construct his or her message around the Burkean concept of identification: the electorate/audience is made to feel that the speaker is "one of their own," and thus qualified to represent them. This political strategy of *argumentum ad populum* finds its paradigmatic form in appeals to national identity: such appeals assert, in essence, "I am like you, and therefore I can speak for you." Representative democracy is thus predicated on an unending process of rhetorical identification, and, though disguised (dis-figured), the figure of the demagogue is ever central to its operation.

And yet, just as Burke asserts that rhetorical "identification is affirmed with earnestness precisely because there is division" (1969: 22), there is an attendant obligation to assert that nationalism is unthinkable without a corollary concept of borders. Despite the political rhetoric of inclusiveness, every trope of Englishness enacts its particular exclusions: even the pinkest of maps has edges. While the metropole by definition conceives of itself as the center (all nationalisms being ineluctably "centric" in their logic), it must do so with recourse to the *concentric* margins of Englishness, that is, to those satellite (post?)colonies whose diminishing orbits increasingly de-

mand that Englishness articulate itself anew (see Gikandi 1996). I will suggest here that with both speeches, what is excluded—in the first case as a
synechdocically present absence, in the second as historically
"other(ed)"—is the age of British imperialism. More polemically, I will further suggest that this exclusion, far from being rectified, is being repeated
and perpetuated by the rhetoric of cosmopolitanism which now, under New
Labour, informs the construction of English nationalism.

Rivers of Blood: The Pragmatics of Powellism

In April 1968, the then Conservative Minister Enoch Powell gave a speech
so inflammatory it led, in the short term, to Edward Heath dismissing him
from the front bench, and in the long term, to Powell's own split from the
Conservative Party and shocking endorsement of their Labour opposition
(even calling on his own constituency of Wolverhampton to follow suit).
Stuart Hall said of this aggressively anti-immigrant address that it represents not only the "enunciation of a specifically defiant policy about race
and the black population by a single person," but also the institution of an
"official racist policy at the heart of British political culture" (1978: 29-30).
     To judge by recent developments, this diseased heart continues to beat
in contemporary Conservatism: during the general election of 2001—
which William Hague fought on a platform of Immigration Policy reform,
despite the electorate being far more interested in matters of health, education, and transport—several Tory ministers refused to sign an anti-racism
pledge. One even claimed, with unmistakable Powellian echoes, that
Britain was becoming a "mongrel nation." Demographically, the phrase indexes a truth about the altered racial mix of British, and English, society,
but the metaphor is pejorative and plays off a concept of the thoroughbred
which few would now publicly maintain.[1] The coda to this episode was predictable in the extreme: another crushing defeat for the Conservatives,
compounded again in 2005 under the leadership of Michael Howard.
Around the issue of Europe—explosive enough to derail even the Iron
Lady and to polarize the subsequent contest for the party leadership—the
Conservative party have had, and are having, a rhetorical struggle with the
concept of cosmopolitanism and its concomitant notion of a cosmopolitics.
It seems that they are losing this struggle. Certainly, the nomination of the
young and deliberately centrist David Cameron as Conservative leader in
November 2005 (he has already been dubbed "Tory Blair") implicitly registers a need to "move on" from a past that is holding the party back. Thus,
it may be that the current abjection of the Conservative party is due to a
rhetorical failure to know its changing audience and the tropes of national
identity with which it is willing to identify. Powell merely verbalized what
had already long been rhetorically forceful within Conservative discourse.

Despite the obvious accusation, Powell has claimed—in his *Biography of a Nation* and elsewhere—that he is *not* a racist. Nonetheless, I suggest the "Rivers of Blood" speech is an example of virulent British Nationalism positing the notion of an embattled island whose (white) purity is threatened by the (black) contaminant of foreign immigrants. There are, of course, glaring contradictions in this discourse of purity, particularly in its presupposition of a certain myth of origin: at that ever-receding wellspring, it becomes apparent that Englishness exercises a strategic amnesia concerning not only the hybridity of its early history[2], but also the impact of imperialism on the racial makeup of its later history. In Powell's astonishing assertion of Empire, "that the nationhood of the mother country remained unaltered through it all" (cited in Gikandi 1996: 78), we can discern a symptom of this repression. And yet, the discourse of purity continues to operate in the rhetoric of English nationalism (and haunts, I suggest, all nationalisms). Indeed, as just indicated, and as we will see with a brief reference to John Major, the trope of an imperiled *white* Englishness continues to operate, particularly within the Conservative discourse, long after Powell's polemic phrasings.

A great deal has been written about the so-called "Rivers of Blood" speech;[3] I therefore propose to concentrate on two specific passages in which Powell employs the rhetorical device of prosopopoeia, in which a character is introduced into a discourse in order to voice its author's intended meaning at one remove. Richard Lanham has defined the term as "The rhetorical exercise known as the speech in character or impersonation" (1991: 124). Clearly a theatrical ploy of citation, prosopopeia is indispensable in the forensic forum of the law courts (as Cicero repeatedly pointed out), and it is in this dimension, as a supplement to artistic proofs, that Powell seems to be using it.

In the two prosopopeic passages on which I wish to focus, Powell portrays himself as merely—or, better, as *only*—the mouthpiece of his constituent's concerns. His call to action in the face of "the rising peril" of immigration is presented as originating within the audience itself: it is surpassingly persuasive to the extent that, as its authors, the addressees must *already* be persuaded. This conflation of persuader and persuadee, addressor and addressee, is a typical strategy of nationalist political discourse, one enabled by the duality of electoral no less than other modes of representation. The play of pronouns which leads to such a conflation moves from the "I" of the speaker to the "we" of the audience, and—crucially in Powellian discourse—opposes itself to a constitutively occluded "them." The circularity of this structure lays bare its metaphysical pretensions and the identitarian logic by which it pursues them. The first passage, which betrays this strategy, is as follows:

A week or two ago I fell into conversation with a constituent, a middle-aged, quite ordinary working man employed in one of our nationalized industries.

After a sentence or two about the weather, he suddenly said: "If I had the money to go, I wouldn't stay in this country. [. . .] I have three schoolchildren, all of them been through grammar school and two of them married now, with family. I shan't be satisfied till I have seen them all settled overseas. In this country in 15 or 20 years time, the black man will have the whip hand over the white man. (Utley 1968: 179–180)

A set of rhetorical identifications are already at work here, in the construction of a paradigmatic Englishness, and, simultaneously, its oppositional other: we note that the constituent is "quite ordinary," neither young nor old, a family man, and—to read the social ciphers of his clipped speech, his lack of money, and the grammar school education of his children—very probably working-class. We are witnessing the construction of an "Everyman." Moreover, inasmuch as he works for "our nation"("-alized industries"), he is anagrammatically coded as a patriot. A few sentences later, all codifying subtlety is discarded when Powell refers to him as "a decent, ordinary *fellow* Englishman" (Utley 1968: 180; emphasis added).

This appeal to a fellowship of Englishman—and the English are legendary for their love of clubs[4]—performs precisely what Kenneth Burke has called the "consubstantiality" of identification:

A is not identical with his colleague, B. But insofar as their interests are joined, A is *identified* with B. Or he may *identify himself* with B even when their interests are not joined, if he assumes that they are, or is persuaded to believe so . . . . To identify A with B is to make A "consubstantial" with B. (1969: 21)

The audience (A) here is being invited by Powell to recognize themselves *in*, substantially, this latter day John Bull (B), to conflate themselves with him, and therefore to impute to him the good, because shared, ethos of patriotism.

Clearly, the term "consubstantiality" is operating in Burke without *ontological* pertinence. A does not *become* B. The substance referred to is quintessentially rhetorical: it is the psychic material of belief or conviction, imaginatively projected, but not empirically shared. Yet even when domesticated within inverted commas, the notion of the "consubstantial" attains the *illocutionary force of the ontological*: the rhetoric of identification—which, at its limit, would persuade difference that it is sameness (identical)—is pseudo-corporeal. Powell's pragmatics of identification would thus imbricate the text of his speech into the weave of the body social (one thinks here of Hobbes' *Leviathan*). However, there is nothing specific to Powell's discourse in the employment of this strategy. Not only is identification the mechanism of political oratory in general, but nationalisms *per se* invariably evoke some mode of the "consubstantial": between the people and the body politic, or (particularly if the nationalism in question is counter-colonial) between the people and the land-as-body,[5] among countless other figurations.

National unity is, therefore, reified as an *organic* necessity, all aberrations from it being couched in topographical terminologies of dismemberment and amputation, or aesthetic criteria —as in Powell's case—of color differentials. While the poststructuralist shall be well placed to unsettle the metaphysics of presence by which such nationalist discourses operate, the theorist of rhetoric must also acknowledge—and, more importantly, *account* for—the rhetic force of these discourses of belonging, especially in their capacity to harness a deep social desire to be with, to be *con*-substantial. Though identification may be the basis of the social contract (the tract here being projected toward an audience in order to render it tractable), it is vital to recognize that the essentialist nationalism by which the signatories of this contract are persuaded to sign, is a con. Powell begins to draw up this con-tract by engendering a positive ethos for his "ordinary," "working," "fellow Englishman" very much prior to his actual discourse, the contents of which will be contentious enough to warrant such careful groundwork. Powell thus uses this cited character to imply that something is drastically wrong if such an honest and hardworking citizen feels compelled to leave the very country of his birth, that is, to renounce his membership to such an exclusive club. The threat which troubles the constituent is one of dramatic inversion: the (colonial) outside is flooding into the (metropolitan) inside, so that "home" is uprooted and dis-placed "overseas." In contrast to the cosmopolitan attitude one might expect to result from the culturally diverse experience of imperialism—during which the "home" was indeed transferred overseas—England is seen to cling to its parochialism. Inasmuch as the sun never sets on the Empire, within that perpetual daylight we can see that this parochialism is structural to the imperial mindset: only cultural violence enables one to remain tenaciously parochial while living "overseas." I shall argue that this tenacity is precisely the trace of the homesickness that accompanied the imperial project: it was then that the notion of a quintessentially rural England, a "green and pleasant land" (which, in point of fact, had not existed since the Industrial Revolution), was charged from afar with the cathectic energy of nostalgia (*nostos*-home, *algia, algos*-pain, sickness).

As it was invested with psychological value, this idyllic vision was also seen as something in need of protection: the notion that "an Englishman's home is his castle" coincided with the adventure of Empire. Hence, Powell's protagonist performs the inversion which, as a crisis, in many ways constitutes the Conservative trope of Englishness: the home is only home to the extent that it is *in danger of becoming unhomely.* That this defensiveness regarding the English home has a long, and literary, lineage is evidenced by Shakespeare's lines in *Richard II*:

This fortress built by Nature for herself
Against infection and the hand of war,
This happy breed of men, this little world;

This precious stone set in the silver sea,
Which serves it in the office of a wall,
Or as a moat defensive to a house.
(Shakespeare 1953: Act VI, Scene 1, 62)

But the inversion hinted at by this constituent is not only, or even primarily, the spatial/proprietorial movement from the outside to the inside of the English home. Most significantly, it involves relations of power. As if an unlikely reader of Hegel, this quotidian Englishman prophecies the movement of the master-slave dialectic, toward what centuries of imperialism have taught him to fear: slave revolt. Managing the threat of such revolts was of course central to the upkeep of empire, so much so that the mentality it created has perhaps permeated the metrolpole's conception of itself. Classical rhetoric defined metaphor as a turning away or deviation from "normal" usage, and it is indeed a putative "normality" that is being overturned here: the image of the black man having the "whip hand over the white man" achieves its rhetorical power solely on the basis of that configuration being in the present, or having been in the past, exactly opposite. The oppositionality of this figure is every bit as stark as the tonalities of black and white which it employs, and it is hard not to discern amidst its binarisms the lurking specter of white supremacism, despite Powell's dubious objections.

The culmination of this passage is highly emotive, but I suggest that Powell only indulges it by distancing himself with the device of the "mouthpiece" (prosopopoeia). I argue that the presence of the "mouthpiece" indexes, despite itself, the fact that the doubleness of representation has its uses even in the putatively "transparent" sphere of representational democracy. One could tease out this doubleness by exposing the unequal relationship of power between the *con-stituent*, and his or her rhetorical *con-stitution*: because elected to represent them, Powell can con-struct his voters using their own voices, for this is what they have entrusted to him by electing him. Ernesto Laclau has written on just this (*necessarily* unequal) relationship:

> ... if the represented *need* the relation of representation, it is because their identities are incomplete and have to be *supplemented* by the representative ... *Ergo*, the relation of representation will be, for essential logical reasons, constitutively impure: the movement from represented to representative will necessarily have to be supplemented by a movement in the opposite direction. (Mouffe 1996: 49)

This "movement in the opposite direction" involves the rhetorical process of identification: Powell therefore persuades his audience by presenting himself as the conduit of *their own discourse*, making it identical with them. In denying the discourse, they deny themselves.

By means of this strategy, Powell figures his discourse not only as the grassroots reportage that befits his political role, but also as an ethical obligation. Thus, to his own question "How dare I stir up trouble and inflame feelings by repeating such a conversation?" he asserts, "The answer is that I do not have the right not to do so." This double negative, coupled with the very last line of the speech (". . . to see, and not to speak, would be the great betrayal"), enacts a subtle ruse which amounts to that well-used defense: don't shoot the messenger! Powell implies that the job of the politician is to listen closely to the Truth of his constituents, to remain heroically focused on that Truth, and to transmit that Truth—even when unpalatable or inflammatory—to those in a position to change it. But the question of whose message it is should not be so peremptorily dismissed beneath this narrative of unproblematic transmission. Particularly if, again, we are to take Laclau's contrary postulation seriously: "The relation representative represented has to be privileged as the very condition of a democratic participation and mobilization" (Mouffe 1996: 49). In this sense, the rhetorical processes of identification through which the political ethos of "I speak for you" is constructed, actually enables, and performs the more violent "I speak you." This is not to suggest that Powell's virulent nationalism is purely a discursive projection, still less a matter simply of his own personal prejudices. Lamentably, we can be fairly sure that he was indeed representing the xenophobic attitudes of a significant proportion of the British people. However, the long-suppressed *epistemological* dimension of rhetoric instructs us that with every mode of "representing" even Truth—*especially* Truth—a certain far from neutral and far from unmotivated inflexion inevitably takes place.

Much the same pattern of rhetorical identification in the construction of a threatened Englishness emerges in the second passage I examine here, again an example of prosopopoeia. In introducing his second prosopopeic character, Powell writes of the "hundreds upon hundreds of letters" he has received from "ordinary, decent, sensible people," who are "rational and often well-educated," and yet who express a "sense of being a persecuted minority." He announces in clear terms that "I am going to allow just one of those hundreds of people *to speak for me*," [emphasis added]. This is a shrewd reversal of the representative role, suggesting humility on the one hand (inasmuch as he is giving up center-stage to allow someone else to speak), and a kinship with his constituents on the other (inasmuch as this stand-in still speaks "for him"). The letter that follows is so brilliantly designed to incite racial animus, while both anticipating and nullifying the logic of its potential refutations, that it is impossible not to read it as an extremely successful rhetorical performance. I quote it in full, since every line moves toward the ingenious repetition and reinscription of that "whip hand" metaphor expressed by the previous "constituent":

Eight years ago in a respectable street in Wolverhampton a house was sold to a negro. Now only one white (a woman old-age pensioner) lives there. This is her story. She lost her husband and both her sons in the war. So she turned her seven-roomed house, her only asset, into a boarding house. She worked hard and did well, paid off her mortgage and began to put something by for her old age. Then the immigrants moved in. With growing fear, she saw one house after another taken over. The quiet street became a place of noise and confusion. Regretfully, her white tenants moved out.

The day after the last one left, she was awakened at 7 AM by two negroes who wanted to use her phone to contact their employer. When she refused, as she would have refused any stranger at such an hour, she was abused and feared she would have been attacked but for the chain on her door. Immigrant families have tried to rent rooms in her house, but she always refused. Her little store of money went, and after paying rates, she has less than two pounds per week. She went to apply for a rate reduction and was seen by a young girl, who on hearing she had a seven-roomed house, suggested she should let part of it. When she said the only people she could get were negroes, the girl said "Racial prejudice won't get you anywhere in this country." So she went home.

The telephone is her lifeline. Her family pay the bill, and help her out as best they can. Immigrants have offered to buy her house—at a price which the prospective landlord would be able to recover from his tenants in weeks, or at most a few months. She is becoming afraid to go out. Windows are broken. She finds excreta pushed through her letterbox. When she goes to the shops, she is followed by children, charming, wide-grinning piccaninnies. They cannot speak English, but one word they know. "Racialist" they chant. When the new Race Relations Bill is passed, this woman is convinced she will go to prison. And is she so wrong? I begin to wonder. (Utley 1968: 187–188)

Again, we are confronted with the image of a home surrounded by dark forces intent upon gaining entry. Through an appeal to *commiseratio*, the protagonist is now figured as utterly vulnerable: the homeowner is female, old, and, as a widower, entirely alone. Yet her loneliness possesses that quiet heroism so admired by the English, since it is born of patriotism: her husband and sons have died for their country, in a struggle monumental enough in the national psyche to require no more specific appellation than "the war." The implication is tragic-ironic: did her husband and sons really sacrifice themselves to protect *this* future? Or, in stark contrast, is the vision of Englishness for which they laid down their very lives being violated, thereby mocking their memory and turning glorious victory into bitter, belated defeat?

But while this citation repeats the image of the besieged home, it also reinscribes the inversion of power consequent upon this siege into a wider economic context. In this passage, the home is very much a marker of property, as well as propriety. The isolated white woman is poor: her house is "her only asset." Yet, the value of this asset plunges through no fault of her own (we are told that she has "worked hard"). This devaluation reaches such an ignominious point that those same frightening "negroes" whom she is struggling to keep at bay turn the tables on her, and are soon in a position to buy her asset from her for a pitiful sum. I suggest this is not only an analogy between the economic depreciation of house prices and the cultural impoverishment of the white English soil by black Asian and Caribbean seeds, not merely the familiar there-goes-the-neighborhood lament writ large. More than this, these fiscal metaphorics insert the issue of blackness into the economy of *class* relations in general. Paul Gilroy has pointed out that the Black and Asian communities in England and elsewhere are so low on the class hierarchy as to fly beneath even the Marxist radar (Gilroy 1987). Here, it is also that the rhetoric of class division is being used, even co-opted, to *articulate* the threat of blackness.

Burke, to return briefly to his thinking on rhetoric (and the relation I am suggesting it has with nationalisms), theorizes a "rhetoric of courtship" by which the mystification of class division is supported and repeated in everyday encounters (1969: 137–142). An entire algebra of etiquette thus marks the rhetorical exchanges between classes: the farmhand who tugs his forelock before the landowner reinforces not only the ostensible hierarchy between them, but the very principle of hierarchy itself:

> The hierarchic principle is not complete in the social realm [. . .] in the mere arrangement whereby each rank is overlord to its underlings and underling to its overlords. It is complete only when each rank accepts the *principle of gradation itself*, and in thus "universalizing" the principle, makes a spiritual *reversal* of the ranks just as meaningful as their actual material arrangement. (1969: 138)

Clearly, this courtly rhetoric serves to shore up the grammar of the status quo. In the account which Powell proffers, it is an entirely opposite rhetoric at work, one of a violent rupturing of the bourgeois sensibilities central to the preservation of England's much-vaunted reserve and quietude (the street becomes filled with "noise and confusion"). These immigrants have no *respect* for *decency* (hammering on her door at the crack of dawn); they are violent (becoming abusive when she will not let them in); they are as filthy as animals (pushing excreta through her letter box); and, significantly, they abuse the right to private property upon which civilized society is built: blatantly, by breaking her windows, or cunningly, by trying to buy the house from her. Burke contends that the Marxist corpus—particularly in *The German Ideology* where Marx addresses questions of alienation and mystification—is in fact a critique primarily of capitalism's *rhetoric* (1969; 101–110). The division of labor institutes the difference which calls forth the need for a rhetoric, and capitalism's response is the mystifying ideology of "naturalized" class difference. In Powell's letter, at least a part of the pathos of the account derives from the breaching of this courtly rhetoric of capitalism—and it is all the more scandalous because these black immigrants are effectively *sub*proletariat.

But there is another, perhaps more devastating, economic decline present in this passage: that of expression. Now the "whip hand" becomes verbal: the terrified widow is lashed and subdued by the term "racialist" as it is brandished by "wide-grinning piccaninnies" who can speak not one other word of English. The force of this term is such that it paralyzes those who would speak *about* race, in any way. Powell thus invokes the tyranny of political correctness to suggest that although this woman has legitimate complaints, there will soon be no adequate tribunal to adjudicate over them. She must therefore suffer alone, and, crucially, without a voice. The linguistic power-reversal implicated here mirrors Powell's earlier proclamation that "those who vociferously demand legislation as they call it 'against discrimination'" have "got it exactly and diametrically wrong" (Utley 1968: 184). An overly liberal agenda has actively obscured the fact that:

> The discrimination and the deprivation, the sense of alarm and resentment, lies not with the immigrant population but with those among whom they have come and are still coming. (Utley 1968: 184)

In trying to wrest the whip back into English hands, then, Powell covertly appeals to a paradigmatic moment of English history. It is a moment which exemplifies the nationalist trope of the cherished-institution-under-threat, the gunpowder plot: "This is why to enact legislation of the kind [that is, against racial discrimination] before parliament at this moment is to risk throwing a match on to gunpowder" (Utley 1968: 184). I do not think it is stretching credulity to argue that the conjunction of the words "gunpowder" and "parliament" are sufficient to evoke in the English imaginary the attempt in 1605 by the Catholic conspirator Guy Fawkes to blow up the Houses of Parliament (another house, this time protecting nothing less than democracy). This might seem a tenuous connection if it were not for the fact that effigies of Guy Fawkes are ritually incinerated every year on Bonfire Night in England, inscribing by repetition the figure of threatened Englishness so vividly portrayed in Powell's besieged widow.

Thus, we have seen that Powell figures Englishness in terms of such binaries as purity/contamination, white/black, inside/outside and, as shown by the two main examples, homely/unhomely. The first terms in each of these pairings are not only privileged—as the grammar of metaphysics dictates—but privileged in exact proportion to the threat posed by their opposites. From this it follows that English nationalism, as formulated in this, and perhaps other, Conservative discourse(s), is predicated on an ideology of paranoia: it is through stressing the threats to its sovereignty that, paradoxically, Conservative Englishness asserts itself most emphatically. In the parlance of a rather twee English jingoism, this is what is called the "Bulldog Spirit": a mixture of tenacity, defiance, and pleasure in the status of the underdog. Thus, England is most English when it is defending itself against overwhelming odds. Furthermore, the England which needs defending from these marauding (and with Powell, black) forces of alterity is, typically, rural, middleclass, and probably based in the south. It is a (non)place which provided the saccharine backdrop for a previous Conservative evocation of purity by Stanley Baldwin:

> The sounds of England, the tinkle of the hammer on the anvil in the country smithy, the corncrake on a dewy morning, the sound of the scythe against the whetstone, and the sight of a plough team coming over the brow of a hill, the sight that has been England since England was land . . . the one eternal sight of England. (Paxman 1999: 143)

It is in order to contrast with these (even in Baldwin's day, ridiculously antiquated) visions of a prelapsarian, agrarian England that Powell paints his counter-visions of urban decay, racial animus, and moral decline.

However, what is notable in Powell's speech is that precisely the historical phenomena which have caused the very influx of immigrants that threatens Baldwin's "Englishness," is nowhere mentioned. I refer, of course, to the age of British imperialism. Could the arrival of his "wide-grinning piccaninnies" be anything other than the backwash consequent upon the original tidal wave of British imperial expansion? Yet the only references to the empire are in the use of the phrase "Commonwealth countries." Simon Gikandi has pointed out this conspicuous omission:

> What is striking in Powell's discourse on the black subject is that the black critical mass has to be rewritten—and demonized—as the primary threat to English national identity without directly associating its presence with England's imperial past. (1996: 71)

However, not only does the presence of blackness synechdocically (that is, by a relation of part to whole) recall the absent presence of empire, but inasmuch as his discourse relies on an essentialist England that *needs* defending, Powell again appeals (despite himself) to a metonym of colonialism. The discourse of purity upon which his scaremongering is parasitic becomes paradoxical when one realizes that this very notion of an English rural and racial purity *was a response to imperialism*, the same imperialism which now—with Powell writing in the late 1960s—threatens to destroy it. Raymond Williams has evoked this dialectic well:

> England's green peace contrasted with the tropical or arid places of actual work; its sense of belonging, of community, idealized by contrast with the tensions of colonial rule and the isolated alien settlement. The birds and trees and rivers of England; the natives speaking, more or less, one's own language: these were the terms of many imagined and actual settlements. (Paxman 1999: 144)

I believe it possible to argue that this vision of a green and pleasant England persists in the Conservative psyche today. Indeed, the nearer one gets to the grassroots of contemporary Toryism in England, the nearer one gets to this puritanical discourse, and the defensiveness and paranoia that go with it (today, reactions to the very word "Europe" serve as a reliable litmus test for this hypothesis).

Trusted tropes are frequently dusted off and paraded in times of turmoil: hence we can read a great deal into John Major's 1993 speech (when the very issue of Europe—site of a forced encounter with cosmopolitanism— was first shown to divide the Conservative party just as much as it does today) in which he said:

> Fifty years from now, Britain will still be the country of long shadows on countrygrounds, warm beer, invincible green suburbs, dog lovers and pools fillers and—as George Orwell said—"old maids cycling to holy communion through the morning mist." (Paxman 1999: 142)

Such transparent yet persistent nostalgia for something that never was has put the Conservative Party well and truly out of touch with most of modern England, for whom mobile phones, cityscapes, and multiracial (if not always multi*cultural*) communities are the overwhelming norm. Though I do not believe that the Conservatives are inherently racist—as today's suffocating political correctness makes it all too easy to suggest—nonetheless their (British Bull)dogged adherence to this nostalgic discourse of purity *does* mean that of all the political parties, the modern day avatars of Powellism who are nonetheless pragmatic enough to reject the extremism of the British National Party or the UK Independence Party, will continue to choose the True Blue of the Conservative Party under which to propagate their own sinister chromatism.

Currying F(l)avor: Overcooking the Rhetorics of Hybridity

I would now like to examine Robin Cook's so-called "Chicken Tikka Masala" speech, delivered to the Social Market Foundation in London on 19 April 2001. For very obvious reasons, this speech stands to Powell's in a relation of exact opposition. Indeed, it is so much like a mirror placed opposite the discourse of purity promulgated by Powell that I will argue it in fact replicates, albeit inverted, the same grotesque amplifications. While on one level I am extremely sympathetic to Cook's redescription of nationalism—particularly when set against the Powellian alternative—at a more fundamental, and I argue more political, level, my overriding concern is to signal the temptation of binarism which its logic holds out, and the fact that Cook surrenders to it. Moreover, Cook's discourse also validates Powell's point about the tyranny of political correctness, in that it trades on a set of familiar liberal clichés which constitute the currency of New Labour's incessantly "worthy" rhetoric. For my purposes here in tracing the tropological evolution of Englishness, the most important thing to note is how diametrically opposed are the concepts that pass as clichés in the two speeches.[6] In their disparity, we are licensed to perceive a genuine shift in national identity.

At first glance, it may seem that Cook's use of (Burkean) identification is exactly counter to Powell's. Certainly he does not have recourse to the device of prosopopeia: there are no constituents presented for/through whom he is speaking. Whereas Powell's was essentially forensic in format, in that it offered proofs and testifying witnesses, Cook's speech is apodictic: what he offers (on a silver platter) is an apparently simple constative description of contemporary British society. And yet, as rhetorician's distrustful of the notion of simplicity, and indeed the constative,[7] one can certainly assert that there are tropes at work here, whose overall effect is persuasive in intent. Furthermore, these tropes operate by a kind of negative identification with, precisely, Conservative discourses of national identity: in what might ludically be termed his *exordium*, Cook structures everything that follows on the basis of a point-by-point refutation of the conservative mythology of a "pure" and "originary" (in this case British) identity under threat:

> Sadly, it has become fashionable for some to argue that British identity is under siege, perhaps even in a state of terminal decline. The threat is said to come in three forms. (Cook 2001)

As we listen to what these three forms are, we can be under no illusions that they constitute an anatomy of long-held Conservative prejudices:

> First, the arrival of immigrants who, allegedly, do not share our cultural values and who fail to support the English cricket team. (Cook 2001)

Cricket—which Gikandi has termed "one of the most exemplary cultural and aesthetic categories inherited from colonialism" (1996: 9)—is here invoking the unjust assertion of Englishness over, yet in the name of, Britishness. But also, it identifies a nostalgic leather-against-willow brand of Englishness with Conservatism. New Labour has consistently enforced this Burkean identification of England's colonial past with the Conservative party (a strategy which, I argue, extends to an oppositional stance toward history in general, even its own, a fact evidenced by its ceaseless appeal to modernity and modernization). The second listed threat confirms that this speech will perpetuate the ploy:

> Second, our continued membership of the European Union, which is said to be absorbing member states into "a country called Europe." (Cook 2001)

This is a reference to the rhetorics of Thatcherism—brilliantly analyzed by Stuart Hall as "authoritarian populism" (Hall and Jacques 1983; Hall 1988)—and their continued influence on Conservative policy toward Europe. This issue is still prohibitive of Conservative solidarity in Britain today, and New Labour never passes up an opportunity to feed on their disarray (even though it too faces a minefield regarding its promised referendum on the subject).

> Third, the devolution of power to Scotland, Wales and Northern Ireland, which is seen as a step to the break-up of the UK. (Cook 2001)

Though there is not room to deal here with the enormous issue of devolution, it is worth noting in passing that New Labour depicts it as very much a *revolution*. In this very speech, Cook implies that the centrifugal force which has lead to the dispensing of representative autonomy to some of the orbiting (post?)colonies of which I spoke in my introduction, actually *reinforces* English identity, thus indicating that the centrism which I earlier imputed to nationalism continues under New Labour. However, for now it will suffice to foreground devolution as a *modernizing* reform which would never have been seen under a Conservative government, against which I suggest Cook sets himself.

Thus, these three basically Conservative grievances, each in their own way predicated upon the discourse of purity which that party *at a certain level* perpetuates, form the template of Cook's subsequent speech. However, as I warned, he does not so much refute them, as invert them. In wishing to distance himself and his party from the xenophobic nationalism of Powell and his successors, Cook pushes the tropological pendulum too far in the opposite direction: against the narrative of an uncorrupted, originary, and historically pure lineage of national identity, Cook uncritically embraces and champions the hybrid, the composite, and the culturally impure. He writes that "the British are not a race, but a gathering of countless different races and communities," and—in exact contradistinction to Powell—that "it is not their purity that makes the British unique, but the sheer pluralism of their ancestry" (Cook 2001). Cook amplifies this pluralism yet further, saying "This pluralism is not a burden we must reluctantly accept. It is an immense asset that contributes to the cultural and economic vitality of our nation" (Cook 2001). Powell is being turned absolutely on his head here: where the "negroes" in his bleak and dystopian scene inflicted economic disaster on the beleaguered white widow, forcing house prices down and ruining her business, with Cook they are an injection of adrenaline into the heart of British industry and commerce. Far from inducing impoverishment, "our economy," he says, "has been enriched by the arrival of new communities" (Cook 2001). Indeed, Cook forms his concept of national identity on the basis of this pluralism. He demands that "we reject insular nationalism and the politics of fear," arguing that "identity is not a finite substance to be shared out between competing loyalties." He even implies a mobile, layered, and schizophrenic nationalism:

> I get impatient when I see opinion polls that ask respondents whether they feel more Scottish or English than British, or more British than European, as if these choices were mutually exclusive. (Cook 2001)

This phenomenon of nationalities-within-nationalities, this Russian Doll effect of subjectivities, represents no problem, it is implied, for the hybrid: s/he simply switches cultural codes as the occasion demands. Such an internationalism is indeed desirable, but I argue that there are (at least) two motivations behind the experiencing of cultural difference: that which is *enforced* by a disparity in wealth and provides the impetus behind immigration, and that which may be called the mobility of the wealthy and which enables a certain "tourism of difference." The one is born of necessity, the other of armchair exoticism. There can be no doubt which of the two is the locus of greater nationalistic friction.

That Cook's enthusiasm for cultural hybridity has an intimate kinship with a parallel enthusiasm for fractured postmodern subjectivities discernible in certain modes of postcolonial theory should not escape our notice. Theory—by no means free of its own buzzwords and modishnesses—thus furnishes political discourse with terms which it can then deploy in a radical, progressive, even supposedly "intellectual" register (although no politician would apply this last term to themselves: in an England which has long prided itself on its pragmatism, it has the resonances of a profound insult). The theoretical notion of hybridity as, for example, expounded by Homi Bhabha, is in this way drained of its problematic and problematizing, political and politicizing, "thirdness," and is made to cover over the rifts it normally exposes: *binaries are depicted as being happy in their binarity*. This sanitization of cultural hybridity by New Labour into a fairy tale of "melting pot" racial harmony should not blind us to the concrete reality of its unceasingly *difficult* nature.

Nor should it blind us to the very specific audience at which Robin Cook's speech is aimed. Cook concedes an indication of this:

> This point [about the enrichment of British Culture by its immigrant influences] is perhaps more readily understood by young Britons, who are more open to new influences and more likely to have been educated in a multi-ethnic environment. (Cook 2001)

This sentiment is in line with a general appeal to youthful, and, moreover, cosmopolitan identifications in the rhetoric of New Labour. Indeed, its projection of a mythology of "Cool Britannia" could serve as the paradigmatic site of its reinscription of the Conservative tropology of national identity:

the passage from an authoritarian, patriarchal, and indelibly imperial "*Rule Britannia*," to an approachable, hip, and post postcolonial "*Cool* Britannia," is the fundamental tropological shift which New Labour have enacted.[8] From an *imperious* rule-by-elite which is essentially vertical in character (the imperial structure in other words), to a cozy, collective contract agreed, horizontally as it were, among friends who speak the same language: this is the movement by which New Labour would persuade its electorate that Britain's imperial past is resolutely confined to that past, and moreover, that that past is the property and responsibility not of themselves, but of the Conservatives. Again, we can detect here a similar play of pronouns to that diagnosed in Powellian discourse: imperialism belongs to *them*, and therefore *not to us*—and, in a Burkean move—*or you* (the electorate).

This point about history and historicity deserves to be expanded, for it conceals the fact that New Labour's insight into multiculturalism engenders a concomitant blindness concerning multiraci(ali)sm. One can detect this in the identifications which "modernizing" New Labour applies to itself: it may not be too far fetched to suggest that New Labour cultivates an analogue with aesthetic modernism's fetishization of rupture, rebellion, and contempt for tradition. The dialectic exposed in Harold Bloom's quintessentially modernist essay, *The Anxiety of Influence*, may go some way to explaining the precursor-successor dynamic between the Conservatives and New Labour. In the very "Newness" of New Labour, one senses an ostensible jettisoning of what has been, a jettisoning with its phases of *clinamen*, *daemonization*, and certainly of *askesis*: for very good reasons grounded in political history (the disastrous economic policies of previous Labour administrations, the association with militant trade unionism, the "Loony Left" image, the hinterlands of the Thatcher years, etc.), Labour did indeed have to reinvent itself to become a viable party of government.

Bemoaning what was then a serious crisis on the Left, Stuart Hall issued clarion calls for just such an ideological overhaul of the Labour party as early as 1987. In a paper entitled "Blue Election, Election Blues" (1988: 259–67), Hall recognized the Burkean process of identification I have extrapolated on here ("Electoral politics—in fact, every kind of politics—depends on political identities and identifications" (1988: 261)), and goes on to define the ways in which Neil Kinnock's electoral campaign of that year failed to help the nation to identify sufficiently with the Labour party to earn their votes. Broadly, his (in retrospect, incredibly prescient) argument is that Labour was mistaken in looking solely to the (especially) Northern working classes for its traditional "core" vote, and in failing to counter the Conservative Party's reputation as the party of wealth-creation. Hall concludes that the Labour party must not confine itself exclusively to traditional welfare issues but embrace *some* of the entrepreneurial values of Thatcherism in order to appeal to the burgeoning middle classes. Significantly, he phrases this exigency in terms of history. After bleakly diagnosing that "there is no evidence that Labour's commitment to traditionalism can construct such a majority" (1988: 266), he asserts—in tones which New Labour and particularly Tony Blair have been echoing ever since—that:

> The question of Labour becoming in a deep sense the majority party of society is therefore not whether it can rally and mobilize its past, but whether it has a convincing alternative scenario to Thatcherism for the future. It cannot build such an alternative by, however honorably, replaying "1945" in 1987. It can only honor its past by aiming to move forward. But to do so it needs a strategy for modernization and an image of modernity. (1988: 267)

In this process of willed misprision which Labour has enacted in reading the text of its own history, it has effectively purged itself of its own past, disavowing, as Hall's piece seems to imply, any temporality but the present and possible future (influence being always harbored by the past). From this *internal* ditching of historical ballast, it would seem that New Labour have extrapolated not an ahistorical, but an anti-historical, outlook. This outlook would cause the oblique separating the past/future couplet to perform also as the oblique separating both the Conservatism/Labour *and* Imperialism/Cosmopolitanism couplets. To state this crudely: the Conservatives cling tenaciously to (albeit a very partial) History, but, with Powell, deny the role of the colonies in the formation of Englishness; New Labour enthusiastically embraces the ex-inhabitants of the colonies and their descendants, placing them, with Cook, at the very fulcrum of national identity, yet deny History the possibility of an entry visa into its carefully policed ideological borders.

To say the least, it would be foolhardy to accept this chiasmatic conceit of New Labour's rhetoric at face value. Postcolonial theorists have been exemplary in demonstrating the persistence of colonial structures of dependence and consciousness long after the removal of their political and administrative facades. Imperialism never was (is) the monolith that Labour's dismissive gesture indicates. It is rather something far too complex to be simply consigned to the "dustbin of history." It would be extreme political naiveté to conflate imperialism with empire, and to imagine the former to have been dismantled along with the latter. For this reason, it remains important to maintain a vigilant critical suspicion regarding *any* enthusiastic championing of the very concepts deployed to deconstruct the nationalist essentialism(s) of colonialism(s), for beneath them an opposite process may well be at work. In fact, it would be possible to argue that New Labour's positive figuration of an unproblematic multiculturalism amounts to the *depoliticization* of *actual*, concrete, multiracialism *under the banner of cosmopolitanism*. In the same way that freedom of speech is sometimes used as a stick with which to beat into silence those who would wish to challenge its promiscuity, liberal choruses of "multiculturalism" can likewise drown out the sounds of empirical racism and concrete, lived inequality. It is once again Burke who encourages a much needed suspicion here:

> In accordance with the rhetorical principle of identification, whenever you find a doctrine of "nonpolitical" esthetic affirmed with fervor, look for its politics. (1969: 28)

I would contend that we need to "look for [or dis-cover] the politics" of Cook's, and New Labour's, uncritical multiculturalism because it implies an—as the rhetorician would argue—*impossible* linguistic scenario of transparency (notwithstanding Cook's exultant image of a happy linguistic multiplicity: "tonight, over 300 languages will be spoken by families over their evening meal"). With New Labour, difference becomes transparent enough to recognize itself, and to be honored *as* difference, which is to say, it is reduced to the order of the same under the undifferentiated, and undifferentiating, proper name called "difference." Again, Burke helps us peer through this transparency at the opacity always already at work behind its obfuscating veil:

> In pure identification there would be no strife. Likewise, there would be no strife in absolute separateness, since opponents can join battle only through a mediatory ground that makes their communication possible, thus providing the first condition necessary for their interchange of blows. But put identification and division ambiguously together, so that you cannot know for certain just where one ends and the other begins, and you have the characteristic invitation to rhetoric. (Burke 1969: 25)

In other words, beneath the identifications that political discourse constructs, the (cool) Rule (Britannia) of the *Agon* continues to operate, and the invitation to engage in a *critical* rhetoric must be answered.

Hence, we must make critical space for just such a reading of the eponymous metaphor in Cook's speech, and the spicy yet all-inclusive "melting pot" he cooks up with it. Despite the fact that he picks (from a long, but selective, menu of National tropes endorsed by New Labour) "Chicken Tikka Masala" as the most *palatable* metaphor for British cultural hybridity, he also thereby betrays the residually imperial inequality inscribed into this distastefully lopsided hybridity:

> Chicken Tikka Masala is now a true British national dish, not only because it is the most popular, but because it is a perfect illustration of the way Britain absorbs and adapts external influences. Chicken Tikka is an Indian dish. The Masala sauce was added to satisfy the desire of British people to have their meat served in gravy.

We are licensed to ask (perhaps saucily): who is doing the compromising here? Who is adapting their national identity? And who is demanding of the other that they accommodate a desire which is not their own, that, indeed, they *serve* it? Moreover, who is in the position of capitalist consumer, who in that of the subjugated worker/producer? And to phrase these questions by their commonality, is this relationship of consumer and producer not locked in all important ways into the hierarchical binarism of colonizer-colonized, a table at which, surely, we have all now eaten our fill? (The question of who is to pick up the bill, however, is too rhetorical to even ask).

Cook would no doubt denegate the charged pathos of these grave questions with the retort that "Legitimate immigration is the necessary and unavoidable result of *economic* success," thereby coding inequality otherwise. The ostensibly charitable discourse of economic liberalism very often snuffs out such demanding questions, rendering the capitalist game one in which everyone is, supposedly, a winner. While the processes of globalization—acknowledged by Cook as being decisive at the beginning of his speech—may well have brought about some material improvements in certain localities, the concomitant epistemic and symbolic violence wreaked upon cultural identities should not be brushed under the carpet. Nor should it be hidden beneath such pseudo-corporate motivational spin as Cook's closing assertion that "We should be proud that those British values have made Britain a successful multi-ethnic society."

Successful? Where? Perhaps, at a considerable push, in London where this speech was being delivered (though even then only, again, as the product of brute economic forces and not at all of some utopian social charter). Indeed, much of New Labour's rhetoric is so metropolitan in character, that it fails to be remotely suasive the moment it extends beyond the M25, a fact which further signals the *partial* universality of its avowed cosmopolitanism. Such a decidedly *metropolitan* claim for a successful multi-ethnic society, for example, looks utterly counterfactual when set against the very serious race riots which ravaged some of England's northern cities, such as Oldham and Burnley, in 2001 (and there have been analogous disturbances in France in 2005). To the victims of racially motivated attacks in these areas, black or white, I doubt that Cook's idealistic rhetoric would carry much weight. Nor can it be denied that the news footage of these riots—bare-chested youths hurling petrol bombs, the burnt out skeletons of overturned cars, police advancing behind riot shields—served to recall in every important way those of Brixton and Toxteth in the early Eighties under Thatcher. Then, the disgruntled communities were largely of Caribbean descent; now they are predominantly of Asian descent. Though twenty years apart, their grievances are very similar: prejudice, unemployment, alienation. However, I would argue that not only does the liberal rhetoric of New Labour impair recognition of this far from multicultural sit-

uation. Perhaps more seriously, its rhetoric of modernization, and the attitude toward history which it betrays, also prevents the recognition of a lam-
entable continuity in racial tension between black and white which is
subterranean to—perhaps even ultimately *indifferent* to—Britain's successive administrations, be they blue or red. It is in these concealed spaces beneath the veneer of institutional politics that a more visceral nationalism,
and racism, seethes and is fed.

In light of this, the rhetorical critic's role becomes one of disassociating
the ideological associations of Englishness with whiteness on the one hand,
and racism/imperialism with (ex)-Conservatism on the other, both discourses which would deny, disguise, or dismiss, the troubling persistence—
from administration to administration—of a racial tension transhistorical
to so-called English cosmopolitanism.

Notes

1. In 2001, a prominent Tory minister was expelled from the party for his involvement
   in the British National Party and his unapologetic racism.
2. See Paxman's chapter entitled "'True Born Englishman' and Other Lies"(1999: 60-76).
3. To cite but a few, Gikandi (1996: 69-83); Gilroy (1990); Foot (1969); and Heffer
   (1999).
4. Ogden Nash famously wrote:
   Let us pause to consider the English.
   Who when they pause to consider themselves they get all reticently
   thrilled and tinglish,
   Because every Englishman is convinced of one thing, viz;
   That to be an Englishman is to belong to the most exclusive club
   there is.
   (Quoted in Paxman 1999: 69).
5. One thinks here of the situation of the landless of Brazil.
6. In the cliché, the critical rhetorician finds the useful contrary of a dead-metaphor: a
   commonplace which advertises itself as such, and thus indicates the topology of the
   field of opinion. A genuinely dead-metaphor is stubbornly invisible.
7. In the radical rhetorics of Paul de Man, for instance, the very notion of the
   constative is an illusion engendered by the allegorical structuration of the text itself.
   For a discussion of this see Gasché (1998): particularly 114-148.
8. That this is also a move from the countryside as locus of nationhood, to the
   cosmopolitan city, was indicated during the height of the Foot and Mouth crisis in
   British agriculture, when Labour were seen as ignoring the concerns of the rural
   regions.

Bibliography

Aristotle. 1991. *The Art of Rhetoric*. Trans. by H. C. Lawson-Tancred. Harmondsworth: Penguin.

Bloom, Harold. 1997. *The Anxiety of Influence*. Oxford: Oxford University Press.

Burke, Kenneth. 1969. *A Rhetoric of Motives*. London: University of California Press.

Cook, Robin. 2001. "Chicken Tikka Masala Speech." [Accessed 19 March 2007] <http://www.guardian.co.uk/racism/Story/0,2763,477023,00.html>.

Foot, Paul. 1969. *The Rise of Enoch Powell: an Examination of Enoch Powell's Attitude to Immigration and Race*. London: Cornmarket Press.

Gasché, Rodolphe. 1998. *The Wild Card of Reading: On Paul de Man*. London: Harvard University Press.

Gikandi, Simon. 1996. *Maps of Englishness: Writing Identity in the Culture of Colonialism*. New York: Columbia University Press.

Gilroy, Paul. 1987. *There Ain't No Black in the Union Jack: The Cultural Politics of Race and Nation*. Chicago IL: University of Chicago Press.

———1990. "Art of Darkness: Black Art and the Problem of Belonging to England." *Third Text*, no. 10 (Spring).

Hall, Stuart. 1978. *Five Views for Multi-Racial Britain* (transcript of talks on Race Relations broadcast by BBC TV). London: Commission for Racial Equality.

———. 1988. *The Hard Road to Renewal: Thatcherism and the Crisis of the Left*. London: Verso.

Hall, Stuart and Martin Jacques. 1983. *The Politics of Thatcherism*. London: Lawrence and Wishart.

Heffer, Simon. 1999. *Like the Roman: the Life of Enoch Powell*. London: Phoenix Giant.

Lanham, Richard A. 1991. *A Handlist of Rhetorical Terms*. London: University of California Press.

Mouffe, Chantal (ed.). 1996. *Deconstruction and Pragmatism*. London: Routledge.

Paxman, Jeremy. 1999. *The English: A Portrait of a People*. Harmondsworth: Penguin.

Shakespeare, William. 1953. *The Tragedy of King Richard II*. C. H. Herford (ed.). London: Blackie and Son.

Utley, Thomas Edwin (1968), *Enoch Powell: The Man and his Thinking*, London: William Kimber.

CHAPTER 9

All the Downtown Tories

Mourning Englishness in New York

Matthew Hart

> By themselves, monuments are of little value, mere stones in the landscape.
> But as part of a nation's rites or the objects of a people's national pilgrimage,
> they are invested with national soul and memory . . . . They suggest
> themselves as indigenous, even geological outcroppings in a national
> landscape; in time, such idealized memory grows as natural to the eye as the
> landscape in which it stands.
> —James Young, *Textures of Memory*

This paper analyses the awkward intersection between English nationalism and global neoliberalism in New York City's British Memorial Garden, which on its completion in 2007, will be dedicated to the memory of the British victims of the September 2001 terror attacks. With the obvious exception of United States citizens, these sixty-seven men and women form the single largest national group of the dead, and with this construction, they will be honored by a memorial that, unique among those on American soil, divides the dead along national lines.

The Garden will be built on the site of a Parks District property at Hanover Square, Lower Manhattan, with the design and fundraising for the project supervised by the British Memorial Garden Trust, a nonprofit organization formed by officers of the St. George's Society of New York, the oldest charitable organization in New York, with long ties to New York's Anglo-American social elite. Featuring a sculpture to "unity" by Anish Kapoor, landscape gardening by Isabel and Julian Bannerman, stonemasonry by Simon Verity, and the imprimatur of royal patron the Prince of Wales, the Garden is an aesthetically and ideologically overdetermined site. Considered as a memorial *qua* memorial, it strives to reject singular monumentality, yet its vision of Britain harks back to the nationalism of the unembarrassed monument. Located at the "Ground Zero" of the "war on terror" and the neoliberal global marketplace, the British Memorial Garden mourns the twenty-first century victims of international *Jihad* through the imperial memory of pastoral Englishness. For in Rupert Brooke's words, quoted on the Garden's official website, Hanover Square is to become "some corner of a foreign field / That is forever England" (Brooke 1915: 115).

Counter-Monuments and National Memory

I am concerned, then, with national culture, memorial architecture, and the way these fields come together in the context of the Anglo-American political and economic "special relationship"—a relationship that has as much to do with the London-New York economic axis (and the British government's willingness to engage in a geopolitical gamble to reorder the Middle East) as with cultural or political fraternity. My epigraph comes from James Young's *Textures of Memory*, an analysis of architectural commemoration in the context of the Holocaust (1993: 2). Discussions about how one should remember the Holocaust necessarily involve questions of ethno-national identity and the concretization of cultural memory in architectural forms; they are thus, despite real historical differences, clearly relevant to the analysis of a project like the British Memorial Garden. Behind Young's Holocaust enquiry lies the insight that, to the extent they remain alienated from the nation, monuments to mass death risk disappearing into or sitting upon the landscape—hypostatized, unreconciled—like so many rocks. As "the objects of a people's national pilgrimage," however, they are transformed into the sacred bedrock of the nation-state. This is particularly important when it comes to the British Memorial Garden, which is designed as a map of Britain in leaf and stone, and quite deliberately aspires toward the status of "indigenous, even geological outcropping in a national landscape." For Young, as an analyst and judge of memorial projects, the naturalization of monumental architectures is innately suspicious, since it attenuates a monument's pedagogical function and identifies the catastrophe of mass death with the salving authority of the nation-state. This problem leads Young to the idea of *anti*-monumentality, which seeks to counter the logic of the becoming-indigenous monument by rejecting the "self-aggrandizing figurative icons of the late nineteenth century, which celebrated national ideals and triumphs" (1999: 2). The anti-monument therefore begins from the *negation* of memorial presence and it is in this light that we can understand something like Horst Hoheisel's entry to the 1995 competition to build a "memorial to the murdered Jews of Europe," in which the German artist proposed blowing up the Brandenburg Gate, grinding its stone into dust, sprinkling the remains over the site, and covering the area with granite. Thus is "a destroyed people" remembered by a "destroyed monument" to German militarism (Young 1999: 1). The political impossibility of realizing such a project is, meanwhile, crucial to its counter-monumental thrust. This is something that Young celebrates in Hoheisel's proposal, even though, as a competition judge with hopes of persuading the German government to actually build the winning entry, he could not vote for it. "The surest engagement with Holocaust memory in Germany," he writes, "may actually lie in its perpetual irresolution" (Young 1999: 1–2).[1]

Young identifies counter-monumental art with "the national ambivalence and uncertainty of late twentieth-century postmodernism" (1999: 2). But the theme of anti-monumentality is, I would argue, largely coterminous with aesthetic and philosophical modernism itself. In *Textures of Memory*, Young quotes Nietzsche asking, "what is the use to the modern man of this 'monumental' contemplation of the past?" and goes on to cite Robert Musil's declaration that "there is nothing in this world as invisible as a monument" (1993: 4, 13). Likewise, in analyzing Maya Lin's 1982 Vietnam Veteran's Memorial, Marita Sturken attends to the many ways in which its refusal of phallic grandiosity make it "unmistakably representative" of a period that includes the infamous postmodernisms of Carl Andre and Richard Serra (1997: 48–49). Yet Sturken elsewhere records that Lin's most moving innovation—carving the names of dead and missing service personnel into the granite surface of the memorial, an act that personalizes the victims at the expense of the narrative of collective sacrifice—was inspired by Sir Edwin Lutyens's 1928 Thiepval memorial to the dead of the Somme (1997: 270n. 29). The postmodern rejection of monumentality appears, then, to involve the realization of a negativity already implicit within modernism. To employ the insights of T.J. Clark, such inter-epochal echoes remind us of the fact that the modernism of Nietzsche, Musil, or Lutyens "was already characterized by a deep, truly undecidable doubleness of mind in the face of the main forms of modernity" (1999: 91). For Clark, "that doubleness was *constitutive*; since modernism is a name not for a stance of Left or Right insurgency or negation, but for a pattern of artistic practice in which modernity's very means of representation [. . .] are put to the test of exemplification within a particular medium" (1999: 91). And this practice comprises a dialectical negativity within the forms of modernist artworks themselves. For while Fredric Jameson understands modernist art as enacting the usurpation of "philosophy's claims to the Absolute"—a moment of sublime hubris that is, in turn, undone by postmodernity's "dissolution of art's vocation"—Clark contends that "modernism was *already* that dissolution and disabusal—but exactly a dissolution held in dialectical tension with the idea or urge to totality" (Clark 1999: 95).[2]

In the case of memorial architecture, we quickly come upon the limit-cases to this position, as Brett Kaplan makes clear in her essay on the trope of "aesthetic pollution" in the design of Holocaust memorials.[3] If Albert Speer's Nazi monumentalism can be classified as a form of architectural modernism, then the "test of exemplification" that it proposes—Benjamin's "violation of the masses" via the "introduction of aesthetics into political life"—is one where the spark of dissolution struggles to survive the over-whelming flood of the Führer's totalizing aesthetic ambitions (Benjamin 1968: 241). Or, to give the point Kaplan's subtlety, the fear of "aesthetic pollution" that so characterizes debates over Holocaust memorial architecture must be understood as a fear of *both* the Nazi impulse to aestheticize politics and the contrary "communist impulse to politicize art."[4] What joins the halves of this dialectic is the demand for autonomous, "unpolluted," memorial and ideological forms, and the fear that the function of Left or Right modernist architectures is to collapse the difference between the memory of a murdered people and the memory of regime aesthetics.

Whatever we think about the status of modernism, this anxiety over the totalizing impulse of politics registers very strongly in the contemporary preference for *memorials* over monuments. Sturken quotes Arthur Danto's statement that, "we erect monuments so that we shall always remember, and build memorials so that we never shall forget" (Sturken 1997: 47). With a monument we "honor ourselves," but by building a memorial we register the fact of irrevocable loss and make concrete the pedagogy of defeat (1997: 48). For Young, the distinction between monument and memorial is not so clear: "there may be nothing intrinsic to historical markers that makes them either a monument or a memorial"—and yet *Textures of Memory* might otherwise be described as the history of a refusal to "allow the past to rigidify in monumental forms" (1993: 3, 15). Young clearly favors artworks that engage the active "work of memory . . . by which minds reflecting on the past inevitably participate in the present historical moment" (1993: 15). Thus, although he is skeptical about any immanent poetics of monumentality, his work implicitly assumes that, as Robert Harbison puts it, monuments—as opposed to memorials—are "engines of false memories" (1999: 22).

And not just any false memories: national memories in particular. The history of monumental architecture demonstrates the centrality of the nation to the logic of public remembering. Among the problems posed by a monument, Savage notes, is the fact that, if it is built in honor of some truly memorable sacrifice or suffering, we should not need to build it at all: "The contrast between heart and stone—between spontaneity and fabrication, feeling and obligation—obviously calls into question the authenticity and efficacy of built forms of remembering" (1999: 15). Into this aporia comes the nation, for the *national* memorial reconciles heart and stone by serving as a "conspicuous sign that a national people understood and valued its own history" (1999: 15). The nation, then, is the privileged collective that explains the otherwise obscure fact of public commemoration, as the memorial to mass death serves to legitimate and naturalize the identity and right of the nation. Sturken argues that memorials participate in the field of national cultural memory, "a field of contested meanings in which [subjects] interact with cultural elements to produce concepts of the nation" (1997: 2–3). In the case of the British Memorial Garden, the collision between nation and memory will be especially severe.

British Gardens and National Cartographies

Perhaps the most obvious feature of the plans for the British Memorial Garden is that it remembers the sixty-seven British victims of 9/11 by building an urban garden shaped like a map of the main island of the archipelago. Even more, by combining the greenery of the English garden with Scottish granite, and by seeding a Manhattan park with plants from royal parks and gardens, the Garden strives to render organic the relationship between its cartography and the soil of the island itself. The Garden's official website contains a number of architectural and landscape drawings that emphasize this quality.[5] Seen from a northeastern perspective, the landscaping frames a central walkway that runs in Pennine fashion up the center of the park, while the decorative borders, constructed from evergreen hedges and topiary, employ the framing devices of the English country garden to map the coastline of the main island. Another pathway to the north suggests the Mersey channel and, thus, the shape of the Irish Sea, the north coast of Wales, and the southwest coast of Scotland. A planted area immediately to the west implies the body of Wales and, as it kicks out at the far western edge of the park, the Cornish peninsula. Yet the most immediately apparent quality of this British map is its excision of Northern Ireland and the many islands that ring the main island, from the Orkneys to Man and Wight.

The Garden is designed to fill the space of the existing park, exploiting Hanover Square's dimensions in order to bring out the island geometry that, one is tempted to say, was long latent within it. Indeed, it is not the first irony of the British Memorial Garden that it is to be built on a public square named after the royal family against which American patriots fought their republican revolution. Hanover Square was formed around 1695 when Abraham De Peyster, a Dutch merchant, built a house at Queen Street (now Pearl Street), on the southern side of the modern park. Bounded over the next decades by development to the north and west, Hanover Square got its current name in 1714, upon the accession of George I to the British throne, and soon became the shopping center of a British New York grown fat on the profits of the Atlantic sugar trade: a famous place to buy dry goods, imported fancies, and slaves (Burrows & Wallace 1999: 124–26). It figured in the history of the revolution, being occupied by British soldiers and loyalists during the war of independence, and was the site of a famous pro-Federalist march in the period of post-revolutionary struggle (Burrows & Wallace 1999: 258, 293). Indeed, revolutionary sentiment led the government of New York to change Hanover Square's name. Following the establishment of the USA in 1787, the square was absorbed into the newly re-named Pearl Street and left nameless until the restoration of the monarchi-cal title in 1830.[5]

The Garden's official history makes much of Hanover Square's links to the British Crown, British New York, and the contemporary expatriate commu-nity. Its symbolic map, however, contains no visible sign of modern trans-At-lantic history; nor, we must note, is it a map of the twenty-first century United Kingdom. Indeed, past and present iterations of the United Kingdom (1801 and 1922) are abandoned in favor of the political map of Great Britain as it arose out of the 1707 Union. The Garden has no place, then, for the province of Northern Ireland, which would seem to present as many prob-lems for the Bannermans' smoothly-contoured, fully contiguous horticul-tural map as it has done for successive Whitehall governments since the establishment of the Irish Free State. And yet this primary historical and ge-ographical erasure conflicts with the Garden's attempt, at many other levels, to include all possible British identities, including the Northern Irish, even though many such identities are only nominally or problematically "British." Witness, for instance, one of the key elements of the memorial—to remem-ber all 67 of the British dead. These victims, from Andrew Bailey to Neil Wright, will be commemorated by the insertion of "national" emblems in the wrought iron railing that runs along the Pearl Street border of Hanover Square. Sitting atop the horizontal anchors of the railings will be obelisk finials that feature the four national emblems of the UK: the English Rose, Scottish Thistle, Welsh Daffodil, and Northern Irish Flax. The obelisk finials can thus be read as part of the Garden's attempt to participate in what his-torians since Hugh Kearney have called "four nations" Britishness (Kearney 1989), and yet the inclusion of the Northern Irish emblem only reaffirms the province's primary exclusion from the mainland of memorial Britishness.

These acts of naming and emblematizing also run counter to the Gar-den's inclusion of a sculpture by Anglo-Indian artist Anish Kapoor, whose work characteristically avoids denotation and the symbolic. Kapoor's design proposes a monolith to Anglo-American unity that utilizes his signature motifs of rough-hewn stone and the creation of holes, hollows, and vortices that, in his recent use of mirrored surfaces, simultaneously draw in and re-flect the viewer's gaze. As Eckhard Schneider puts it, "the viewer [of Kapoor's sculptures] experiences a simultaneity of fullness (color) and void (the extinguished reality) in a state of critical balance" (2003: 23). Homi Bhabha explains that Kapoor sculpts "too much emptiness to be invisible, too much absence to be mere vacancy" (1998: 35). One can see these qual-ities in the sketches that are, so far, the only public record of the sculpture, and which suggest how Kapoor's sculptures, with their ceaseless oscillation between present absence and absent presence, might form a powerful part of a counter-memorial to those lost in an act of apparently nihilistic political violence. As Germano Celant writes about the mirrored sculptures, such as the massive structure recently unveiled in Chicago's Millennium Park:

> They live out the vicissitudes of a dialectical existence in which the sublime co-exists with the everyday, the object is affirmed in its environment, fullness is reflected in emptiness, the real lives in harmony with the abstract. Something happens in the void, and this something eludes our grasp, for it does not really coincide with one thing or another, one space or another, one position or another. (Celant 1996: xxxvi)

Considered as the work of a postcolonial British artist, Kapoor's sculpture should be understood as a career-long critique of the idea of the origin or the home; or, as Bhabha puts it, as a poetics of the transitional object:

> The shape of the void and the sign of emptiness must be conceived of in a logic of doubling; like the transitional object, they are unified at the point in space and time of their separation and differentiation. Such a mode of representation does not contain, deep within its being, an 'object' that unfolds, in its own time, to reveal its unitary presence. (1998: 36)

It is in this sense—as much as through the obviously exotic imagery of his early pigment sculptures, with their evocation of "primary color in its raw state" and sacralization of the everyday (Celant 1996: xx)—that Kapoor's art engages with his Indian heritage and the discourse of the postcolonial. And yet his poetics of the transitional object fits awkwardly with the accidental otherness of the British Memorial Garden, which longs for the unitary presence of the British landscape and yet succeeds only in revealing the missing parts of that far off land.

This logic of memory and forgetting adds up to an awesome nostalgia, as in the contribution of Simon Verity, who is in the process of carving a memorial pathway that incorporates the names of the UK counties, London boroughs, and overseas dependent territories. These engraved granite slabs will surround the garden, tracing the coastline; by displacing the victims' names to outside the bounded whole of the nation they will only reinforce the sense that the Garden is more interested in mourning a certain vision of Britain than the sixty-seven dead. The embrace of geography is, once more, compromised in space and history. Verity explained to the Glasgow *Herald* that, for reasons of space, his granite flagstones will be arranged out of order: "Nairn, for example, will be on the north-west coast of this map of Britain, somewhere about Gairloch" (Ross 2004: 28). Even worse, the pathway will repeat the very colonial condescension that its inclusiveness was surely meant to prevent. For although counties have a stone to themselves, and London boroughs nestle two to a slab, the names of dependent territories are to be engraved on the commas that separate the master nouns of the home nations. Reduced to punctuation, colonial dependencies like Montserrat are simultaneously denied the independence of their grief and rendered epiphenomenal to the narrative of British imperial collectivity. In the calculus of suffering, this is doubly bitter, given that with the death of New York City firefighter Keithroy Maynard, Montserrat (population 13,000)[6] lost as many of its countrymen as Northern Ireland (population 1.69 million) and half as many as Wales (population 2.92 million).[7]

Of course, whatever symbolic disjunctions it might reveal, this comparative arithmetic of loss is not a little crude. Read sympathetically, the Memorial Garden's inclusion of Montserrat is an act of generosity: a reminder that Britain's island story is, in fact, a story of many islands and not a few continents. Surely the point is not to foster invidious comparisons but to proclaim that the losses of one part of Britain are felt and remembered by all. Still, the Garden's incessant desire to anatomize the limits and extent of Britishness makes one wonder why its every inclusion excludes, and every embrace, belittles. The answer to this question lies, I eventually conclude, in the ideological contradictions of contemporary English Toryism, but I must first say something more about the Garden as a map.

In *Out of Place*, Ian Baucom investigates how the logic of the "locale" serves as a "disciplinary and nostalgic discourse," a "*lieu de memoire* that purports to testify to the nation's essential continuity across time" (Baucom 1999: 4–5). The problem with England is that, given its long possession of a vast overseas empire, its history is not one of "expansion and contraction" but of "cultivated confusion": "The empire [. . .] is less a place where England exerts control than the place where England loses command of its own narrative of identity" (1999: 3). One can say something similar about Great Britain as about the empire, for if the ungovernable human and topographical difference of colonial life undid the autotelic narrative of Englishness, then the 1707 Union created a space and identity that suppressed the expression of English political nationalism as the price of Greater Britishness. Place, then, is a condition of national sameness; it is the predicate of simultaneity, of the nation as a synchronic unity, but place also undermines historical unity. As Cairns Craig puts it, regarding Anglo-Scottish relations: "The imposed unity of the state and its culture that is modeled on the singularity of the direction of time is undone by the multiplicity of space, which continues to generate otherness" (Craig 1996: 205).[8]

It is in this light that we can think again about maps as forms of control. Baucom describes the British Survey of India (begun 1767) as "a vital element in the English attempt to control the empire less by occupying it than by knowing it, classifying it, and rendering it visible" (1999: 93). The maps generated by colonial surveyors thus offer the imperial government the "seductive [. . .] fiction of fixity, of ordered, visible, and bounded space" (1999: 94). Likewise, the Ordnance Survey of Ireland (begun 1824) must be seen not simply as a military enterprise, in which the topography of an often-hostile country was rendered knowable to British warships and artillery, but as a form of discipline in which "colonial space must be transformed sufficiently so as to no longer appear foreign to the imperial eye" (Said 1994: 226).[9] We can sense, here, some of the historical embarrassment that the memorial cartographer might feel in recharting the territory of imperial Britain; and yet the problem for the British Memorial Garden is that the mainland of Britain is already, ineradicably, mapped. When it comes to Britain, cartography is not so much an exercise in seeing and fixing the unknown, as a process of remapping previously charted territory: the island is too well known, so that every mapping is a remapping, every iteration a reiteration.

This problem animates art like that of Layla Curtis, whose *The United Kingdom* (1999) was purchased for the inaugural hang of the Tate Modern Gallery at Bankside, London (see figure 1). Curtis graduated from Edinburgh College of Art in 1998, the year of the referendums on devolution, and the

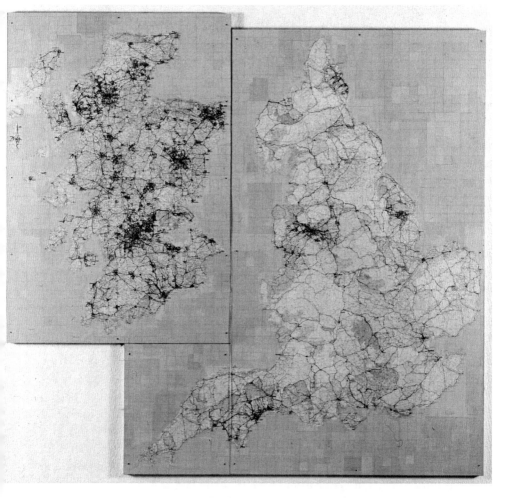

Figure 1. Layla Curtis. 1999. *United Kingdom*. Collage on paper. 2050 x 2260mm. Tate Gallery, UK.

cultural politics of the devolving UK from the unmistakable context for this work. *The United Kingdom* is a collage made from a road map, a feature that is most immediately obvious in the checkered surface of the seas that still surround the islands. From a distance, the map appears to follow the contours and coastlines of the main island. Look more closely, however, and one notices that Curtis has transposed the usual topography, places, and place-names of the island. Manchester and Glasgow have swapped positions, as (more shockingly) have London and Aberdeen; the English south and midlands have become almost entirely rural; Scotland is mottled by the appearance of scattered English towns and suburbs. Though beautiful as all maps, the collage depends for its effect on a version of Freud's *Unheimlich*—we might call it the cartographic uncanny. The reordering of the map is at once aesthetic, psychological, and didactic, causing one to reconsider the links between industry and landscape, town and country, margin and center, as well as the role of cartography in ordering national myths and imperatives—and then there is the Utopian charge of imagining a nation as a chaotic space that we might reorder to fit alternative ecologies and political structures. *The United Kingdom* is the perfect figure for the confusion that marks contemporary British cultural identities, not least because its title cannot help but draw attention to Curtis's critical excision of Northern Ireland, Man, and the Channel Islands. In these gaps, Curtis offers us a negative image of Britain's dependence on—and debt to—various "overseas" locations and dependencies: an essential supplementary symbol for the glut of "British" names, loyalties, and locations.

Pastoralism and the Neoliberal City

If the national symbolism of the Garden is so thoroughly overdetermined, what does it really encourage us to remember? The Garden's symbolism, it is time to admit, is heavily weighted toward the English metropolitan center. London is the only city whose boroughs merit special enumeration, while the designs suggest that the Garden's artistic anchor, Kapoor's unity sculpture, will be placed on a spot consistent with London's location on the map of Britain—as if the void at its heart might teleport New Yorkers back to the Ground Zero of imperial hegemony. If we return to the unsavory demographics of death, we see that this metropolitan bias is strangely appropriate, if incommensurable with the Garden's more ecumenical cartographic gestures. By my calculations, fifty-six of the sixty-seven British dead (83.6 percent) lived or were born in England.[10] In this group of fifty-six, I can establish a hometown or county for forty-five men and women, thirty-one of whom came from London or the Home Counties, eight from the north and midlands, and seven from the south and southwest.[11] If we are to ignore, as the idea of a "British" memorial implies, the fact that many of the victims were long resident in North America and several were naturalized citizens of the US or Canada, the Garden's geographic biases reflect, with uncanny precision, the demographic dominance of England, which, according to the 2001 census, also makes up 83.6 percent of the UK population. What these figures distort, however, is the relative demographic weight of the metropolitan southeast, which for all London's density accounts for just three in ten of England's population.[12]

This pattern recalls a key fact of the 9/11 attacks in New York: the predominance of financial services companies as tenants of the World Trade Center and the strong link between Manhattan and London as world financial markets. By far the majority of the British victims worked in this sector, with Cantor Fitzgerald, EuroBrokers, Aon Insurance, and Risk Waters accounting for more than half the dead. Predominantly English, white, professional, college educated, and well paid, the British dead of September 11 represent the elite of the Wall Street/Square Mile axis. And yet, rather than *explaining* the British Memorial Garden's version of pastoral Englishness, this knowledge renders it even more symptomatic of the crisis in contemporary Toryism. To reveal one final element of its nostalgic Anglocentrism, Verity's flagstones represent not the disposition of the counties in 2001 but, rather, as they existed before the 1972 Local Government Act.[13] The Memorial Garden will refer, then, to the extinct counties of Rutland and Westmoreland, but not to large administrative regions such as Greater Manchester or Merseyside, which—we can only conclude—are at once too modern, too urban, too "ethnic," to carry the weight of English grief.

Over-layering a geographic bias that is explicable, if not excusable, in demographic terms, the Garden includes the ghost of an ancient and aristocratic Englishness that vanished with the empire. Its topography aspires to a form of indigenous pastoralism—an ideology that, as Krishan Kumar argues, was central to the emergence of an English nationalism previously subsumed within British unionism and imperialism, which demanded that "English identity had to find objects other than the English nation on which to fasten" (Kumar 2003: 179). Prior to the end of the nineteenth century, English nationalism *as such* was impossible: "For the English in their empire, as for the Austrians and Russians in theirs, empire offered an identity that lifted them above 'mere' nationalist self-glorification" (2003: 193). English pride, privilege, and chauvinism remained powerful forces, as Kumar's pronoun "their" and the commonplace identification of the "British" empire with the process of cultural and linguistic Anglicization make plain. But it is only in the context of a heady *fin de siecle* historical brew that the encompassing identity of Britishness became sufficiently degraded for the emergence of an Englishness that might parallel Scottish or Irish nationalisms:

> Faltering confidence in empire; the decline of religion, and the identities it had sustained; changing perceptions of the national enemy; the rise of cultural and ethnic nationalism; all these worked to undermine the primacy of the British identity that had been established in the wake of the Unions of 1707 (Scotland) and 1801 (Ireland), following upon that much earlier incorporation of 1541 (Wales). Not that British identity by any means collapsed; far from it. But there was now room [. . . .] and a felt need, for some expression of English national identity. (Kumar 2003: 202)

It is worth emphasizing the relative weakness of this English nationalism and the concurrent persistence of Britishness as a national-political identity that, from the perspective of the *fin de siecle*, was yet to experience the late imperialism of 1914 to 1918; the Anglo-Celtic alliance of the Labour movement; the new solidarities of the Welfare State; and the postcolonial development of "Black British" identities that, however controversial, remain inassimilable to insular ethno-nationalisms.[14] Indeed, the sclerotic or belated nature of English nationalism underwrites many of the best analyses of modern British political identities and has proved a staple of the British New Left. For Perry Anderson, it is not Englishness but Britishness that, in 1964, forms the "Origin of the Present Crisis": "a general malady of the society" in which "Britain appears an archaic society, trapped in past successes" (P. Anderson 1992: 43). And yet in Anderson's explanation, the failures of British "social imperialism" are the result of a specifically *English* history of cultural blockage in which, following the bourgeois revolution of the Civil War and the constitutional upheavals of 1688, English mercantile capital failed "to constitute itself as an internally compact or autonomous political force" (1992: 19). Likewise, in Tom Nairn's classic 1977 account of British "break-up," both "Ukanian" constitutional underdevelopment and postcolonial racism of the sort associated with the 1968 marches in support of Enoch Powell are linked symptoms "of *an absence of* popular nationalism among the English," who possess "no coherent, sufficiently democratic myth of Englishness [. . .] where mass discontents can find a vehicle" (Nairn 1981: 294; italics in original). Nairn's theory of nationalism has often been critiqued; yet his basic point about the enigma of English nationalism is surely borne out by the way that, in the British Memorial Garden, hegemonic Englishness can still hide behind the shrubbery of imperial Britishness.[15]

One of the strengths of Kumar's sociology of the "moment of Englishness" is that it registers the limitations of Anglo-nationalism without reducing it to an ideology of place, different from "ethnic" nationalisms. On the contrary, the history of Anglo-nationalism includes the racial notion of

Anglo-Saxonism; and yet this racial theory was simultaneously limiting and expansive: part of the ideology of imperialism that was transferred to settler colonies in North America, Australasia, and Southern Africa.[16] English pastoralism, then, can be seen as the force that bound and located this traveling racial theory—though it is a force that depends on the prior subcategorization of rural experience. The version of country life that emerges out of the *fin de siecle* is not one of northern wilderness or industrialized agricultural production: it is calm, green, and, like the British Memorial Garden, ringed by hedges and pathways; a healing redoubt against the irresistible depredations of the city. We can observe this quality in a text like E. M. Forster's 1910 novel, *Howards End*:

> If one wanted to show a foreigner England, perhaps the wisest course would be to take him to the final section of the Purbeck Hills, and stand him on their summit, a few miles to the east of Corfe. Then system after system of our island would roll together under his feet . . . . Nor is suburbia absent. Bournemouth's ignoble coast cowers to the right, heralding the pine trees that mean, for all their beauty, red houses, and the Stock Exchange, and extend to the gates of London itself. So tremendous is the City's trail! (Forster 2000: 142–43)

This is a highly partial national vision, predicated on a southern and rural vantage point. It shows us a pastoral England threatened to the south and east by urban and suburban encirclements, so that even Forster's vision of the country's insecurity depends on the primary erasure of the industrial cities and mining villages of the north and west. Forster's urbanism is metropolitan; his capitalism is imperial and mercantile, not industrial. The pathway that leads from gated London to the alien forests of Bournemouth is the trail of the City and Exchange, not the dirty smoke trail of coalfields or steelworks. This limiting nostalgia clearly predicts the harmonious resolution of *Howards End*, which sees the bourgeois Wilcoxes and bohemian Schlegels united by the magic of property—the properly bequeathed English country seat realizing its promise as a synecdoche for England and Englishness, resolving the contradictions of an imperial economy in which the pleasures of home depend upon the expropriation of land and labor in the rubber plantations of Nigeria.

This is to put things in Saidean terms and draw attention to the geographic displacements of imperial fictions and the constitutive relations between pastoralism and the trade and territory it renders invisible.[17] And yet English pastoralism has survived the transformation of the imperial economy; indeed, it is undergoing something of a recrudescence, confirming Kumar's sense that the forms of Anglo-nationalism, like Hegel's Owl of Minerva, tend to fly at dusk, "when their subjects, as practical concerns, are at the point of dissolution" (2003: 197). This, at least, is the subtext of Roger Scruton's *England: An Elegy* (2000), which talks of England and the English in the past tense, as things forever lost to cultural, political, and institutional Bolshevism. Scruton's writing is full of a certain type of English grief, occupying a tonal range between George Orwell's ambivalent carica-ture of the Blimp and a tragic figure like Christopher Tietjens, Ford Madox Ford's "last English Tory"—another patriot of country life and the "shared sense of membership" in communities that possess some essential difference from the "artificial states left in [the] wake of collapsing empires"(Scruton 2000: 6).[18]

Scruton has long been known as a writer on philosophy and as a Tory commentator, increasingly concerned with country ways.[19] In *England: An Elegy*, he repeats the sentiment, common to Left and Right writing on Eng-lishness, that:

> Ideas of race, tribe and religion, which have played a dangerous part in conti-nental politics, have also shaped English identity. But [. . .] England was first and foremost a place—though a place consecrated by custom. There thus grew on English soil a patriotism not unlike that from which the word 'patriotism' de-rives—the patriotism of the Romans, in which the homeland, rather than the race, was the focus of loyalty. (Scruton 2000: 7)

These sentences establish the keynotes of Scruton's lament. Note their basic qualification between England and Europe; their disengagement from the formative complexities of Anglo-Celtic relations; their reverence for the consecrating power of custom; and their invocation of a culture that grew—organic, autochthonous—on English soil. Indeed, Scruton's central argument depends upon an abstracted form of what Baucom explains as the *ius soli*: the "law of the soil" (Baucom 1999: 8–9). Scruton congratu-lates the (dead) English for the fact that "for seven centuries there was no other official test of Englishness than the fact of being born here," and ex-plains the post-1945 amendments to that principle as "emergency mea-sures," motivated not by racism but by the natural anxiety caused by "the disruption of an old experience of home, and a loss of the enchantment which made home a place of safety and consolation" (Scruton 2000: 7).

In arguing thus, Scruton never explains why an England become home to the citizens of the former empire is necessarily transformed into a place of disenchantment, danger, and cold comfort. Rather, this rhetoric con-nects with his persistent evocation of England as "a place domesticated by its indigenous law" (Scruton 2000: 234). The soil of England is powerful stuff: legislation is built upon it, grows from it, works upon it like some cru-cial element in a self-sustaining ecosystem. The elegiac analysis of Eng-land's law therefore leads inexorably to an obituary for its countryside. Scruton believes that "English culture entered the modern era with an im-movable commitment to the pastoral," and bemoans the fact that today, "the passion that educated English people devote to the *idea* of rural life is not matched by any creative interest in the *fact* of it" (Scruton 2000: 242). Yet his vision of the English pastoral is, like Forster's, an attenuated and semi-feudal thing: it is built around the obsolete ideology of the country house, "in which hierarchy was softened by neighborliness, and wealth by mutual aid"; it is redolent of the long-extinct "tradition of the yeoman farmer" and the brutalized "living fence" of the English hedgerow (Scruton 2000: 238–41).

It is here that we see how Scruton's elegy for the cultural geography of the squirarchy connects with the British Memorial Garden—another memorial to English death, framed by hedges, and littered with extinct symbols. Scruton complains, "where you see hedges that have grown straggly [. . .] you know that the land is passing" (Scruton 2000: 241). The irony is that the limited sovereignty of English country life has been compromised for years by the very forces of capital and empire at which Scruton can gesture—but only that. England has never been England, entire to itself, since at least the time when a British colonial government gave a German monarch's name to a Dutch city square built on Lenape Indian land. As Baucom explains, apropos of the vaunted simplicity of the *ius soli*: "If British history were the history of a stably bordered nation, then the rule would indeed be [...] simple. But Britain's borders, to put it mildly, have been far from stable, and the 'rule,' consequently, far from simple to apply" (Baucom 1999: 8). The pastoral rootedness of England has long been complicated by the elasticity of England's borders, while, in an era of global neoliberalism, the search for new markets, materials, and labor power undoes the native entrepreneurialism that Scruton celebrates as the gift of a legal sovereignty that was "objective, permanent, and part of the furniture" (Scruton 2000: 9).

Scruton maintains that from England's *Heimlich* law stems an individualistic "disposition to affirm the right and responsibility of individual action in all spheres of social life"; thus follows the indigenous, even geological, nature of English capitalism (2000: 10). The revolutionary and imperial force of economic liberalism is, then, also an English and Tory power. But herein lies the impossibility of pastoral Toryism in an age of neoliberalism, in which, as Wendy Brown has noted:

> In contrast with the notorious *laissez faire* . . . of classical economic liberalism, neoliberalism does not conceive either the market itself or rational economic behavior as purely natural . . . . Far from flourishing when left alone, the economy must be directed, buttressed, and protected by law and policy as well as by the dissemination of social norms designed to facilitate competition, free trade, and rational economic action on the part of every member and institution of society. (Brown 2003: para. 10)

Political parties and agents of all kinds are implicated in the regime of neoliberal economic management. This is something that Scruton recognizes, though only dully. He asks of his socialist father's commitment to the English *genius loci*, "if he identified [the forces that were disenchanting England] with big business, and big business with the Tory Party, was he wholly wrong?" And he says of New Labour that it is "committed to 'globalization', indifferent to the fate of rural England" (Scruton 2000: 256–57). But though he argues that England is a not "an enterprise but a country," Scruton can never identify the muddy roots of its great experiment in the market and empire as the very thing that has leached the money, population, and enchantment out of the countryside.

To appropriate a sentence by Stefan Collini: "the [political and economic] forces that are destroying all that [English Toryism] loves are the forces [it] is ideologically committed to supporting" (2001). It is this paradox that, in the end, provides the surest link between the recrudescence of English pastoral ideology and the transplanted country memory of the British Memorial Garden. They both suffer from English grief, where the commitment to global capitalism sustains the "special relationship" between the neoliberal cities of London and New York but which, in its destruction of the cultural and economic basis of pastoral English identity, long ago extinguished the eternal flame of Brooke's "forever England."

Notes

1. It is worth noting that, even in this retelling, Hoheisel's project presumes a level of negativity that Young's does not. Whereas Hoheisel offers a politics of destruction and absence, Young engages in a liberal act of inclusion, recruiting Hoheisel's radicalism through discourse, while not acting on its behalf.

2. The object of Clark's critique is Jameson's *The Cultural Turn*, wherein one finds the phrase "dissolution of art's vocation to reach the Absolute" (Jameson 1998: 84); see Clark (1999: 95).

3. Kaplan (2003). The fact of a limit-case would not bother Clark in the least: "I shall operate with a loose and capacious notion of modern art, and spend a lot of my time (not all) on limit cases; the assumption being that in these the pressures and capacities of a particular mode of representation (maybe we should call it a family of modes) will tend to be clearest, just because the capacities are pressed to breaking point. 'Limits' in this case does not mean edges" (1999: 7).

4. Kaplan (2003: 6). Witness Daniel Libeskind's language as he disparages one of his rivals for the commission to build on the site of the destroyed WTC: "Towers of learning? The phrase sounded as if it had been lifted from Stalinist literature!" (2004: 170).

5. See the photographs and drawings, especially the "Initial Artist's Impression," at <http://www.britishmemorialgarden.org/development.html>. 27 Jan. 2005. The following paragraphs draw on F.J. Sypher, "Hanover Square in the British Colonial Period." Publication of the British Memorial Garden Trust. 21 Dec. 2004. <http://www.britishmemorialgarden.org/history.html>. 27 January 2005.

6. "Montserrat." *World Encyclopedia*. Philip's 2004. *Oxford Reference Online*. Oxford University Press. Univ Illinois-Urbana Champaign. 05 Jan 2005. <http://www.oxfordreference.com/views/ENTRY.html?subview=Main&entry=t105.e7758>. This and all other information about the national origins of the dead were gleaned from a number of news archives, most notably CNN and *The New York Times*.

7. This and all other 2001 Census information from UK Resident Population Statistics, Office for National Statistics. 05 January 2005. <http://www.statistics.gov.uk/CCI/nuggest.asp?ID=760&Pos=3&ColRank=2&Rank=896>.

8. Both Baucom and Craig owe their analysis of the temporal/diachronic and spatial/synchronic axes of national identity to Benedict Anderson's *Imagined Communities* (1992). I am doubly indebted.

9. See also, in this context, the seminal Foucauldian account of cartography as a tool of governmentality by J.B. Harley (1989).

10. Of the remaining eleven victims, four were from Scotland, two from Wales, and one from Northern Ireland; four came from the postcolonial Caribbean but emigrated to the United States without ever living in the UK, making them highly nominal Britons.

11. In ethnic terms, of the total group of sixty-seven victims, fifty-nine were Caucasian, the exceptions being: two men of Indian origin (both ex-Londoners); two men of Afro-Caribbean descent, one of whom emigrated to New York from London, the other from Birmingham; and four men from Montserrat, Guyana, the British Virgin Islands, and Bermuda. These numbers (88 percent white; 12 percent South Asian or Afro-Caribbean) represent a more ethnically diverse range than the British population as a whole, where only 7.9 percent of Britons are non-white.

12. A rough formula—the true ratios are 31 out of 45 (68.9 percent) victims with a given British home location in London or the southeast, rather than 15,172,736 out of an English population of 49,138,831 (30.9 percent).

13. The 1969 Royal Commission on Local Government Reform in England and Wales was chaired by Lord Redcliffe-Maude and paved the way for the 1972 Local Government Act that eliminated some of the historic counties of England and Wales.

14. In this context, see the repeated discussions of the label "British" in Samuel (1998), especially 49. For a critique of the idea of national history that underwrites the historiography of Samuel and his History Workshop collaborators, see Gilroy (1993: 63–73).

15. For critiques of Nairn, see for example Smith (1998: 49–55); Pocock (2000: 41–52).

16. Kumar (2003: 206–7). For an alternative account of Englishness as an 'ethnicity,' formed in and through a globalizing world system, see Stuart Hall (1997: 173–87).

17. My model, here, is Said's classic analysis of Austen's *Mansfield Park* (1994: 80–96).

18. For Tietjens' southern and pastoral vision of England (which somehow overpowers his Yorkshire roots) see Ford's 1924 novel *Some Do Not*: "This, Tietjens thought, is England! A man and a maid walk through Kentish grass fields: the grass ripe for the scythe . . . . Each knew the names of birds that piped and grasses that bowed . . . . In the hedge: Our Lady's bedstraw, dead-nettle, bachelor's button" (Ford 1950: 105). For Orwell's Blimp see, e.g., "My Country Right or Left," where he argues for "the possibility of building a Socialist on the bones of a Blimp" (1968: 592).

19. The biographical note to *England: An Elegy* notes that Scruton "lives in Wiltshire where, together with his wife, he runs an experimental farm."

Bibliography

Anderson, Benedict. 1992. *Imagined Communities: Reflections on the Origin and Spread of Nationalism*, rev. ed. London: Verso.

Anderson, Perry. 1992. *English Questions*. London: Verso.

Baucom, Ian. 1999. *Out of Place: Englishness, Empire, and the Locations of Identity*. Princeton, NJ: Princeton University Press.

Benjamin, Walter. 1968. *Illuminations*. Trans. by Harry Zohn. New York: Schocken.

Bhabha, Homi. 1998. "Anish Kapoor: Making Emptiness." In *Anish Kapoor*. London, Berkeley, & Los Angeles: Hayward Gallery & University of California Press: 11–41.

Brooke, Rupert. *The Collected Poems of Rupert Brooke*, ed. George Edward Woodberry. New York: Dodd, Mead, & Co., 1915).

Brown, Wendy. 2003. "Neo-liberalism and the End of Liberal Democracy," *Theory & Event*, vol. 7, no. 1. 1 February 2005. <http://muse.jhu.edu/journals/theory_and_event/v007/7.1brown.html>.

Burrows, Edwin G. and Mike Wallace. 1999. *Gotham: A History of New York City to 1898*. Oxford & New York: Oxford University Press.

Celant, Germano. 1996. *Anish Kapoor*. London: Thames and Hudson.

Clark, T. J. 1999. *Farewell to An Idea: Episodes from a History of Modernism*. New Haven: Yale University Press.

——. 2000. "Origins of the Present Crisis." *New Left Review* 2 (March–April): 85–96.

Collini, Stefan. 2001. "Hegel in Green Wellies." *London Review of Books*, vol. 23, no. 5 (8 March). 5 January 2005. <http://www.lrb.co.uk/v23/n05/coll01_.html>.

Craig, Cairns. 1996. *Out of History: Narrative Paradigms in Scottish and British Culture*. Edinburgh: Polygon.

Ford, Ford Madox. 1950. *Parade's End*. New York: Knopf.

Forster, E.M. 2000. *Howards End*. London: Penguin.

Gilroy, Paul. 1993. *Small Acts: Thoughts on the Politics of Black Cultures*. London: Serpent's Tail.

Hall, Stuart. 1997. 'The Local and the Global: Globalization & Ethnicity." In Anne McClintock, Aamir Mufti & Ella Shohat (eds.) *Dangerous Liaisons: Gender, Nation and Postcolonial Perspectives*. Minneapolis: University of Minnesota Press: 173-87.

Harbison, Robert. 1999. "Half–Truths and Misquotations: A Skeptical Look at Monuments." *Harvard Design Magazine* 9 (Fall): 20–22.

Harley, J. B. 1989. "Deconstructing the Map," *Cartographica*, vol. 26, no. 2 (Summer): 1–20.

Jameson, Frederic. 1998. *The Cultural Turn*. London: Verso.

Kaplan, Brett Ashley. 2003. "Aesthetic Pollution: The Paradox of Remembering and Forgetting in Three Holocaust Commemorative Sites." *Journal of Modern Jewish Studies*, vol. 2, no. 1: 1–18

Kearney, Hugh. 1989. *The British Isles: A History of Four Nations*. Cambridge: Cambridge University Press.

Kumar, Krishan. 2003. *The Making of English National Identity*. Cambridge & New York: Cambridge University Press.

Libeskind, Daniel. 2004. *Breaking Ground*, with Sarah Crichton. New York: Riverhead.

Nairn, Tom. 1981. *The Break-Up of Britain: Crisis and Neo-Nationalism*, 2nd expanded edition. London: Verso/New Left Books.

Orwell, George. 1968. *Collected Essays, Journals and Letters, Vol. I: An Age Like This, 1920–1940*. Sonia Orwell & Ian Angus (eds.). London: Secker & Warburg.

Pocock, J.G.A. 2000. "Gaberlunzie's Return," *New Left Review* 5 (Sep–Oct): 41–52.

Ross, David. "How to Pave from Caithness to NYC." *The Herald* (8 Nov. 2004): 28.

Said, Edward. 1994. *Culture and Imperialism*. New York: Vintage Books.

Samuel, Raphael. 1998. *Island Stories: Unraveling Britain: Theatres of Memory*. Vol. II, Allison Light (ed.). London: Verso.

Savage, Kirk. 1999. "The Past in the Present: the Life of Memorials." *Harvard Design Magazine* 9 (Fall): 14–19.

Schneider, Eckhard. 2003. "Anish Kapoor—My Red Homeland." In *Anish Kapoor: My Red Homeland*. Bregenz, Germany: Kunsthaus Bregenz: 16–41.

Scruton, Roger. 2000. *England: An Elegy*. London: Chatto & Windus.

Smith, Anthony D. 1998. *Nationalism and Modernism: A Critical Survey of Recent Theories of Nations and Nationalism*. London: Routledge.

Sturken, Marita. 1997. *Tangled Memories: The Vietnam War, the Aids Epidemic, and the Politics of Remembering*. Berkeley, CA: University of California Press.

Young, James E. 1999. "Memory and Counter–Memory: The End of the Monument in Germany." *Harvard Design Magazine* 9 (Fall): 1-10.

Young, James E. 1993. *Textures of Memory: Holocaust Memorials and Meaning*. New Haven & London: Yale University Press.

NOTES ON CONTRIBUTORS

Vivian Bickford-Smith is a Professor in the Historical Studies Department at the University of Cape Town. He has published extensively in the area of nineteenth- and twentieth-century South African history, with a focus on racial/ethnic identity and experience, particularly Englishness. Much of this output has been on Cape Town history including: *Ethnic Pride and Racial Prejudice in Victorian Cape Town* (Cambridge, 1995), *Cape Town the Making of a City* (Cape Town, 1998) and *Cape Town in the Twentieth Century* (Cape Town, 1999). More recent contributions include: "Revisiting Anglicisation in the Nineteenth Century Cape Colony," *Journal of Imperial and Commonwealth History*, 31:2 (May 2003), 82-95 and "The Betrayal of Creole Elites, 1880-1910" in Philip D. Morgan and Sean Hawkins (eds.), *Black Experience and the Empire* (Oxford, 2004).

Bridget Byrne is a Lecturer in Sociology at the University of Manchester. Her most recent publication is *White Lives: The Interplay of "Race," Class and Gender in Everyday Life* (Routledge, 2006).

Enda Duffy is an Associate Professor of English at the University of California Santa Barbara. He is the author of *The Subaltern Ulysses*, a pioneering book on the postcoloniality of James Joyce's texts, and numerous articles. He is coediting a collection of essays on Joyce and Walter Benjamin and has recently completed a study of the experience of velocity in modernist culture, *The Speed Handbook*.

Sheila Ghose is a Ph.D. candidate in the English Department, New York University, USA, where she is working on a dissertation on redefinitions of Britishness. She received her B.A. from Stockholm University, Sweden, and her M.A. from the University of Wales, UK.

Matthew Hart received his Ph.D. from the University of Pennsylvania and is currently an Assistant Professor of English at the University of Illinois, Urbana-Champaign. His essays have appeared in *Postmodern Culture*, *Review*, and a forthcoming volume on T.S. Eliot's international reception. He is currently working on two book projects: *Nations of Nothing But Poetry: Late Modernism and Vernacular Sovereignty*, and a collection of essays on British politics and culture since 1979.

Graham MacPhee has taught at universities in Britain and the US, and is currently Assistant Professor of English at West Chester University of Pennsylvania. He is the author of *The Architecture of the Visible: Technology and Urban Visual Culture* (Continuum, 2002), and has published widely on the philosophy and culture of modernity, including recent articles in *Angelaki*, *Literature and Theology*, and *New Formations*.

Geoffrey Nash is a Senior Lecturer at the University of Sunderland where he specializes in Victorian and postcolonial writing. His latest book is *From Empire to Orient: Travelers to the Middle East 1830-1926*.

Prem Poddar is Associate Professor in Postcolonial Studies at the University of Aarhus. In addition to numerous essays, he authored *Violent Civilities* and edited *A Historical Companion to Postcolonial Literatures*. He is currently working on a reference book on postcolonial Europe.

Colin Wright gained his Ph.D. at the University of Nottingham where he is now Director of Undergraduate Studies in the Department of Critical Theory and Cultural Studies. He is founding editor of the journal, *Situation Analysis: A Forum for Critical Thought & International Current Affairs*, and the author of *Psychoanalysis: An Introduction* (2006), and *Philosophy, Rhetoric and Ideology: Towards a Sophistic Democracy* (2006), and coeditor, with Cristina Demaria, of *Post–Conflict Cultures: Rituals of Representation* (2006).

Index